Opsey

(negative / positive forms)

Redefining freedom pp 18, 21

Freedom to / from — Isaiah Berlin

Two sides of democracy — timely? visit?
— "no guarantee" → rebel choice!

Globalism p. 177

Native Intyponing of Human "Right" p. -161

Opposition to new warfare is similar to
opposition to global environmental governance
(p. -162)

About Island Press

Island Press is the only nonprofit organization in the United States whose principal purpose is the publication of books on environmental issues and natural resource management. We provide solutions-oriented information to professionals, public officials, business and community leaders, and concerned citizens who are shaping responses to environmental problems.

In 1994, Island Press celebrated its tenth anniversary as the leading provider of timely and practical books that take a multidisciplinary approach to critical environmental concerns. Our growing list of titles reflects our commitment to bringing the best of an expanding body of literature to the environmental community throughout North America and the world.

Support for Island Press is provided by Apple Computer, Inc., The Bullitt Foundation, The Geraldine R. Dodge Foundation, The Energy Foundation, The Ford Foundation, The W. Alton Jones Foundation, The Lyndhurst Foundation, The John D. and Catherine T. MacArthur Foundation, The Andrew W. Mellon Foundation, The Joyce Mertz-Gilmore Foundation, The National Fish and Wildlife Foundation, The Pew Charitable Trusts, The Pew Global Stewardship Initiative, The Rockefeller Philanthropic Collaborative, Inc., and individual donors.

Environmental Governance

Environmental Governance

THE GLOBAL CHALLENGE

Lamont C. Hempel

ISLAND PRESS

Washington, D.C. ◆ Covelo, California

Library of Congress Cataloging-in-Publication Data

Hempel, Lamont C.
    Environmental governance: the global challenge / Lamont C.
    Hempel
        p.   cm.
    Includes bibliographical references and index.
    ISBN 1-55963-447-2 (cloth: acid-free paper). — ISBN
1-55963-448-0 (pbk.: acid-free paper)
    1. Environmental policy. I. Title.
HC79.E5.H457   1996
333.7—dc20   95-39224
                                                        CIP

Printed on recycled, acid-free paper ✪

Manufactured in the United States of America

10   9   8   7   6   5   4   3   2

Contents

Chapter 9   Cornucopians, Catastrophists,
            and Optimizers   226

Preface

As humanity prepares to enter the twenty-first century, the world is experiencing the ecological strain produced by twentieth century thinking. The onslaught of environmental statistics, darkly portrayed, has left many people with a sense of numbness or helpless resignation. In an average day, an estimated 260 thousand people are added (net) to the world's population, 30–100 species of plants and animals are prematurely extinguished, over 90,000 new motor vehicles take to the road, 57 million metric tons of carbon dioxide are released to the atmosphere from the burning of fossil fuels, over 42,000 hectares (162 square miles) of tropical forest are destroyed, 68 million tons of topsoil are lost to erosion, and 38,000 children under the age of five die from hunger or contaminated drinking water.

Statistical portraits of this type help to convey the enormity of the environmental challenge but not the pathos that it represents, especially when the collisions of people and carrying capacities occur in faraway places or future times. We have arrived at the millennium with the means to remake ourselves and the world but without the ecological wisdom to do so safely and sustainably. The poet Gary Snyder has captured the resulting environmental anxiety in a passage from his poem "For the Children" (*Turtle Island*, 1974).

> *The rising hills, the slopes,*
> *of statistics*
> *lie before us.*
> *the steep climb*
> *of everything, going up,*
> *as we all*
> *go down.*

Snyder's solemn air of inevitability permeates the writing and speeches of many environmentalists, and yet the signs of change have seldom been more ambiguous. It is hard to gauge who will be more instrumental in shaping the next century: the people organized to exploit the environment or the people organized to protect it. And what should we conclude about the vast majority of people whose lives seem to be organized to do both? The outcome appears highly uncertain, especially if one is willing to credit humanity with a dual capacity for incremental adaptation and paradigmatic transformation. People have adapted incrementally to ever-worsening environmental conditions, but they have also marveled at the pictures of their fragile planet taken from space, and some, transformed by the experience, have vowed to preserve its ecology for future generations. Many recognized instantly that the biosphere, that delicate membrane of life that covers the earth, represents the ultimate battlefield on which the fate of the world will be decided.

This book is about the struggle to protect the biosphere, and the public policies and institutions involved in that struggle. Its purpose is to examine the challenge of global environmental awareness and governance within an evolving international system and to identify promising directions for the design of future policies and institutions. Most of the book is devoted to the identification and management of transboundary and transgenerational environmental change. Governance, rather than government, is its focus; policy synthesis, rather than analysis, is its primary goal. The global and regional issues that are addressed in the book (e.g., greenhouse warming, ozone depletion, and declining biodiversity) are treated as part of an interacting set of environmental challenges that are likely to reach critical proportions within the life spans of most children born today.

The author's orientation is that of a conceptual "carpenter" who builds frameworks for understanding some of the momentous changes in global ecology that are underway, as well as the political and economic reforms that will be required to manage them. As such, this book is intended to aid in the reconceptualization of both problems and opportunities for environmental governance. It is future oriented but grounded in contemporary debates about environmental protection. Although based in political science, the plan of the book is multidisciplinary in design, drawing on concepts and tools from ecology, economics, law, business, sociology, philosophy, international relations, and related fields. Ethical concerns and cultural considerations are treated within the context of the continuing North–South dialogue on sustainable development.

Environmental governance has been a neglected topic. The media attention given to environmental problems has tended to emphasize catastrophic events, controversial individuals, or interest-group conflict. Telegenic stories about crises and dramatic personalities predictably tower over "visually impaired" stories about policy content, issues of process, institutional design, or incentive structures needed for cooperation. The typical reader of this book is much more likely to know something about Bhopal, Chernobyl, the *Exxon Valdez*, or the Antarctic ozone hole than about such things as environmental harmonization in world trade, the principle of common heritage, or the workings of the Global Environmental Facility. Dramatic events always appear more interesting than the complex forces and institutions that give rise to them. Open and effective governance, however, requires that people connect events with driving forces, policy content with process, and individual opinion leaders with institutions. It requires that they understand not only what is happening to the environment and why, but also the feasible policy responses and political processes needed to reverse the destruction. How members of a society organize power and authority over their lives is intimately connected with how they organize power over nature. By tying environmental improvement to the art of governing, the challenge of ecological sustainability can be seen for what it really is—a challenge to traditional notions of national security, national sovereignty, and individual freedom.

The principal thesis of this book is that global changes in ecology and in political economy (e.g., expanded cross-border trade and investment) are beginning to foster a devolution of power and authority away from the nation-state and toward greater reliance on supranational, regional, and local levels of governance. A new and more environmentally oriented world order is likely to emerge as a result, either by design or by force of circumstance. Its political institutions will be "glocal" in character, their dual nature reflecting both global and grassroots implications of a biosphere in crisis and an economy that is straining to expand world markets. While political power is likely to remain concentrated among nation-states far into the twenty-first century and perhaps beyond, the adequacy and legitimacy of the state-centric system will come under increasing attack. Rapid population growth alone may ensure that governing among nation-states becomes more complicated—particularly as tensions grow between geriatric institutions and an increasing pediatric population. Ceding some national environmental sovereignty to supranational entities and revitalized communities may encourage needed experimentation with global forms of federalism and local forms of self-reliance, but few expect the state to wither away in the process. Strong states, in fact, may be indispensable, at least initially, for achieving a politically acceptable form of global environmental governance.

Many other important arguments and theses are addressed only superficially in this book. The penalty for thinking big and "coloring outside the lines" is that comprehensive, disciplinary analysis becomes impossible. A more telling criticism of the book is that even some of the central arguments and theses are not fully developed. The conceptual frameworks are presented without detailed instructions for operation. Moreover, no formal, quantitative models are presented. To the charge of empirical "softness" the author must plead guilty, while begging the reader's indulgence. This book is not intended to be a tightly constructed, incremental addition to the technical literature on environmental politics and policy. Its aim is reconceptualization. Attention to detail and comprehensiveness are worthy goals, but their blind pursuit can interfere with the goals of discovery and understanding. To stimulate and provoke thought, it may be necessary to take risks in offending the conventional wisdom. As the American sociologist George Homans once observed: "To overcome the inertia of the human intellect, it is sometimes more important that a statement be interesting than that it be true." While this book strives for truth, it stops short of making hard evidence the arbiter of content and approach.

Plan of the Study

In the chapters that follow, every effort is made to emphasize the important environmental choices that confront the world's governments at all levels, and to examine the political and socioeconomic considerations that will be involved in making those choices. In chapter 1 the problems of global environmental change and governance are introduced, along with the concept of *glocal* design. Three ongoing and unplanned global experiments—atmospheric, biological, and political—are presented for the purpose of illustrating the basic challenges of environmental governance. Chapter 2 examines the significance and possible legacy of what are to date the two most important focusing events for global environmental action: the 1992 Earth Summit and the 1994 Cairo Conference on Population. The chapter reviews the principal achievements and failures of these meetings of world leaders, paying special attention to the policy and institutional changes that resulted and to their significance for framing future environmental negotiations and strategies. In chapter 3, a qualitative model of environmental threats and driving forces is developed for the purpose of delving deeper into the causes of the problems examined at the Earth Summit and at the Cairo Conference. Three distinct perspectives of environmental destruction are explored and then linked to a set of eight major driving forces of environmental change. The model, applied in chapter 4 to the case of greenhouse warming, is used to illustrate how each of the driving forces operates with respect to the global atmospheric experiment introduced in chapter 1. The case also demonstrates the difficulty of converting environmental science into public policy. Chapter 5 addresses the institutional and procedural obstacles that currently inhibit design, adoption, and implementation of effective environmental policies. Here the principal concern is with the *process* of international policy making. The objective is to understand how the process influences policy outcomes. To assist in this endeavor, a lifecycle model of international environmental policy making is constructed, highlighting the roles of scientists, advocacy coalitions, policy entrepreneurs, domestic political institutions, the media, and international organizations in shaping policy outcomes. The political challenge of reforming and redesigning this process is examined in chapter 6. Three major approaches are explored: (1) development of a limited world federalist system, (2) confederal reform of the United Nations and its affiliated agencies, and (3) expansion or extension of existing models of international and regional treaties and regimes. Using a "political ecology" framework, each approach is assessed for its promise of securing greater international cooperation in the face of cross-national differences in wealth, cultural values, and political and technical capacities to respond to problems. Chapter 7 provides a political economy context for evaluating how environmental needs and demands are likely to fare in a world increasingly influenced by transnational business organizations and by the global movement of capital. It reviews some of the most promising market-based measures devised thus far to improve global environmental quality. In chapter 8, the ethical requisites of global environmental governance are examined more fully, using the concepts of common property, common equity, common security, and deliberative democracy. Finally, the exercise is brought to a close in chapter 9 with an examination of three competing visions of future environmental politics—cornucopian, catastrophist, and optimizer—and their implications for environmental governance. The author's vision of a glocal society is then developed further, using the themes of ecological literacy, sustainable communities, and "earthkeeping" politics.

In attempting to capture the mixture of change and continuity that characterize global environmental politics today, this book is necessarily sweeping in its perspective. It is more than a little thin in its attention to the nuances of international environmental law, diplomacy, and regime formation. For readers in need of this understanding, I have included a short section on suggested readings, featuring works by authors who are better at bringing out this level of detail. I make no apologies for departing from the microspecialization of my academic profession. We need books about global environmental dilemmas that are interdisciplinary and future oriented, that push the boundaries of standard political and economic thinking, that focus on the institutional agents of reform, and that provide plausible models for reconceptualizing the problems and processes involved in environmental governance. If this is such a book, I have achieved what I set out to do. If not, I must share responsibility with the people listed on the following pages, all of whom influenced my thinking and forced me to discard the narrow but comfortable views that used to fortify my claims to scholarship.

Acknowledgments

Works of this kind invariably represent the intellectual gifts of many different people. I owe a special debt of gratitude to friends and colleagues who offered comments and suggestions at various stages of the manuscript preparation. Guiding members of the professoriat include Michael Black, Lynton Caldwell, John Cobb, Sheldon Kamieniecki, Tom Horan, Dan Mazmanian, Tom Rochon, Susan Sell, Burns Weston, and Ned Woodhouse. I am also indebted to many fine environmental professionals and activists who took the time to comment on portions of the manuscript and to discuss issues that needed to be addressed. Robbie Nichols offered valuable editorial advice on the first draft of the manuscript. Dianne Dillon-Ridgley provided practical insights about environmental diplomacy and helped me make the most of my role as an observer at the 1992 Earth Summit. Efforts to reconceptualize the environmental problems and opportunities addressed in this book were greatly assisted by long discussions, some beginning in the early 1970s, with John Rodman, Joan Hartmann, Paul Shepard, Frank Tugwell, Jyoti Duwadi, Nancy Atkinson, and T. Lindsay Moore, Jr., Denis Hayes, and Amory Lovins warrant special mention as sources of inspiration as well as information.

No work of this kind would be manageable without the help of some fine research assistants. Elizabeth Ng deserves to be singled out for her tireless work in tracking down leads and contributing background information and analysis. Of the many current and former students who helped shape my thinking and presentation, I give special thanks to Doris Fuchs, Daniel Press, Matthias Kaelberer, Mark Stuart, and Bill Munn. I also wish to thank Island Press' Stacye Spencer and her former colleagues, Peter Prescott and Nancy Olsen, for their fine effort and encouragement on this project. Finally, to my wife, Marilyn, goes the most heartfelt thank you of all. Her work on issues regarding women and population has greatly informed my thinking. Her uncompromising view of environmental peril has challenged my complacency. At the same time, her love and support has sustained my hope for a better world.

Environmental Governance

CHAPTER 1

Between Two Centuries

In his acceptance speech for the 1949 Nobel Prize for Literature, William Faulkner sadly observed that only one question really mattered: "When will I be blown up?" (Nobel Prize Committee, 1971: 7–8). It was a poignant moment, rich with irony and full of dark forebodings about the technologies of annihilation. Although he went on to say that humanity would somehow endure, even prevail, Faulkner's question was a haunting reminder of life's fragile hold in the atomic age.

Today we express guarded hope that the nuclear arms race that began in the middle of the twentieth century has run its course. But even as some dream about "the end of history," a new set of alarms is sounding about potentially irreversible changes in the global environment—changes that in their own way remind us of the solemn question Faulkner posed nearly forty-five years ago. Holes in the ozone layer, global climate change, swelling human population, toxic pollution, vanishing rainforests, overfishing, desertification, acid rain, mass extinction, and eroding topsoil: All are part of an interlocking set of slow-motion crises that may eventually surpass nuclear war as the most plausible threat to civilization on earth.

We live in a period of transition between two centuries—the passing one shaped largely by world wars and ensuing cold wars; the emerging one shaped principally by ecological limits, redistributive politics, and the global reach of technology. To be sure, military threats are not going to disappear, even in the face of rising global economic integration. Regional conflicts may rivet world attention for many years to come, especially if the spread of biological, chemical, and nuclear weapons threatens to expand those conflicts.[1] Still, it is conflict with Mother Nature that is most likely to erupt on a world war scale. And it is ecological thinking, not armaments, that may offer the best hope for bringing about a sustainable world peace.

As the political climate between East and West has thawed, the physical climate has shown signs of overheating. The changes that comprise the first trend give us hope that the second trend can be reversed. But setbacks in political cooperation are inevitable, and hope may be short-lived. Looming across the horizon of future environmental progress are the shadows of greed, resurgent nationalism, and ethnic unrest.[2] Extremism, both national and subnational, lurks in every corner of the globe, ready to amplify its power through modern technology. We find ourselves warily groping for more cooperation, compelled by ecological limits to rethink our economic and energy behavior, and at the same time terrorized by the ability of a single individual or small group to set fire to the paper-thin bridges of cooperation that we are building. The paradox is that as the need for global cooperation grows stronger, so does the power to prevent it.

Despite the new ecological and political realities, the search for cooperation is thwarted at every turn by interests and institutions that benefit from the accelerating struggle for advantage in material wealth and power. The world's most educated societies continue to invest their best minds in the pursuit of quarterly profits, legal sufficiency, military supremacy, and technological innovations that cater to instant gratification. Unfortunately, the priorities that guide this use of human resources, and the related consumption of natural resources, are premised on an unsustainable vision of economic growth that fails to distinguish adequately between quantitative and qualitative indicators of value. What makes the vision unsustainable is the presence of ecological limits; what perpetuates it for the time being is excessive faith in technology and the fact that ecological limits will impinge on future generations much more than they do on the present, thus shifting the burden of adjustment or deprivation to those who are now politically powerless.

Given the economists' penchant for discounting the future, the engrossment of businessmen with quarterly earnings, and politicians' preoccupation with the next election cycle, it is not surprising that modern societies are ill-prepared to resolve environmental problems that unfold over decades and even centuries. Somehow, decision-making processes must be developed that give due consideration to the long-term consequences of insatiable human wants and rising ecological needs. Institutions must be developed that enhance collective and individual capacities for deferred gratification while curbing reliance on deferred maintenance of our engineering and biological infrastructures as temporizing answers to budgetary woes. If our society fails to do this, future generations may regard our lack of ecological foresight with far less tolerance than we reserve for our own ancestors, who wiped out the buffalo and ancient forests. For unlike those who tamed and plundered the "endless" frontier, we know better; increasingly we know that ecosystems are fragile, and that our policies and lifestyles promote serious ecological risks and potentially irreversible losses, the costs of which will be shifted to those not yet born.

Unfortunately, recognizing that we leave heavy footprints on the planet has not yet convinced most of us to walk with lighter steps. Pushing back the temporal horizons that currently confine political and economic decision-making will help dispel environmental complacency, but rapid mobilization seems unlikely, given the gnawing scientific doubts that accompany many environmental fears. Right now, global environmental problems do not strike most observers as clear and present dangers, at least not to our species. The argument that environmental threats will soon loom larger than economic or military ones is simply not credible to those who remember the Great Depression, Auschwitz, or Hiroshima. So maybe there *is* an increase in future skin cancers as a result of depleted ozone; and maybe the climate *does* change in ways that cost us money and comfort; and maybe the loss of rainforests, whales, and a smog-eaten Parthenon or Sphinx *will* leave a nostalgic void from time to time. But why should we treat these environmental impacts with any greater concern than we treat the challenges of building a competitive workforce, defending democracy, or developing free and fair world trade? Why, indeed, should we act in advance of scientific confirmation that many of the feared environmental threats are real?

The answers to these questions will almost surely become clearer in the next century, but at present they leave room for much uncertainty and speculation. At stake is the planet's life-support system, which may be threatened in thousands of ways that are too subtle, silent, or fragmented to hold people's attention or to divert that attention from personal and international competition for wealth and power. One need not pander to Malthusian or apocalyptic thinking to ask in all seriousness whether the biosphere as we know it can survive another century like this one. As former Mexican president Carlos Salinas de Gortari argued, "If we don't address the issue of global ecology, we won't have to worry about the other issues" (Branigin, 1990: A18). While such views may underestimate the human ability to muddle through each new crisis and nature's ability to repair or adapt to the damage people inflict, the arguments should not be dismissed simply because they trade on fears about human survival. Survival, after all, can refer to values other than physical existence that are just as precious as life itself. Presumably, it is not biological survival of the human species that is in danger so much as it is the moral or spiritual survival of what it means to be *human* and to be part of a complex living community. We cannot count the ways in which human identity, imagination, and aesthetic appreciation depend on the richly textured landscape of nonhuman nature. What but unbridled hubris could let us think that what we consider human nature will survive if we despoil all of nonhuman nature?

Ecological estrangement of this type may contribute to the rising anomie and urban violence being reported throughout much of the world. Vivid examples can be found in the devastating riots that gripped Los Angeles in the spring of 1992. The riots may reveal almost as much about the effects of imposed isolation from nature as they do about the consequences of racial and class discrimination. Amidst the concrete rubble and smog-filled roadways of the inner city lies an ecological wasteland that contributes in subtle but profound ways to the misery of its human inhabitants. While ethnic and class polarization can rightly be said to be the proximate causes of the urban unrest, human separation from the natural world remains a hidden but potentially powerful source of despair and alienation, especially where large segments of the underclass have lost hope of finding any compensating form of material progress, religious faith, or positive cultural identity.

The events in Los Angeles may be flashpoint indicators of the fateful connection between ecological and social forms of poverty. They remind us that the twin problems of economic privation and lost biological wealth are not confined to the "Third World." Moreover, they demonstrate that the conditions that give true quality and dignity to human life are deteriorating across much of this planet in ways that reduce the survival value of our species to a matter of mere biological necessity. While continued survival as *Homo sapiens* may be possible for hundreds or thousands of more centuries, survival as moral individuals and communities— as *Homo humanus*—is already threatened by the growing amount of irreversible harm knowingly inflicted on the natural world and, by extension, on other human beings.

Designing the Future

In many ways, we are like modern-day Matthew Arnolds—wandering between two worlds, one that is dying and the other "powerless to be born" (Arnold, 1867). Societal transitions typically commence without clear destinations, or even clear departure points, and the present transition is no exception. The future we are moving toward is, in part, an echo of the past, but it is neither dictated by economic and technological determinism nor impervious to political design. In the words of John Schaar (1993):

> *The future is not some place we are going to but one we are creating. The paths to it are not found but made, and the activity of making them changes both the maker and the destination.*

This book is about the momentous political choices that will shape the environmental future of our planet and the quality of life that it makes possible. The focus is on global environmental governance and on the local political arrangements needed for its success. Global governance, as used here, does not imply centralized world government.[3] It refers instead to the people, political institutions, regimes, and nongovernmental organizations (NGOs) at all levels of public and private policy making that are collectively responsible for managing world affairs. Environmental concerns are only the latest in a series of threats to international security and development that have called attention to the potential need for laws and institutions that operate beyond the zones of sovereignty. Frank Judd, a member of the British Parliament and former Minister for Overseas Development, puts it this way:

> *The 21st century could easily see a terminal environmental and ecological crisis for humanity. The issues of resources and populations are already threatening. We probably have little more than 25 years in which to get a grip on things. Global governance is about how we effectively mobilize all those elements of society that can contribute to its organization. Formal government is part of this, but it is much wider. Parliaments, popular assemblies, NGOs, businesses, and professional associations all have a crucial part to play. So also do many other people who get together spontaneously or systematically to take control of their own lives and do something about them. Global governance embraces the whole exciting patchwork of institutions, processes, and people which together make society. (Commission on Global Governance, 1994: 3)*

Although the successful design of global environmental governance will depend a great deal on the efforts of national leaders, the design itself is likely to relegate nation states to a position of declining influence in world affairs. The principal thesis of this book is that political institutions will have to become increasingly "glocal" in design if they are to cope successfully with growing biospheric crises. Both global and local ends of the political spectrum must be strengthened in order to achieve effective environmental governance. This means that some of the environmental authority currently reserved by sovereign states may have to be redistributed to supranational entities and to local communities, simultaneously. The process through which this redistribution takes place is likely to involve some form of world or regional federalism.

The reasons for developing supranational authority are straightforward. Environmental problems are increasingly transboundary or global in scope and significance, yet governance remains sharply fragmented and territorial. Less obvious, however, are the reasons for simultaneously empowering local communities. Here, the rationale has to do with facilitating social learning about sustainable lifestyles (Milbrath, 1989), protecting the social fabric of technologically driven societies (Etzioni, 1994), and improving government performance through civic involvement (Putnam, 1993). I argue that it is only by reestablishing the primacy of community in political life that the social and environmental sensibilities needed to manage the global reach of technology and capital are likely to emerge. The ease with which billions of people can now communicate and trade with one another makes the comprehensible scale and sense of place afforded by local communities indispensable for balancing the freedom of global interaction with the responsibility of civic engagement. As explained in chapter 9, communities provide needed social "roots" for people who are increasingly preoccupied with the use of technological and economic "wings."

Global environmental protection begins at the community and bioregional level—the level where complex living systems are most interdependent and vulnerable (Orr, 1992; Sale, 1985). Local watersheds, ecosystems, and microclimatic conditions are among the primary objects of bioregional protection, and their alteration by human activities is much easier to understand from the vantage point of local communities than from the macro perspective of global ecology. Moreover, if it is true that global threats to the environment require supranational policy responses, the empowerment of local communities may provide needed checks and counterbalances to reassure citizens interested in democracy that environmental stewardship does not necessarily imply authoritarian forms of global government.

The relationship between strong communities and effective governance has been documented in numerous studies. For example, a long-term study of 20 Italian regional governments by Robert Putnam (1993) revealed a strong correlation between the development of civic community and successful government performance.[4] Northern Italian regions have much stronger traditions of citizen participation and communitarian thinking than those of southern Italy, and this civic advantage was demonstrated to be partly responsible for northern Italy's superior economic and political performance to that of the south. Previous studies of civic culture (e.g., Almond and Verba, 1965: chapter 11) have produced similar evidence showing that community participation and associational membership are important factors in developing the political trust and cooperation needed for effective democratic governance. The politics of place—that is, the conduct of public life within spatially defined communities—appears to be a powerful, albeit neglected, element in the democratic design of environmental governance. According to some observers (e.g., Kemmis, 1990), meaningful citizen empowerment and political engagement may be impossible without a community-centered sense of place.

One cannot emphasize the promise of community without noting the political and environmental risks that it raises. Without global coordination, community empowerment may simply be another term for political fragmentation. It may promote dangerous forms of parochialism and isolationism. Some forms of community life can stunt human development just as severely as disease and war. Many small, homogenous communities have been a source of debilitating conformity in times past. Often dominated by a single family or economic interest, some of these communities have allowed their natural environments to be exploited with a ruthlessness and wastefulness that exceeds, in per capita terms, the worst environmental transgressions or regulatory omissions of national governments. In the United States, many cities and counties have weaker environmental quality standards than the federal government. Similarly, in Europe and other regions, conflict over environmental protection often begins with local communities objecting to more stringent national or regional standards and programs.

The point of the community restoration argument is not that it guarantees ecological improvement; but rather that it permits rooted engagement and face-to-face deliberation of a type and scale that may foster ecological learning and, under the right conditions, adoption of more sustainable lifestyles. To be sure, the definition of community used here (and elaborated in chapter 9) does not extend to today's megacities, with their tens of millions of transient and poorly integrated inhabitants (Fuchs et al., 1994). Nor does it extend to the idea of "virtual" community, so attractive to those who use computers as the principal means of human interaction (e.g., Rheingold, 1994). From the standpoint of ecological learning, cyberspace is a poor substitute for the physical realities of community life. It consists of electronic information that is produced by remote and faceless sources that mock the politics of place. Although the potential environmental benefits of the information revolution are very impressive, the forms of human interaction inspired by this revolution may undermine the goals of community that sustain environmental action at the grassroots.

A central premise of this book is that only by linking community ecological values with democratic design of policies and markets can the goals of environmental governance be realized in a sustainable fashion. While it may be tempting, in the interest of time, to dispense with citizen education and community-based democratic deliberation and somehow construct the kind of enlightened authoritarian government that can act decisively on behalf of environmental protection and restoration, such forms of friendly "eco-fascism," in the name of sustainability, are themselves unsustainable and symptomatic of the instrumental thinking that has led to our present set of biospheric crises. If effectiveness of environmental governance depends in part on political legitimacy, then not even the most eminent and benevolent environmental scientists should be allowed to assume the role of planetary managers.

But what if it is true that democratic policy making is too incremental and cumbersome to do what is necessary, let alone sufficient, to protect a bioregion or the biosphere? Such trade-offs between legitimacy and effectiveness confound and divide environmental advocacy groups. For those who respect present boundaries of political feasibility, effective environmental governance means incremental reform of the nation-state system, perhaps leading in a century or more to some limited form of world federalism. Their radical counterparts argue that only a rapid and large-scale conversion of state-centric, military-industrial economies into global, regional, and community-based civilian economies can prevent massive eco-destruction. Roderick Nash (1989: 150), for example, argues that incremental "reform environmentalism" is worse than doing nothing because it offers only symptomatic relief, while allowing the underlying problem to fester. Occupying the middle ground are all those who believe that incrementalism is likely to operate in combination with sudden bursts of change—"punctuated equilibria" (Baumgartner and Jones, 1993: 3–24)—with the result that the huge gaps between legitimacy and effectiveness, and between environmental necessity and sufficiency, may be closed within a few decades. Regardless of who is right, however, redesign and conversion efforts are unlikely to flourish unless the values and aspirations that have guided twentieth-century development are widely reexamined in light of the unacceptable environmental costs they have created.

If the foregoing assessment of global environmental problems and response strategies is correct, future governance structures will differ appreciably from those that have been utilized until now. Major political institutions, policies, and markets will have to be deliberately altered to facilitate greater international cooperation. As noted previously, portions of sovereign state power will have to be redistributed to both ends of the governance spectrum—local and global. But what if our future history is written without "punctuation marks," except for the "period?" What if reform of environmental governance depends on gradual enlightenment and on agenda-setting events that occur too late to prevent ecological ruin?

Because of the concentrations of wealth and power lodged in the present international system, nonincremental design changes and power-sharing arrangements have little prospect in the short run of being adopted by peaceful means or in a manner that makes for sustainable outcomes. As a result, pragmatic political reformers and designers will have to overcome opposition from both the entrenched interests in the status quo and the environmental vanguards of alarmed citizens. Many environmentalists will properly point out that the scope and urgency of global environmental problems appear to demand rapid response strategies. But the basic truth is that human response rates are determined less by the need for action than by the complexity of cultural, political, and economic institutions through which action is organized. Large-scale action is constrained by the hands of history, habit, and political design.

The argument being advanced in this book is *not* that incremental action is preferred or that it will be sufficient to avert ecological disasters; it is merely that such limited action may be all that the conditions of political feasibility permit at this juncture of human history. Punctuations in the political equilibria are almost certain to occur, but their timing and direction are likely to be unpredictable and difficult for environmental reformers to manipulate. In the absence of appropriate focusing events and open policy "windows" (Kingdon, 1984: 176–178), insisting on radical departures may only strengthen the resolve of entrenched interests to stand firm in their opposition to change (Lewis, 1992: 6). As many business leaders point out (e.g., Ohmae, 1990; Schmidheiny, 1992), the sources of radical change are more likely to be found in the unintended consequences of technoscientific development and world trade than in the products of democratic deliberation about environmental protection. In fact, developments in technology and trade liberalization may have much more influence on the design of future global governance than developments in environmental awareness. The point is to make sure that strong environmental goals are harnessed to changes wrought by technological innovation and world trade. It is the effort to link environmental concern, technology, and trade that provides what is perhaps the best hope for constructing a global governance structure that will respond to emerging environmental threats before it is too late.

Global governance, in this context, clearly does not imply a unitary world government. In fact, arguments will be developed in subsequent chapters for treating global environmental problems through a combination of market-based mechanisms, worldwide atmospheric and oceanic regimes, regional trade and security regimes, a reformed United Nations, strengthened local governments, and a greatly expanded role for NGOs. The focus remains on governance because it is the deliberative mechanism or process for making authoritative political choices about the future health of our planet. The institutional structures and values used in governance will in large part determine the degree of protection reserved for ecological wealth in a rapidly changing global economy.

Clearly, the growth of regional and global markets will influence the design of future governance. But economic considerations must not be allowed to dominate political reason. As important as markets and terms of trade are in shaping future environmental conditions, they are nevertheless derivatives of politics and probably always will be. Conversely, as important as politics is in shaping markets and trade relations, it is alliances of transnational corporations that increasingly shape the distribution of political and economic power. Citizen involvement on a global scale, organized primarily at the local community level, is clearly needed to keep both forces in check. Based on the premise that there is no such thing as a free market or free trade, only designed markets and designed trade, the central question becomes how to foster cooperation within and between groups of ordinary citizens, businesses, and governments for the purpose of designing policy, institutions, and markets that will improve global environmental quality.

Having introduced the fundamental design challenges of future governance, it is important to examine more fully the environmental dilemmas that appear to make such extraordinary design efforts necessary. The climatological and biological changes that human activities have wrought are inescapably linked to the governance problems identified in the preceding discussion. Together, they constitute a set of global experiments that will shape much of the twenty-first century's environmental and political agenda. They are experiments in the interaction of human and natural systems that surpass all previous experiments in rearranging life on earth, including the combined influence of past wars. Unlike these previous tests, however, humanity cannot afford to fail in conducting its present experiments. "We have only one earth on which to experiment" (Stern, 1992: 271).

Dangerous Experiments

Our world of 5.6 billion people, perhaps soon to be 10 billion, is embarked on a precarious adventure that will test the elasticity of earth's carrying capacity.[5] Edging along the conceptual chasms that divide modern economics from ecology, it will pit human ingenuity and foresight against human greed, apathy, and procreative freedom. In the course of this adventure, human societies will complete three massive, unplanned, and unpredictable experiments—the first geophysical; the second biological; and the last political. They are unwitting experiments in the sense that they involve implicit tests of human foresight and response capacities that risk either ecological or sociopolitical ruin. The results of any one experiment could shape the quality of life on this planet for many centuries to come. The first experiment, described by the late Roger Revelle (Revelle and Suess, 1957) as a geophysical experiment of global dimensions, will test the limits of the earth's atmospheric integrity in the presence of increasing concentrations of greenhouse gases and ozone-depleting chemicals. The second experiment will test the planet's biological resiliency in the face of mounting human threats to natural diversity among species. The final experiment, a two-part test of democracy and national sovereignty, with profound implications for future environmental quality, will reveal whether science and politics can be joined democratically in the transnational management of an increasingly complex technoscientific world.

While no one really knows how any of these experiments will end, or whether the human experimenters will come to regret their involvement, it is highly probable that the preliminary results will become available within the next few decades. As a result of the geophysical experiment, we will discover whether earth's climate and its atmospheric mechanisms for filtering deadly radiation from the sun are sufficiently resilient to withstand cumulative changes in atmospheric chemistry caused by fossil fuel combustion, deforestation, agricultural expansion, and ozone-depleting chemicals. In the biological experiment, we will find out what happens to our planet's self-regulating biosphere when it is overrun by a human species with an enormous appetite for land, water, and other natural resources. From the political experiment—the one that holds the key for deciding how long and how far the other two experiments will be allowed to go—we will learn whether it is possible to reconcile political freedom and ecological sustainability in a viable form of democratic governance.

Experimenting with the Atmosphere

The preliminary results from each of these experiments, while considered ominous by many experts, are nevertheless open to wide interpretation. The global-warming debate is perhaps the best example of this. While most scientists agree that the average surface temperature of the earth has warmed roughly 0.5°C (0.9°F) during the twentieth century, and that it is likely to continue warming due to increased atmospheric concentrations of greenhouse gases, there is significant disagreement about the rate and magnitude of resulting climate changes and about their impacts on the natural world. Signals of climate change are embedded in a background of "noisy" atmospheric chemistry and physics, making accurate interpretation of subtle changes very difficult. Many scientists foresee serious consequences from greenhouse warming for food and energy production, water resources, human settlements, and the maintenance of ecosystems. These include increased frequency and severity of storms and droughts, reduced forest productivity, ocean flooding and increased saltwater intrusion in estuaries, loss of wetlands and other wildlife habitat, changes in species composition, and a myriad of other problems resulting from synergistic changes in temperature, precipitation, wind patterns, sea level, ocean currents, and cloud behavior. But other scientists counter that climate changes, if they occur at all, are likely to permit incremental adaptation without straining either human ingenuity or foresight. Some nations and world regions, they argue, will benefit from changes in climate, while those that experience net losses will find that they have plenty of time to prepare for a less favorable climate. In the long run, according to this view, technological society will prove as resilient to climate threats as the physical earth has been to the ravages of fire and ice.

But even if the greenhouse skeptics are right about the capacity of our technology to cope with changes in climate, there is strong evidence that nonhuman nature is quite vulnerable to such changes. This is the point at which the geophysical and biological experiments converge. The maximum migration rates of many plant and animal species may not be fast enough to keep pace with human alterations of climate. Many types of forest, for example, require centuries to adapt to changes in temperature and precipitation that greenhouse forces could impose in as little as three or four decades.[6] Hence, if the geophysical experiment turns out badly, it is almost certain that the biological one will, too.

The potential race between climate change and species adaptation calls attention to the fact that the near-term rate of climate change may be much more important than its long-term magnitude. In other words, sudden economic and biological dislocations caused by a rapid climatic transition may prove to be far more costly than the aggregate impacts of a much larger but slower change in climate. The Intergovernmental Panel on Climate Change (1990), a U.N.-sponsored group of prominent scientists and diplomats from over 100 nations, estimates that further increases in global mean temperature from 1° to 5°C (1.8° to 9°F) can be expected in the next century, depending on the preventive measures adopted by emitters of greenhouse gases. While the projected average temperature changes seem small relative to the daily, seasonal, and year-to-year variations in "normal" weather, the amplification of these global changes through the complex coupling of atmosphere, oceans, and lithosphere could trigger a chain of destructive climatic events that would exceed anything that life on earth has encountered during the past ten thousand years. As many environmental writers are fond of pointing out, an increase of just 2°C would mean a warmer earth than human beings have ever experienced. Jonathan Weiner, author of *The Next One Hundred Years* (1990: 8), puts it this way; "Infants born today may experience more change in their lifetimes than the planet has undergone since the birth of civilization."

Experimenting with Biodiversity

Among the most sweeping changes already being felt are changes in the planet's biological composition. Forecasts of declining biodiversity and ecological collapse brought on by growth in human population and increasing per capita consumption have, like forecasts of climate change, produced lively debate among scientists and policy makers, especially with regard to possible effects of this growth on world food supplies, water resources, and forest products. The difference, of course, is that the results of the biodiversity experiment are already widely visible (Myers, 1990).

The World Bank (1992) estimates that world population will reach 12.5 billion before stabilization is achieved nearly a century from now. Already we are adding nearly one hundred million individuals each year to our population base, most of them as infant members of a permanent underclass. While most eyes are trained on the human consequences of

poverty, pollution, and resource consumption resulting from this population growth, by far the greatest impact may be on the millions of species
with whom we share the planet.

Ecologists view the loss of natural diversity as a process of biological
erosion, in much the same way that many anthropologists view declining
cultural diversity as a loss of social wealth and a withering of the collective human imagination. Stopping or slowing biological impoverishment
requires not only the ability to identify species that are in jeopardy but
also the political will and administrative capacity to implement recovery
programs that protect them. Unfortunately, only about 1.5 million of the
estimated 10–50 million species in existence have been identified and formally named, let alone assessed for viability or offered protection (Mc-
Neely et al., 1990). Millions of undiscovered species may disappear before we can identify and study them, particularly those found in the
vanishing moist tropical forests. While the natural or background rate of
extinction for vertebrates is estimated to range from roughly 90 species
per century (Raup, 1986) to as few as perhaps a dozen species every million years (Wolf, 1987), human activities have increased the natural rate
by hundreds and perhaps thousands of times. For insect species, such as
forest beetles, the rates may be much higher. Total anthropogenic extinctions will probably pass the one million mark by the end of this century. During the next few decades, some scientists fear that as much as
25–50 percent of the earth's genetic storehouse may be destroyed (U.S.
National Science Board, 1989).

This represents an irreplaceable ecological loss, as well as a potentially
enormous economic cost in terms of medicinal drugs, biological pest
control, and sources of food and other products or services that might
have been provided by or extracted from these extinct species. Unfortunately, there is no credible way to quantify the costs involved in mass extinction. Placing a value on biological diversity is extremely difficult because of the intangibles involved and because of human ignorance about
the ecological services that such diversity provides. While economists
have attempted to measure the monetary worth of a few select diversity
factors—for example, the contribution to annual GDP of wild resources
harvested for human consumption (Prescott-Allen and Prescott-Allen,
1986)—no one can begin to place an aggregate value on the contribution
of these and other biological resources to the maintenance of ecosystems,
water cycles, soil protection, and other natural features and processes.
Even the scientific, educational, and recreational values that human beings attach to biodiversity are seldom quantifiable beyond a handful of
select species. Human societies, for whatever reasons, have chosen to
exist on an incredibly narrow genetic base. Food growers, for example,

rely on just seven of the known eighty thousand species of edible plants to feed most of the world (Tobin, 1990). Medical researchers have sampled only a tiny fraction of exotic plant species that may yield cancer-treatment substances, despite the growing threat of extinction facing many of these species and despite estimates that one out of ten will prove useful in cancer research (Wilson, 1985: 701). We simply cannot know how important it may be for our own future prospects to protect species that currently have no monetary value associated with them. Hence the economic risk of continuing the global experiment in extinction.

Beyond the economic values afforded by biodiversity, there are profound ethical and social reasons for protecting other species from the destructive impacts of human development. A reverence for other life forms, a belief in the intrinsic or "existence" value of all living or sentient beings (i.e., the right to exist independent of human notions of utility), and a deep appreciation of ecological interdependence are all examples of fundamental tenets found in many religious and cultural traditions. In most of these traditions, the desire to transcend anthropocentric boundaries is a powerful one. It involves the need to encounter life on its own terms rather than as part of a man-made environment in which even the so-called "wild" creatures are managed in accordance with the needs of scientific research, natural resource planning, park maintenance, and ecotourism. Natural diversity and nonhuman "otherness" may be bound up in some fundamental way with healthy human development, cognition, and sensory alertness (Shepard, 1978). Our very identities and sense of wholeness may depend on encounters with other life forms, encounters that make possible a clearer understanding of the place of the human self in nature. Thus, to engage in the permanent destruction of unique gene pools that have taken millions of years to develop is more than an act of hubris; it is ultimately self-destructive. It is, as Richard Tobin (1990: 14) reminds us, "the only irreversible ecological change that humans can cause."

Experimenting with Democracy

In contrast to the biological experiment, the political experiment is fundamentally concerned with endangered "species" of governments or systems of governance. It is an experiment that will test the ability of democratic processes and sovereign nations to survive in a future of fast-moving science, unforgiving technology, and global economic integration. In particular, it will test the capacity of democratic nations to resolve highly technical, transnational problems and dilemmas, without sacrificing either citizen participation or the popular belief in national autonomy. Chief among the problems and dilemmas that could under-mine both democracy and the nation-state system are the changes occurring in the global environment. The scientific complexity that colors the debate about the atmospheric and biodiversity experiments has already compounded the technocratic challenge to democratic governance featured in the political experiment. Similarly, the negotiations among nations about how to manage these experiments have focused increasing but reluctant attention on the need for some form of transnational governance. Because attempts to solve global environmental problems invariably collide with the narrow self-interests of a state-centric system, few nations are prepared to follow the logic of collective environmental action to its political conclusion. As a consequence, the tensions between global science and national politics over how to interpret and manage results from the first two experiments are almost certain to affect the results of the third.

In simplest terms, the political experiment involves an attempt to reconcile twentieth-century forms of governance with twenty-first-century environmental constraints and global market incentives. The experiment proceeds along two dimensions of choice about governance, each of which may heavily influence future environmental quality: the choice between democracy and technocracy in managing ecological risks, and the choice between national and supranational (or glocal) institutions in managing transboundary environmental problems. The first choice deals with the tensions between scientific expertise and politics in deciding how to protect the environment; the second deals with the tensions between national sovereignty and cross-national cooperation in extending that protection globally.

The Technocratic Challenge

While a larger role for science in environmental policy making will almost surely improve strategies for responding to the dangers posed by climate change, ozone loss, and mass extinctions, it may exacerbate the perceived dangers posed by technocracy. The rise of technical expertise in contemporary policy making is already a source of concern for many who fear that increasing reliance on science will undermine democracy. Their fear is not that scientists are hungry for political power, but rather that the growing complexity of economic, technological, and environmental problems will thrust experts more and more into public decision-making roles, thereby further eroding participation by uninformed or scientifically illiterate citizens. While technocracy in its crude form may be very improbable, there are subtle varieties that cannot be easily dismissed. One such form has been described by Jurgen Habermas (1971) as a "decisionistic society" in which access to expertise becomes the principal source of power for political elites. The problem with this kind of society is not that scientists replace elected representatives, but that they increasingly define the agendas and alternatives needed to govern, thereby reducing bargaining and compromise as major components of the democratic process. In the words of political scientist Frank Fischer (1990: 20), "Politicians still choose one policy option over another, but it is increasingly the experts who shape the deliberative framework within which they must choose."

Issues of global environmental change appear to be tailor-made for debates about technocracy. They are perhaps the most complex scientific and political problems that humanity has faced since the advent of atomic energy. John Kemeny, the scientist who chaired the presidential commission investigating the nuclear accident at Three Mile Island, could have just as well been investigating the greenhouse, ozone, or biodiversity problems when he concluded that Jeffersonian democracy can no longer work in an age of Big Science and untamed technology; that "it is no longer possible to muddle through. The issues we deal with do not lend themselves to that kind of treatment. . . . [T]he world has become too complex" (Kemeny, 1980).

While Kemeny's controversial views are limited to Jeffersonian democracy, some of the technical experts who have examined the interlocking nature of global environmental problems question whether any truly deliberative form of democracy is capable of responding in time to avert disaster. The atmospheric and biodiversity experiments present a formidable challenge for self-governing societies because participating citizens must not only grasp increasingly technical arguments in order to make informed decisions, but they must do so far in advance of educational feedback about the results or consequences of their decisions. In the case of greenhouse warming, climate changes that can be unambiguously linked to anthropogenic greenhouse gases may have a lag time of many decades before becoming visible. Scientists who are used to dealing with change on epic time scales are presumably in a better position to exercise foresight in such cases than are discount-driven economists, politicians, and business leaders. But as scientific expertise and technical knowledge continue to replace property and armies as bases of political power, one can expect escalating conflict between the property-rich stakeholders of the old system and the information-rich stakeholders of the new. As the planet's citizens become more sharply divided on the basis of scientific literacy, concern about global atmospheric and biological changes may also divide increasingly along the lines of the few who are literate and the many who are not. In the process, our political experimenters may record a further erosion of public faith in the ability of democratic institutions to confront issues involving high levels of scientific and technological complexity. The alternative—placing our faith in technocratic planetary managers—seems even more problematic, especially in light of previous arguments about community empowerment and glocal thinking.

The Challenge of Transnational Governance

Although democracy may survive and even thrive in future tests imposed by global environmental change, the nation-state system is likely to become increasingly endangered. In fact, the deepest and most immediate challenge posed by the political experiment is the question it raises about the concept of national sovereignty. Reliance on national boundaries, laws, and institutions for purposes of environmental management is likely to prove inadequate when so many environmental threats arise from supranational or transboundary forms of pollution, resource depletion, and "ecosimplification" (loss of ecological diversity). While it is unclear whether this may eventually lead to new supranational institutions, to some radical form of political decentralization, or to some hybrid of both (e.g., "Think globally but act locally"), there is little prospect that the nation-state system will remain unchanged. The lure of world federalism may grow in the post–Cold War world, but it is by no means inevitable or necessarily desirable. It seems much more likely that future political power, at least during the transition to something more stable, will be shared by supranational institutions, regional trading blocks, weakened national governments, and legions of enterprising community, NGO, and private-sector actors. Uncertainty about changes in politics will prove to be just as great, if not greater, than uncertainty about changes in climate or in the distribution of species. The only certitude is that national institutions will have to undergo rapid and broad transformation if sharing of power is to be encouraged and if global, regional, and local aspects of environmental protection are to be addressed through effective cooperation.

The problem of building transnational forms of governance to supplement or replace the nation-state is clearly daunting if one considers the redistribution of power and wealth that is involved. To provide the global management that is needed, the struggle for military and economic advantage among sovereign nations must be sharply limited. An atmosphere of cooperation must be cultivated that goes far beyond what has been achieved thus far by the United Nations and other prominent international institutions. Furthermore, the countermobilization of subnational political forces must be addressed and constructively channeled. To this end, the promise of small-scale community governance could be restored up to a point by encouraging more decision-making and responsibility at the local level, provided that certain national, regional, and global interests, such as ocean fisheries management, were safeguarded from parochial local actions or preemptions.

Since virtually all nations are "amateur" experimenters when it comes to designing transnational (and to some extent, subnational) institutions, even sincere efforts to manage international competition for wealth and power may turn out badly. How, for example, could transnational representation in governance be determined? By linguistic, religious, or cultural affinity? By employing natural boundaries, such as river basins, biomes, air sheds, or climate zones? By formally trying to represent the concerns of future generations? Or should criteria used in the design of present international institutions be employed, such as military might, population, wealth, territorial size, or economic development potential? After all, any agreements to build transnational regimes will presumably have to start with international negotiations that reflect the interests and power of national governments.

The changes that appear needed at the local, national, and supranational levels are unlikely to come about merely because environmental sanity invites them. Not even the efforts of Earth Day activists to create a sense of impending crisis or global catastrophe are strong enough to overcome the dead weight momentum of apathy or the entrenched interests of nationalism and consumerism. It appears that something more will be needed in order to make the global environment an integral concern of human governance; something that can harness basic concerns about individual liberty to those involving global ecology.

Redefining Freedom

Against the backdrop of the Cold War, human freedom appeared, ironically, as the protectorate of nuclear arsenals. It represented, in Isaiah Berlin's (1969: 118–172) term, a negative form of freedom—freedom from "X" (e.g., foreign domination) rather than freedom to do "Y" (e.g., to realize human potential). While the two notions of freedom may be difficult to distinguish on close inspection, they have in the past signaled an important relationship between security and liberty. "Freedom from" thinking, with its emphasis on military strength and alliances, was thought to be a necessary condition for "freedom to" thinking to flourish. Thus the United States and other industrial democracies with large defense budgets were quick to assume the responsibility for developing and preserving international freedom. Paradoxically, while government activism in foreign affairs thrived in the name of liberty, in the domestic sphere, government activism was typically viewed as the principal threat to human liberty. Domestically, "freedom from" thinking meant the absence of government constraint or intervention, while "freedom to" conceptions were tied to economic growth and, often reluctantly, to the expansion of the welfare state.

We are now moving into a period in which neither security nor liberty may be fundamentally tied to military power or even to social-welfare programs. Increasingly, ecological challenges to freedom are supplanting many of those imposed by authoritarian or intrusive governance. The coercive consequences of climate change and ecological ruin may be no less threatening in the long run than government restrictions on individual liberty. If freedom means merely the absence of government constraint, either in the form of international communism or domestic "Big Brother," then recent trends involving the collapse of communism and the decline of centralized governance (or alternatively the rise of political "gridlock") portend a future of expanding human freedom. Although regional conflicts may intensify—perhaps as a result of hegemonic decline—the overall threat to human freedom should subside under the growing influence of global markets and supranational actors, such as the United Nations. From this perspective, freedom will be secured as both a means and an end of progress. Still, the rumblings from ecology give us pause. While in the old order freedom was often defined deterministically as an aspect of social progress, in the emerging order freedom can be defined as the preservation of meaningful choice—the choice to breathe clean air, to experience wilderness, to bear children who will not overcrowd the planet. It is a freedom that fundamentally depends on the preservation of healthy ecological systems. Moreover, it is a freedom that transcends individual and national self-interest, for it implies the preservation of choice for future generations as well.

That humanity is capable of making life-enhancing choices is less in doubt than whether worsening environmental conditions permit the time that it will take to make these choices democratically. The preservation of meaningful choice implies the choice of meaningful forms of democracy, but nothing about democracy implies that people's choices will be either timely or wise. Cynics argue that nature and human nature are locked on a collision course, and that scientific progress and democratic reform will merely delay the inevitable. But such cynicism seems unduly hopeless in an era of serious ozone diplomacy, Earth Summits, and international agreements on population stabilization. People are neither the brutish atoms in collision that Hobbes lamented nor the angelic altruists portrayed by certain romanticists. Human nature is somewhat malleable, its shape determined in limited but important ways by whether the prevailing social, economic, and political systems are designed to bring out cooperation or conflict, ecological awareness or consumer fetishism.

Sustainable democracy, like sustainable development (discussed in chapter 2), will require personal and institutional changes that strengthen our capacities for both cooperation and ecological awareness. Failing to accomplish this objective will place an enormous burden on technology to succeed where reforms in politics, lifestyles, and institutions could not. Technological salvation, however, seems exceedingly doubtful. We have only to consider the unforeseen consequences of chlorofluorocarbons— once touted for their environmental virtues—as evidence of the dark shadows behind well-intended technological innovations. The quest for ecological freedom is in fact an invitation to renounce unbounded faith in technological solutions and in the ability of nature to heal itself. While new technologies will unquestionably be needed to repair or mitigate the environmental damage inflicted by old ones, it is highly improbable that advances in technology alone will be able to preserve the kind of choices that will matter most in the next century. In fact, some advances, such as genetic engineering to lengthen human life spans, may greatly reduce the important ecological choices available in the future, even as they expand individual human choices. What is needed most, therefore, in addition to environmentally safe technologies, is the ability to distinguish between choices that preserve ecological integrity and those that do not, along with the political will to pursue them.

A Thematic Roadmap

Before turning to the choices themselves, and the governing processes by which they are made, it is useful to alert the reader to what lies in store in the remainder of the book. The objective is to identify where the present themes and arguments are leading, and to foreshadow some of the conclusions that will be drawn.

For most of modern history, public policies and decisions for the protection of ecological integrity have been made by actors and institutions that were organized on the basis of cities, subnational regions, and nation-states. National conceptions of economic self-interest have largely determined the political boundaries of environmental action, while community and regional development aims have tended—in industrial societies, at least—to confine or constrict those boundaries. International environmental decision-making is a relatively recent phenomena, especially with regard to multilateral (as opposed to bilateral) agreements. It has ushered in a new era of global and regional diplomacy, but the resort to sovereign immunity by nations opposed to particular measures has greatly limited the effectiveness of the resulting agreements.

Despite these limitations, prospects for international environmental cooperation have improved rapidly in the past decade. Several widely heralded international conferences have taken place in recent years that have helped set an agenda for global environmental action. The most important of these meetings, the 1992 Earth Summit and the 1994 Cairo Conference on Population, symbolized the hopes and frustrations of global environmental thinking in the midst of a transition from a bipolar to a multipolar world. The Earth Summit represented an unprecedented effort to engage world leaders in collective action on the tightly linked problems of ecology and economic development. The Cairo Conference attempted to engage their commitments to stabilize human population growth. Together, the two conferences created the most ambitious and complex agenda for global environmental governance ever attempted. In the next chapter, we shall examine the components of that agenda, and the controversies and challenges that it continues to raise for global environmental governance. The examination, however, serves merely as a departure point for further analysis about how to move beyond these promising initial steps.

The United Nation's attempt at priming the international community to respond to environmental and population problems served mainly to call attention to the *need* for action rather than to the capacities of participating governments to act and to achieve a successful outcome through cooperation. In later chapters, the concern with global agenda setting gives way to a concern with the efficacy of policy-response strategies. A fundamental premise of this book is that present governing arrangements are wholly inadequate to meet the challenges of mounting global and regional environmental threats. These arrangements fail to structure policy responses that can overcome the legacies of colonialism, Western cultural hegemony, and the "lowest common denominator" politics of international cooperation.

Designing environmentally sustainable societies appears to require a wholesale redesign of today's governing institutions. Sweeping reform, however, will be difficult without a compelling vision of the future, together with the political "architecture" needed to support it. Much of what follows is devoted to the development and testing of such a vision, and to an examination of the political-design considerations involved in its construction. The guiding vision and the political design to implement it are presented as essential for undertaking meaningful action on global and regional environmental problems. Action, however, is contingent on knowledge. It must be driven and informed by more than vision alone. A major objective of this book is to demonstrate why the resolve to act must be accompanied by a deeper understanding of the causes of environmental destruction and by a more coherent grasp of the ethical, political, and economic forces that influence the design of institutional and policy responses. Getting the causal theory right (the subject of chapter 3) is the indispensable first step in developing successful policies and institutions. It is the basis for good design.

The emphasis on political design is meant to call attention to the role of institutions and procedures involved in making transnational environmental policy. While substantive issues are addressed throughout this book, the primary concern is with the environmental policy-making *process* and its connection with such themes as national sovereignty, democracy, civic community, "glocalism," supranational federalism, ecological learning, and the role of science in policy formation. Contemporary issues of environmental diplomacy are purposefully embedded in both empirical and normative discussions about North–South conflict, political "ecology," and international political economy. Environmental problems are treated largely as symptoms of underlying pathologies of governance and of the human values that guide it. The main assertion, once again, is that we cannot achieve environmental sustainability unless we first get our political institutions and communities in order. The fate of the polis presages the fate of the earth.

Saving the biosphere begins with restoring the ideal of civic community. Both missions require political competence. Developing political competence, however, requires a very demanding combination of knowledge, integrity, and hope. Without an informed and hopeful view of governance—one that simultaneously strengthens local and global levels of political authority—there is little prospect of dealing with transboundary environmental problems in a timely and effective manner. Establishing a competent *glocal* political order is the central challenge of environmental governance for the coming century. Unfortunately, such an order may require decades to prepare and cannot be achieved through skilled leadership alone. Public confidence in the efficacy and legitimacy of political institutions will have to be restored along the way. But how can this be accomplished?

Today, the general political outlook in much of the world is characterized by mulish cynicism and abject apathy. Meaningful choices about governance are arguably in short supply. Global thinkers, such as the world federalists, invite ridicule by cynics for their seemingly naive grasp of international politics and power. At the other extreme, radical communitarians are accused, sometimes justly, of wanting to return to the isolationist ideals of an agrarian past, one that is rooted in parochial small towns or villages. Neither end of the governance continuum commands more than a small fraction of the power wielded at its center by the nation-state. Regional arrangements, which offer many advantages over the solo operations of independent states, nevertheless remain limited by geography and by the logic of strategic state alliances. Cooperation and compliance are heavily dependent on how well the short-term self-interests of participating states are served by regional membership. Such arrangements appear to be, at best, transitional or complementary steps to a glocal political order, particularly if environmental threats are global in scope.

Regardless of whether one chooses a local, national, regional, or global framework for political design, the success of the design, democratically speaking, is manifested in its power to elicit public trust and participation. Trust and participation in environmental governance, I argue, begins at the local community level. Accordingly, a major theme of this book involves the need for an environmentally enlightened form of community empowerment. National, regional, and global political authority must be better balanced and integrated with local levels of governance. Restoring a sense of civic community, and the opportunity for democratic deliberation that it affords, is perhaps the most promising way to blunt the growing cynicism and apathy that afflict modern politics at all levels. Moreover, such communities provide a fundamental connection to the physical environment—one that could prove to be essential for developing ecological foresight and understanding.

If it is true that major, community-based political reforms will be necessary to improve and maintain global environmental health, how can the needed reforms be achieved? In the eight chapters that follow, a variety of themes and arguments will be explored in hopes of providing some answers to this question. A brief preview of the most salient of these themes and arguments may assist the reader in understanding the logic of the book's organization and contents. With that purpose in mind, I have prepared the following list of key ideas and proposed reforms, all of which are developed to varying degrees in subsequent chapters. Together, they represent a large sample of the critical design elements that I believe will be necessary for achieving effective political reform on a global basis.

Design Elements of Environmental Governance

- Better causal theories about how and why environmental destruction occurs, including theories about the influence of core human values, amplifying forces (such as population growth and modern technology), consumptive behaviors, and the driving forces of political economy

- Greater cooperation of scientists, ordinary citizens, and political leaders in bringing about the democratic conversion of environmental science into public policy

- Revitalization and empowerment of local communities, and improved understanding by citizens of the bioregions in which their communities operate

- Experimentation with limited forms of supranational federalism and other institutional reform measures to facilitate "glocal" environmental management

- Greater participation by nongovernmental organizations in the formation, implementation, and monitoring of environmental policies and programs

- Rapid development of culturally sensitive population stabilization programs and incentives, followed by programs that encourage negative population growth

- Redistribution of financial resources from industrialized to developing countries and regions through fair trade practices, government and nongovernmental aid packages, and appropriate technology transfers

- The empowerment of women through education, political participation, access to credit, reform of inheritance laws, and improved nutrition and health care

- Enhanced public-private sector cooperation in the design of "green" markets and market incentives

- Strengthened environmental regulation of world trade in order to protect threatened natural resources and major ecosystems;

- Expansion of community-based worker's rights, minimum wage provisions, environmental health and safety programs, and right-to-know laws to balance the growing power of corporate strategic alliances

- The development of a set of international norms — common heritage, equity, security, and deliberative democracy — based on an ethical framework that weaves together principles of ecological sustainability and economic sufficiency

- Educational reform and the development of ecologically literate citizens, armed with a hopeful view of the future and with an environmentally coherent understanding of human freedom, interdependence, and personal responsibility

Some readers may wonder how and why empowering women, redistributing wealth, and other such measures will improve environmental governance. The answer, in a nutshell, is that environmental governance cannot advance without simultaneous progress in the social and economic life of civil society. Those who would design planetary-management regimes without worrying about sexism, racism, and poverty may be suffering from the technocratic illusion that environmental problem solving can be separated from social problem solving; that technical know-how is more important than political legitimacy in governing the biosphere.

The design objectives for improving environmental governance are ultimately about how to bridge political authority and ecological interdependence in the service of justice and sustainability. Without a better means of social learning and political consensus, no amount of environmental handwringing will save the planet from the growing tide of humanity. While many of the design elements listed earlier require further illumination and development, they at least provide a skeletal framework of sorts for connecting the policy "parts" to the desired "whole" of governance. Regardless of their adoption feasibility or development potential today, each one deserves careful consideration under different scenarios of political and environmental change. Designing our political future will never be possible in any complete or linear sense, but that fact should not dissuade us from trying to imagine a better form of environmental governance and attempting to plan some of the major steps for achieving it.

In essence, this book attempts to expand people's sense of what is politically possible, to probe the weaknesses of the current international system, and to suggest promising alternatives that offer the possibility of sustainable living. Others have attempted this but usually with a more modest set of reforms in mind (e.g., Young, 1994; Susskind, 1994). They typically focus on incremental improvements in public education, institution building, and collective action. For example, Peter Haas, Robert Keohane, and Marc Levy (1993) argue that successful environmental governance requires three fundamental tasks: (1) increasing environmental awareness and concern, (2) increasing the political capacity to act in a timely and multilateral fashion, and (3) enhancing the contractual environment for international agreements. By political capacity they mean the availability and strength of financial, bureaucratic, technical, and educational tools of policy making, especially at the national level. The term "contractual environment" refers to the bargaining forums, diplomatic procedures, and monitoring, accounting, and verification services that facilitate making and keeping international agreements. While I regard the work of these authors as very important to the study of environmental governance, I want in my own work to look beyond the state-centric system and to challenge readers to consider more demanding political reforms and levels of environmental awareness. My argument is not only that we must be prepared to move to a glocal structure of governance, but that we must reconceptualize some of our most precious ideas and values in doing so. We must rethink what freedom means in a finite world that now adds nearly two million people (net) every week. We must reform the immensely powerful institutions that make possible the conversion of long-term ecological wealth into short-term capital. And we must rebuild the spirit of civic community on which the future of ecological learning and democratic deliberation may depend.

Notes

1. Bilateral tensions between nations such as Iran and Iraq, Pakistan and India, and North and South Korea take on much more significance as the spread of sophisticated weapons of mass destruction proceeds with the help of scientific advances and black-market sales of weapons and plutonium stockpiled in the former Soviet-bloc countries. For a discussion of the gravity of this situation, see William E. Burrows and Robert Windrem, *Critical Mass: The Dangerous Race for Superweapons in a Fragmenting World* (New York: Simon & Schuster, 1994).

2. On the issues of resurgent nationalism and ethnic unrest, see Daniel Patrick Moynihan, *Pandemonium: Ethnicity in International Politics* (New York: Oxford University Press, 1993).

3. Governance encompasses much more than the organizations we refer to as "governments. It involves the institutions and symbols that make possible collective choices about how people shall live. Some scholars (e.g., Rosenau and Czempiel, 1992) go so far as to suggest that the key to success in world politics is the development of "governance without government."

4. Robert Putnam (1993) measures civic community on the basis of membership in community organizations (sports clubs and cultural associations), preferences in voting behavior, participation in referenda, and newspaper readership. His indicators of government performance are cabinet stability,

budget promptness, breadth of statistical and information services, legislative reforms and innovations, provision of day-care centers and family clinics, industrial policy techniques, agriculture spending capacity, local health unit expenditures, housing and urban development priorities, and bureaucratic responsiveness.

5. Ecological carrying capacity is a function of at least three key factors: (1) the *assimilative* capacity of ecosystems and bioregions (e.g., the ability of marshes to absorb and break down certain harmful pollutants), (2) the *regenerative* capacity of natural systems (e.g., forest regrowth after fires), and (3) the technological expansion or *substitution effect*, whereby man-made artifacts can be used in place of damaged natural amenities (e.g., growing food hydroponically in order to cope with topsoil erosion).

6. Studies of North American forests (e.g., Zabinski and Davis, 1989) suggest that many tree species will not be able to migrate as fast as climate regimes. For a discussion of the possible impacts, see Daniel Botkin and R. A. Nisbet, "Projecting the Effects of Climate Change on Biological Diversity in Forests," in *Global Warming and Biological Diversity*, R. L. Peters and T. E. Lovejoy, eds. (New Haven, CT: Yale University Press, 1992).

CHAPTER 2

Earth Summit or Abyss?

We owe the world to be frank about what we have achieved here in Rio: Progress in many fields, too little progress in most fields, and no progress at all in some fields.

—Gro Harlem Bruntland, Prime Minister of Norway, 1992

When future environmental historians look back at the final decade of this millennium they are likely to record at least two events that were pivotal in the development of global environmental awareness: the 1992 U.N. Conference on Environment and Development and the 1994 U.N. Conference on Population and Development. The first and most important event, in terms of agenda setting, was known as the "Earth Summit." It was organized explicitly to address issues of environmental governance. The population conference devoted much less attention to environmental concerns. Both conferences, however, represented political turning points in ecological thinking.

There were of course many other focusing events in the late twentieth century that contributed to international environmental concern. Most, unlike the environment and population conferences, were neither planned nor solicited. Examples include the Chernobyl nuclear accident, African droughts and famines, ozone holes over Antarctica, the *Exxon Valdez* oil spill, the toxic calamity in Bhopal, the fiery clearing of Amazon rainforest, the ravages of acid rain on European forests and monuments, and the plight of lead-poisoned children in Silesia (Poland).

The U.N.-sponsored conferences on environment and on population were in some ways a response to the growing realization that these incidents of environmental destruction, and their interactions with demographic change, were increasing in both salience and frequency. In this chapter, we shall examine the global agenda-setting functions of these conferences, paying particular attention to the first and largest of the world meetings—the Earth Summit of 1992. Both conferences provided institutional focusing events and international policy windows through which to preview twenty-first-century issues of environmental governance. Together, they serve to frame the key dilemmas and response strategies that are now emerging from the study of international environmental politics and policy.

The Spectacle of 1992

Beset by the twin specters of too little shared development and too much shared destruction, representatives from 178 nations met in Brazil in June 1992 to outline the environmental dimensions of a new world order. Several thousand high-level delegates, including 118 heads of state and government, attended the historic meeting, dubbed the "Earth Summit." It was held, appropriately enough, in a setting renowned for its extreme ranges of wealth and topography—Rio de Janeiro. Officially known as the United Nations Conference on Environment and Development (UNCED), the two-week gathering of the world's most powerful political leaders attracted eight thousand delegates, nearly nine thousand journalists, approximately three thousand accredited observers representing nearly fourteen hundred nongovernmental organizations, and another fifteen to twenty thousand foreign visitors and nonaccredited NGO representatives who participated in the Global Forum—a series of separate meetings, exhibitions, and nonbinding negotiations timed to coincide with the official deliberations of government delegations.

Never before in history has an international conference approached in scale and in scope the dimensions of the Earth Summit. To its critics, however, few historical events can rival the Rio summit's record of timid leadership and missed opportunities, especially when measured against rising global needs and expectations. Faced with an agenda of more than one hundred environmental policy issues, more than a thousand pages of negotiating texts, and the unprecedented security requirements of the assembled presidents, prime ministers, and other VIPs, the organizers of the summit understandably wanted to be remembered more for what they overcame politically than for what they achieved in policy terms.

Twenty years earlier, the United Nations had taken the first small step in developing global environmental awareness by organizing the Stockholm Conference on the Human Environment. Its chairman, Maurice Strong of Canada, was asked to continue the skillful leadership he displayed at Stockholm by presiding over the preparations and negotiations for the Rio conference. Strong accepted the challenge with great determination to make the Earth Summit an action arena for many of the transnational ideas and policies that had failed to take root in Stockholm two decades earlier. Encouraged by the infectious optimism that followed the collapse of Cold War politics, Strong set out to make the summit a turning point in diplomatic history. What he and his staff could not foresee, however, was how quickly the political vacuum left by the breakup of the Soviet Union would be filled with ethnic strife, recessionary pressures, and an inability or unwillingness to redirect the so-called "peace dividend" to matters of social and environmental security.

An Agenda for Century 21

At the top of the summit's agenda were six key items: a "Rio Declaration" setting forth twenty-seven principles for sustainable development; a seven hundred–page, nonbinding action plan, known as "Agenda 21" (United Nations, 1992); the funding strategies and commitments required for implementation of the action plan; global treaties on climate protection and on biodiversity, and a set of proposed guidelines for forest management. While the proposed treaties attracted intense media scrutiny and generated most of the political controversy, it was the action plan and its funding obligations that drew most of the delegates' time and attention.

Agenda 21 was intended to stimulate cooperation on more than 120 separate initiatives for environmental and economic improvement, each of them commencing by the turn of the century. Having devoted forty chapters to issues ranging from soil erosion to the creation of a U.N. Commission on Sustainable Development, the action plan represented the most comprehensive framework ever devised by governments for global environmental policy making. It arrived at the summit as a controversial draft document, requiring careful negotiations to remove literally hundreds of bracketed items—words and numbers in the text identified by one or more negotiating parties as inappropriate or unacceptable. The Forest Principles alone contained seventy-three separate sets of brackets. Every chapter's finance section ("Means of Implementation") arrived bracketed because of disputes over who should pay, how much, and for how long. The entire chapter on the atmosphere was bracketed by Arab countries fearing that its repeated mention of energy conservation and renewable energy development would work against their economic interests. The chapters dealing with biodiversity and biotechnology, intergovernmental institutions, legal instruments, technology transfer, freshwater resources, and population were likewise subject to heavy bracketing. In the case of population issues (chapter 5), the Vatican successfully lobbied against a controversial provision calling for "universal access to family planning services and the provision of safe contraceptives." Direct references to family planning and contraceptives were omitted in favor of language encouraging responsible decisions about the number and spacing of children. Two years later, as we shall see later in this chapter, these controversies over language were revisited and expanded at the U.N. Conference on Population and Development in Cairo.

Despite the numerous disagreements over ideas and the wording used to express them, the delegates to the Earth Summit were ultimately able to settle most of their differences in a series of "contact group" meetings, which were arranged to give each of the parties objecting to the draft language an opportunity to work out compromises in a closed, intimate atmosphere. Not surprisingly, some very promising and environmentally needed measures were sacrificed in order to win broad agreement. The resulting final draft of the action plan, although ambitious by historical standards, contained a large gap between the language of goals and the language of implementation. The action items endorsed in the plan were actually rather tepid when measured against the needs for action identified in the conference's preparatory documents. Seasoned diplomats were not surprised by this outcome, but the disappointment among many of the environmental nongovernmental organizations was palpable. Of particular concern was the fact that political support for implementation of these measures began to wane almost before the ink had dried on the final agreement. Unlike the hopeful anticipation and momentum of "New World" thinking that carried the summit through a difficult three-year organizing process, the momentum created by the adoption of Agenda 21 was too weak to overcome the friction of rising political fragmentation and setbacks in international peacekeeping efforts. The road from Rio was plagued at the outset by cross-traffic and congestion in the form of regional conflicts and growing political upheaval in the former Soviet Union and Yugoslavia, the Middle East, Somalia, South Africa, and more than a dozen other hotspots. Moreover, the greater controversy and specificity associated with the draft climate and biodiversity treaties tended to divert media attention away from the importance of Agenda 21.

Treaty Making

The atmospheric and biological experiments introduced in chapter 1 drew their first full-fledged international policy response at Rio. The Framework Convention on Climate Change and the Convention on Biological Diversity emerged in the weeks leading up to the summit as the front-page stories of the conference. Their adoption during the final days of the meeting was hailed as the Summit's leading accomplishment. The news media covered the ratification process and the follow-on negotiations over implementation and strengthening of the conventions. The climate convention, which was signed by over 150 nations, entered into force on March 21, 1994, ninety days after its fiftieth ratification had been registered. The biodiversity convention, which was signed by 165 nations and the European Community, took effect December 29, 1993, ninety days after its thirtieth ratification. Elements of both conventions, as we shall see, provoked strong opposition from the U.S. delegation.

Climate

The climate convention's "ultimate objective" (Article 2) was the stabilization of atmospheric concentrations of greenhouse gases. As part of a framework treaty of general goals and principles, however, this objective was not tied in any direct way to the means required for its realization. Instead, each party to the convention was left to its own devices and schedule to incorporate the goal of stabilization into its policies and actions. Negotiations for climate protection took place as part of a two-step process of initial framework building, to be followed eventually by concrete policy measures known as "protocols." The framework convention's only specific action requirements (Article 4) were that all parties prepare national inventories of anthropogenic emissions, as well as contingency plans for dealing with climate change. Otherwise, the convention consisted mostly of broad pledges to control greenhouse gases; to promote international cooperation in greenhouse science, policy, and technology transfer; and to consider the impacts of various domestic policies and actions on climate stability. The convention called upon developed country parties to take the lead in adopting climate change prevention and mitigation policies. In the spirit of this treaty provision, most of the industrialized countries pledged to reduce their greenhouse gas emissions by the year 2000 to 1990 levels. The U.S. delegation, having unilaterally and successfully insisted on changes that removed targets and timetables from the convention, promised only to improve the nation's greenhouse gas abatement efforts in a voluntary, open-ended manner—a policy that was later revised and strengthened by the Clinton administration. A formal review of the adequacy of such voluntary actions was included as one of the follow-on requirements of the treaty. As with the assessment of voluntary reduction programs, most of the hard policy choices about climate change were deferred for consideration at the first meeting of the parties, which took place in Berlin during late March and early April of 1995.[1]

Biodiversity

Unlike the final text of the climate convention, the biodiversity convention stepped on political "toes" with almost reckless abandon, at least in the view of U.S. negotiators. The principal provisions of the biodiversity treaty went to the heart of sensitive land-use, biotechnology, and sovereignty issues. Foremost on the minds of environmental leaders was the provision that each party establish "in-situ" conservation measures (Article 8), including designation of protected areas and restoration of degraded ecosystems. In contrast, most of the political leaders attending the summit were more concerned about the economic implications of proposed changes in biological resource management. Although there was broad support in principle for the protection of threatened habitat, and for the regulated collection and use of genetic materials, the commercial concerns about access to—and property rights in—rare plant and animal species tended to drown out concerns about diversity and ecology. Developing countries complained bitterly that many of their unique genetic resources—especially native plants—were being exploited by biotechnology, agribusiness, and pharmaceutical firms based in developed countries, with little or no economic returns accruing to the host countries. Worse yet, some of the genetically engineered products of this exploitation (e.g., medicines and hybrid seeds) were allegedly sold at enormous profit by these firms to poor Third World residents who were being asked to forego their own development in order to preserve the genetic base for such enterprises.

Representatives of the biotechnology industry complained almost as bitterly about the efforts of developing countries to undermine intellectual property rights with respect to plant and animal materials, and to apply instead self-serving notions of sovereign control over these living materials. Led by the U.S. negotiating team, opponents of the biodiversity convention insisted that rights to intellectual property not be overridden by provisions for country-of-origin protection and technology-transfer requirements. They also insisted that the financing mechanisms for implementation of the treaty be changed to avoid the volatile situation in which simple majority rule determined how much each donor country was obligated to pay. In the end, the opposition forces were unsuccessful in removing what they perceived as fatal flaws in the treaty language, but only the United States refused to sign the convention. This created the single largest note of discord heard during the summit's proceedings. Although ostensibly the loser in the contest, the United States was widely perceived to have been victorious in removing the wind from the convention's mainsails.

The Retarding Lead

The summit and the intense preparations that preceded it could be likened to a climbing expedition in which the mountaineers, all linked by a frail rope, were forcefully confronted with the advantages and disadvantages of interdependence. Split into coalitions of the rich and the poor, the participants spent much of their time arguing about how to finance the climb and about which members were most prepared to lead. Reaching an impasse, the expedition eventually succumbed to the law of the "retarding lead," a political accommodation whereby the most cautious and powerful members got to set the pace and to determine the route to the summit.

The United States, as the lead climber, won little respect in Rio for its courage or sense of direction. President Bush arrived at the summit amidst angry and widespread criticism of his administration's opposition to binding targets and timetables for reducing greenhouse gas emissions and his previously announced refusal to sign the biodiversity treaty. Because of the White House's highly publicized positions, the United States was branded the "skunk at the picnic," out of step and out of favor with the rest of the world. But United States obstinacy was not the only drag on progress at the summit. While Bush's positions on the climate and biodiversity treaties officially isolated the United States from its traditional allies and from the other nations of the globe, there is little doubt that his administration's views were privately shared by a number of other world leaders. Part of the evidence can be seen in the meager funding commitments that many of the wealthy nations made to implement the treaties and to enact the hundreds of other provisions agreed to as part of Agenda 21. Of an estimated $600 billion per year—$125 billion in external aid—needed to carry out the global environmental actions that were endorsed in principle at Rio, less than $5 billion was pledged by the participants. By comparison, UN members were collectively spending an average of that amount every 44 hours on national military preparedness.

Many Third World representatives interpreted the lack of financial commitment by their wealthy counterparts as a sure sign that the world's economic and military powers were not about to let environmental protection become a lever for redistributing wealth. Most of them had arrived in Rio with a strong interest in improving terms of trade and securing more grants in aid, loans, and favorable foreign investment. One of their most important objectives was to persuade wealthy nations to accept a previous and largely ignored U.N.'s goal of annually transferring at least 0.7 percent of GDP to needy countries in the form of official development assistance (ODA). Some of the delegates argued that much of the increased aid could be earmarked for environmental purposes. The conference began and ended, however, with little hope that the 0.7 percent ODA goal would be met by more than a handful of donors. Only four donor countries currently meet or exceed this level of aid: Norway (1.04 percent), Sweden (0.97 percent), The Netherlands (0.94 percent), and Denmark (0.94 percent). The United States provides less than 0.2 percent of its GDP in official development assistance, placing it last among the eighteen OECD donor nations.[2]

At the Earth Summit, as in most international diplomacy, a simple (and simplistic) geopolitical distinction was used to characterize global power and wealth: the so-called "North–South" divide. The North, led by the Group of Seven (G-7) nations—United States, Japan, Germany, Britain, France, Italy, and Canada—controls most of the money and power, while the South, or G-77 nations (actually numbering over 125 countries), controls most of the people and impoverished lands. The environmental-funding implications of this division were constantly under examination at the Rio conference. The effect of the retarding lead on financial transfers from North to South was a hot issue for delegates from the South, but not everyone condemned the outcome. Some feared that aid from the North would invariably become unwanted intervention—that is, "eco-imperialism." At the same time, many delegates from the North feared that money or technology transferred to the South for environmental purposes would never reach its intended target.

Sadly, no amount of government-to-government financial assistance can guarantee that sufficient funds will trickle down through swollen bureaucracies, and in some cases kleptocracies, in order to attack the roots of poverty, overpopulation, and ecological destruction. Furthermore, even if funding targets can be reached quickly and efficiently, the provision of external funding and technology for environmental protection will often prove to be less important than internal social and policy changes, such as land reform. Cultural and religious factors may also play a decisive role. For example, the empowerment of women may provide the single most effective population-control measure in many countries.

But educating girls to the same degree as their male cohorts and extending the rights of women to own and inherit property may require domestic social and political changes that are far harder to obtain than the foreign aid needed for family planning and reproductive health programs.

The North–South Divide

If there was a singular failure of the Earth Summit that warranted gloom, it was the unwillingness of the overconsuming rich and the overpopulated poor to accept responsibility for their own contributions to global ecological destruction. Instead, they tended to blame each other. Many industrialized nations were eager to seize on Third World population growth and tropical deforestation as the critical issues of the day, while developing nations pointed accusingly at the destructive lifestyles of the rich and powerful nations of the North (Miller, 1995). Although population issues were downplayed on the official conference agenda—ostensibly to await debate in September 1994 at the International Conference on Population and Development in Cairo—they were a frequent topic of conversation in the unofficial meetings and hallway encounters that comprised much of the real business of the summit. Deforestation, on the other hand, was inserted high on the agenda by the United States just before the conference opened, thereby provoking angry responses from tropical timber-exporting countries, led by Malaysia, that succeeded eventually in blocking the U.S. proposals for action.

Placed on the defensive by population and deforestation arguments, many of the G-77 countries openly complained that the United States and some of its industrial allies were using the UNCED meetings as a way to shift attention from their own environmental failings to those of the developing countries. Malaysian Prime Minister Mahathir Mohammed (1992:B7) warned against "making the South the scapegoat for the ecological sins the North committed on the road to prosperity. . . . At Rio, the eco-imperialism of the North ought to be put to rest once and for all."

From a realist's perspective, the industrialized nations were not wrong to call attention to overpopulation, but they failed in many cases to recognize their own overpopulated condition in terms of unsustainable consumption levels. More important, they failed to address adequately the role of poverty—and their own role in perpetuating it—as a powerful driving force behind Third World population growth. In the case of deforestation, their admonitions to the Third World appeared hollow and steeped in hypocrisy. Having replaced most of their own ancient forests with tree plantations, farms, and parking lots, many industrial countries were in no position to champion forest preservation. Their cause, however legitimate, could hardly have seemed more sanctimonious.

Most Third World leaders, for their part, refused to acknowledge that government corruption and strategic neglect were rampant in many developing countries and that not all of the environmental problems of the poor could be blamed on colonial legacies or on a lack of official development assistance. Having earlier lost a bid to bypass the World Bank and International Monetary Fund for environmental funding, these leaders grudgingly approved a plan to steer funding through the Bank's Global Environmental Facility (GEF), which was established in November 1990 as a $1.3 billion pilot funding project, managed jointly by the Bank, the U.N. Environmental Program (UNEP) and the U.N. Development Program (UNDP). The GEF was expressly designed to funnel loans for combating transboundary environmental threats to the atmosphere, biodiversity, and water resources, but many Third World representatives complained that its purview was too narrow (e.g., it neglected desertification) and that its grant and concessional funding was controlled by a handful of nations from the North. Besides, they argued, the GEF's funding levels were utterly inadequate to meet present needs. In response to these concerns, the scope of the GEF was broadened to encompass additional target issues, wider national participation in decision-making, and increased funding levels. These concessions, however, were viewed by Southern delegates as being adequate.

Despite the modest steps to strengthen the GEF, delegates from North and South continued to accuse each other of manipulating the summit's agenda and proceedings for selfish purposes. Nowhere was this more apparent than in the debate over the relationship between environmental quality and economic development. Many countries in the South feared and resented the prospect that additional environmental standards would hinder or preclude their own rapid development—forever closing, perhaps, the South's opportunity to reduce the income gap with the North. In their view, only success in fostering development could encourage environmental protection. Representatives from the North countered that only by attending immediately to environmental problems could development for *both* North and South be made sustainable in the future.

For many attending the conference, the debate was fundamentally about the presumed trade-offs between international equity, environmental quality, and national development. It was not enough to examine the relationship between environment and development in the abstract, they argued, especially when that relationship varied widely with income, geographic location, and cultural characteristics. The burden of investment in environmental protection was clearly on the shoulders of the North, but the return on that investment depended in large measure on the self-control and self-denial exercised by the South in foregoing environmentally destructive forms of development.

Sustainable Development

The Earth Summit, like the Stockholm Conference of 1972, provided an international framework for action that far exceeded in scope and ambition all prior initiatives in environmental governance. It also attempted to provide a mobilizing vision and motivational ethic that would persuade billions of individuals to take more responsibility for their environmental misdeeds and to welcome, or at least tolerate, added regulation of behaviors and forms of development that were deemed incompatible with the goals of environmental protection. This combination of vision and environmental ethics, however, failed to overcome the entrenched interests of powerful political and economic institutions. In a sense, the Earth Summit represented a familiar situation in which legal frameworks for policy making were developed ahead of ethical frameworks (see chapter 8). Declarations of principles sometimes served as hollow instruments for rationalizing policy choices ex post facto rather than as ethical pillars on which to base such choices. As a consequence, the normative synthesis of environmental accountability and economic welfare that was attempted at Rio often degenerated into tiresome political and legal debates over ecology versus growth.

To the extent that any mobilizing vision and ethical framework was established, it was embodied in the principle of *sustainable development*.[3] This concept became the most popular means at Rio for weaving ethical and action goals together. Defined as development that "meets the needs of the present without compromising the ability of future generations to meet their own needs" (World Commission on Environment and Development, 1987: 8), sustainable development became the dominant theme of the summit from its very inception. It represented a politically expedient compromise between the forces of economic growth and those of environmental protection. Environmentalists enthused over the word *sustainable*, while many business and government leaders praised *development* as the final word. However awkward the pairing of these words may have seemed, their combination signified a rare convergence in ecological and

economic thinking. Agenda 21 represented the most striking manifestation of this convergence, but there were many other programs and policies that emerged with sustainable development as their professed goal.

The concept of sustainable development is based on the belief that
human progress must conform to basic ecological precepts and human
needs in order to endure. All of the world's microchips, space shuttles,
and breakthroughs in biotechnology cannot replace sustainability as the
ultimate measure of progress. Like the idea of progress, however, the
concept of sustainability suffers from a certain confusion of ends and
means. Just as it is appropriate to ask "progress for whom and for what
end?", it seems fitting to question whether sustainability is truly an end
or merely a necessary means to some higher end. Sustainability, after all,
can imply the continuation of societies, beliefs, and practices that are un-
just or incompatible with other cherished values. For example, some have
questioned whether a consumer society is, or should be, sustainable
(Ekins, 1991). Even ecological sustainability is problematic. For example,
sustaining a healthy lake as a stable aquatic ecosystem means reversing
the natural process of eutrophication that slowly turns lakes into marshes,
and marshes into forests.

Part of what makes an individual's life precious is the knowledge that it
is unsustainable. The same is true, ultimately, of the biosphere and its
collective forms of life. Science teaches that neither living species nor the
earth itself are permanent fixtures, at least not when considered in terms
of geological time. From rainbows to breathtaking sunsets, what gives
poignancy to beauty is the knowledge that it seldom lasts. What must be
sustained is the biogeochemical system that generates such beauty.
Hence, the object of sustainability thinking is not preservation or en-
durance so much as it is *wholeness*. Sustainability is ultimately about ideas
and forms of human organization that cohere ecologically and that do
not require linear notions of time for their validation—only a deep sense
of harmony and connectedness. By providing the organizing framework
for this sense to develop, sustainable development and, better yet, sustainable *communities* (described in chapter 9) offer a means of collective
hope and transcendence that help make the personal sacrifices required
for future environmental improvement more worthwhile.

This sounds good, but skeptics may point out that sustainability thinking can be carried too far, at least from the perspective of planetary stewardship. If sustainable development is an end, rather than a means, of
ecological survival, what objection can there be to proposals to eventually
abandon a ruined earth in favor of space colonies that re-create nature's
vital amenities in a "can."[4] Man-made environments, after all, may per-

mit consumer societies to flourish long after earth has ceased to support complex life-forms. Technological prowess of this type may even invite environmental deterioration on earth in the expectation that options for artificial life-support systems will develop. Biosphere II, a U.S. experiment in developing artificial, self-sustaining microenvironments, appears from this perspective to be a sophisticated step in the direction of sustainable development.[5]

Despite all of these concerns and considerations, sustainable development emerged from the Earth Summit with a large following in the international diplomatic community. Although the term is viewed by many environmentalists as an oxymoron, sustainable development need not imply an end to entropy or the acceptance of limitless material growth. It can be contrasted quite nicely with the "development-as-destruction" process that has in the past devoured nature's capital in order to produce fleeting forms of man-made capital. As with the postmaterialist notion of progress, sustainable development refers to development that is largely qualitative or self-limiting in nature. It can conceivably encompass most of the important objectives of global environmental governance. And despite suffering from abstraction and oversimplification in day-to-day usage, it offers a useful bridge for connecting environmental concerns with social and economic well-being. It also promotes a much needed reconceptualization of the traditional goals of economic growth, national security, and human freedom in light of the interests of future generations. To be truly sustainable, however, development must satisfy more than these goals. It must also attend to issues of social and cultural diversity and the trade-offs that they imply between different forms of sustainability.

Participants at the Earth Summit engaged in sometimes heated debate about how to make sustainable development a concept that had real meaning across different cultures and perspectives on human–environmental improvement. At least four types of sustainability were given consideration: environmental, social, cultural, and economic. *Environmental* sustainability requires that industrial and agricultural development conform to the expandable but limited carrying capacities of biotic communities. *Social* sustainability requires that just and informed citizens participate in the governance and improvement of human communities. *Cultural* sustainability requires that people partake of the educational and social opportunities inherent in a multicultural, multilingual world, while respecting and tolerating, up to a point, its political and ethical differences. Finally, *economic* sustainability requires that environmental costs be included in consumer prices and that wealth be shared more equitably.

Just as development cannot be sustained without environmental progress, prosperity for the rich may not be sustainable without the progress of the poor.

These notions of sustainability are merely a starting place for guiding environmental action. Skeptics question how such lofty ideals can be operationalized or made politically feasible. They should be reminded, however, that the ideals sketched in Rio represented attempts at reconceptualization, not prediction. The only thing harder than forging international consensus around such ideals is developing adequate environmental protection in their absence. Fortunately, an initial framework for global environmental action is now in place, thanks to the Earth Summit. What remains to be seen is whether the summit's organizing principle of sustainable development can imbue the actions pledged at Rio with elements of personal responsibility and social commitment. Anything less could make the substantial political progress represented by Agenda 21 and its companion agreements a hollow achievement of what is necessary, not what is sufficient.

Assessing the Summit's Success

Like the famous Stockholm conference of 1972, the Rio summit was supposed to inaugurate a new era of international ecological responsibility. It was to have marked not only the end of a negotiating process and the beginning of an implementation process, but also the start of a global transition to a new century of sustainable development. Predictably, much of what the environmental community hoped for did not materialize. In part this was a result of greed and of the recalcitrant leadership style displayed at the summit by the United States and some of its key allies. But there were other important reasons. First, the timing of the summit left much to be desired, what with an American presidential election looming, a far-reaching recession underway, and the rise of "donor fatigue" gripping many wealthy nations as a result of simultaneous efforts to underwrite the 1991 Gulf War, to address Third World poverty and disaster relief, and to rebuild the Eastern European and former Soviet economies. Other reasons for stunted progress can be attributed to the scientific uncertainty that permeated key UNCED debates about climate protection and biodiversity, and the diverting clash that occurred between North and South over the "side issues" of fair trade and development assistance. Perhaps the most important reason, however, stemmed from the difficulty of addressing global problems through international coalitions. In a world divided into nearly two-hundred sovereign nations, environmental cooperation is clearly limited by what political scientists call the "complexity of joint action" and the "lowest common denominator" (LCD) effect.[6] The joint action problem arises in decision processes that involve multiple veto points or "clearances." Generally speaking, the more clearances, the less chance of meaningful agreement or of successful implementation. The LCD effect typically results from efforts to avoid the joint action problem by designing compromises based on the demands of the least supportive party to a negotiation—that is, by finding what is acceptable to the party most unwilling to bargain.

To those alarmed about the state of the global environment, the summit in Brazil seemed to confirm the political axiom that time is short and change slow. For a planet sorely in need of a giant leap for ecology and mankind, the summit provided only a small step. While radical environmentalists complained that a small step was politically worse than no step at all, moderates argued that the symbolic importance of the summit vastly outweighed the lackluster achievements of the participating government leaders and delegations. Some, such as Lester Brown of the Worldwatch Institute, predicted that the summit and what it symbolized would some day be remembered as a critical turning point in international efforts to balance ecological and development concerns. Meanwhile, seasoned diplomats argued that any immediate claims or predictions about success or failure would be premature. As Geoffrey Palmer, former prime minister of New Zealand, remarked, "It will take at least five years to find out if what was said at UNCED, or left unsaid, will make any real difference to the world" (Palmer, 1992b).

Ultimately, judgments about what was accomplished in Rio depend to a large degree on whether the summit is viewed as an event or as a process. As an event, the summit can be seen as a spectacle of political posturing and "photo-ops" designed to divert attention from the weak and underfunded treaties that it produced. As a process, however, the summit offers a much more hopeful image. From this vantage point the most important achievements of UNCED were not the treaties or what they symbolized, but rather the framework for action that was provided by Agenda 21. Out of the deliberations that led to the action plan came new institutions, policy proposals, and financing mechanisms that will provide a much surer footing for future environmental governance. Most notable, perhaps, was the agreement calling for establishment of a UN Commission on Sustainable Development (CSD) to provide a new oversight and coordination mechanism for implementation of Agenda 21. Composed of representatives from fifty-three nations, the commission was formally established in New York in February 1993 to monitor progress on the agreements reached in Rio and to report their findings to the U.N.'s Economic and Social Council (ECOSOC). Although currently short on power and funding, the commission may someday emerge as a major instrument in the redesign of global and regional environmental governance.

Another important accomplishment of the summit was the expansion of environmental knowledge that resulted from the extensive preparations for the summit. In addition to dozens of international studies about climate change, habitat loss, and other key issues, more than 140 national reports on the state of the environment were prepared for the conference. Even more importantly, the UNCED process mobilized and expanded a worldwide network of environmental organizations and individuals who are likely to play pivotal roles in future global monitoring and political action. Confronted with the growing incapacity of governments to resolve many environmental dilemmas, representatives of private and nonprofit organizations observing the summit vowed to pick up the slack left by government negotiators, finance ministers, and complacent heads of state. Several thousand of these representatives participated in the "NGO Forum," a shadow summit of sorts, in which they negotiated unofficial treaties and strategies that mirrored the deliberations, but not the results, of their government counterparts. Many others staffed exhibits and information booths at the Global Forum. There, amidst the carnival acts, prophets of Armageddon, and environmentally correct T-shirt salesmen, they engaged in what may have been the most productive business of the entire summit: connecting environmental activists and entrepreneurs with networking organizations, exchanging ideas and strategies for mobilizing political action, and renewing faith among members of grassroots environmental groups that environmental protection was a cause worth dedicating one's life to. Perhaps the best expression of the idealism of these NGO participants could be seen in the dozens of banners they paraded through the streets of Rio proclaiming, in Gandhi's words, "If the people will lead, the leaders will follow."

By fostering thousands of personal contacts and the cross-national and cross-cultural sharing of environmental perspectives, the Earth Summit contributed vitally to improved understanding of the diverse opinions that currently divide the world community and impede environmental cooperation. The debate and discussion that took place along the way energized global environmental thinking to a greater degree than ever before. Temperate and tropical, rich and poor, male and female, and black, white, brown, and red—each perspective or voice reminded all who would listen that while the world was now ecologically indivisible, it remained highly fragmented with respect to politics and human values.

The Cairo Conference

Following close on the heels of the Earth Summit was another global summit of sorts: the 1994 International Conference on Population and Development (ICPD) in Cairo. Evidence of political and cultural fragmentation following the Earth Summit did not deter many environmental activists from transferring their hopes to the Cairo Conference as a vehicle for restoring global momentum on environmental issues. Many environmentalists, especially those from the North, regarded overpopulation as the leading cause of environmental destruction around the world. They hoped that the lack of emphasis on population stabilization at the Earth Summit would be more than compensated by the issue's commanding presence in Cairo. Envisioning the ICPD as a policy springboard for action on a host of population-related problems, they were anxious to find in Cairo the global consensus that had eluded them in Rio.

Arguments about overpopulation are easy to grasp statistically but much harder to interpret socially, politically, and environmentally. We know that world population has grown more in the last 4 years than it did in the first 400,000 years of *Homo sapiens* existence, but the uneven distribution of this growth has led to conflicting views about growth-induced environmental impacts. Over 90 percent of this growth is taking place in countries that collectively account for less than 20 percent of the world's monetary wealth. As noted earlier, the South has justifiably complained that per capita consumption rates among the rich are more reliable indicators of many types of environmental destruction than aggregate population growth among the poor. In other words, rapid population growth in developing countries appears to be less damaging than slow to moderate population growth in industrialized nations. While the strength of these arguments and their influence on global environmental thinking will be examined in the next chapter, it is sufficient for the time being to observe how the Cairo Conference helped frame these arguments and how the resulting program of action has served to link the roads from Rio and from Cairo.

The third in a decennial series of U.N. population conferences, the Cairo ICPD represented the first time that a major international meeting on population issues produced strong and widespread agreement on all but a few controversial measures. Previous international meetings in Bucharest (1974) and Mexico City (1984) had resulted in weak international commitments to develop family-planning programs and related population stabilization measures. Because of their opposition to abortion, the use of contraceptives, and the rhetoric of population "control" carelessly proclaimed by many industrialized nations, the Vatican and various developing and communist nations insisted on compromise language in each of the prior conference agreements. In the case of the Bucharest meetings, a coalition of the Vatican and Soviet-bloc countries managed to prevent many promising stabilization measures from reaching the final agenda. In Mexico City, the U.S. delegation, following the lead of President Ronald Reagan, downplayed the importance of population growth and refused to assist in funding family-planning programs that included abortion services. By the time the Cairo Conference opened, a new opposition coalition had formed between the Vatican and fundamentalist Islamic nations—one that promised to re-create many of the impasses encountered in previous meetings and negotiations.

Despite sometimes fierce opposition, however, the Cairo Conference managed to build bridges over many of the obstacles that had proven to be insurmountable in Bucharest and Mexico City. Its sixteen-chapter Program of Action went far beyond earlier action programs and population policies. For one thing, the Cairo Conference changed the framework of debate from conventional issues of family planning to broader questions of reproductive health, empowerment of women, and integration of population policy with environmental policy and development strategies. Although the Vatican initially succeeded with the news media in portraying the conference as a summit on abortion, most of the delegates firmly rejected this characterization and formed large informal coalitions to demonstrate how isolated the Holy See and its allies had become. Members of the Women's Caucus, many of them veterans of the Earth Summit, lobbied aggressively at the three preparatory meetings and at the conference itself to pressure delegates into supporting reproductive health and women's empowerment themes as the overriding issues of the conference.

Despite threats of terrorism and sabotage from fundamentalist Islamic groups, the conference ended peacefully and productively on September 13, 1994. Representatives from 183 nations declared their consent (some with reservations) to a program of action that aimed to stabilize human population by the year 2020, to provide greater equality for women, along with improved reproductive health care, and to address seriously the issues of migration, family reunification, AIDS, and teenage sexuality as part of global population policy. Maher Mahran, Egypt's population minister and an obstetrician by training, noting that he had never been involved in such "a difficult and protracted delivery," joined Nafis Sadik, U.N. undersecretary in charge of population programs, in declaring the conference the most successful international meeting in U.N. history.

In contrast to the Rio experience, most of the five thousand NGO representatives attending the conference voiced enthusiasm for what had been accomplished. Adding to their enthusiasm were announcements by many of the donor countries—especially the United States, Germany, and Japan—that they would substantially increase their funding for population programs.[7] Unlike the hundreds of billions of dollars needed annually to implement Agenda 21, the population forces at Cairo estimated that only $17.5–21.7 billion would be needed to implement the ICPD program of action. Although few of the donor countries had made any progress following Rio in meeting the U.N. target for official development assistance—0.7 percent of GNP—the goal was nevertheless reaffirmed by many of the participants at Cairo.

For all of its success and sense of accomplishment, the ICPD, like the Earth Summit, largely failed to integrate demographic, environmental, and economic development issues. Many of the environmental activists participating in the Cairo Conference complained that their issues were slighted or even ignored in the battle over abortion issues and in the effort to reach consensus on population stabilization. The Indian delegation, for example, opposed making any environmental connections at the Cairo Conference on the grounds that such linkages had presumably been explored at the Earth Summit. They, like many other developing countries, urged that the goal of equitable development be the sole standard for measuring progress in population matters. Environmental NGOs quickly became aware that most of the ICPD delegates viewed rapid population growth foremost as a social and economic problem.

But as one environmental participant noted, the environmental benefits of population stabilization occur whether or not there is an explicit recognition of their linkage. The real challenge was to ensure that Cairo's program of action, like Rio's Agenda 21, would receive affirmation from domestic policy groups and finance ministers back home.

That environmental issues sometimes got lost in the debate was not in itself evidence that the international policy agenda has become overloaded; only that some compartmentalization is necessary when dealing with huge, multifaceted problems. Most of the ICPD participants understood that solutions to one problem (e.g., deforestation) depended heavily on progress toward solving another (e.g., migration). For women's groups in particular, the key to both environmental protection and population stabilization lay in the empowerment of women. At the Cairo Conference, they made this point strongly, although somewhat elliptically in the case of environmental protection. Many hoped that the fourth world conference on the status of women, held in Beijing twelve months later, would solidify and clarify their position.

The ICPD represented an important step in a sometimes controversial U.N. strategy for building a new world order. The success of the strategy depended on the successful linkage of issues about environment, population, development, the empowerment of women, and human rights. The Earth Summit provided the foundation on which to build international consensus for the first link in the strategy: environment and development. The World Population Conference in Cairo, the World Human Rights Conference in Vienna (June 1993), the World Social Development Summit in Copenhagen (March 1995), and the World Conference on Women in Beijing (September 1995) were designed to connect the remaining themes of reproductive responsibility, social equity, and women's empowerment with the ideal of a world order based on sustainable, just, and democratic development. To the degree that the environment–population–development linkage was poorly drawn at Rio and Cairo, the U.N. strategy was rendered weak at its base. That it was developed at all, however, marked a major turning point in international policy making.

Conclusion

In weighing the Earth Summit and the Cairo Conference symbolic accomplishments against the inadequate policies that emerged from the deliberations, it is tempting to declare victory for form over substance, political summitry over ecological sufficiency. If history is a useful guide, however, the real accomplishments of these meetings are still quietly emerging in the form of enabling institutions and strengthened environmental coalitions that can prepare the way for genuine policy reforms to follow. Women activists from all over the world used the Rio and Cairo Cons as forums for empowerment. The passion and commitment generated by their experience are unlikely to permit a return to the *status quo ante*. In general, the same can be said for NGO participants, many of whom recognized the growing opportunity to supplement and to help steer government programs in these issue areas. Even the hard-bitten critics of the U.N. conferences granted that some progress was achieved.

Unfortunately, plodding progress is not satisfying if a perception of crisis dictates that only sweeping transformation will suffice to resolve the problem. Many environmentalists, ambivalent about the progress they observed, left Rio and Cairo convinced that the conferences' legacy would prove to be "too little, too late." They bemoaned the fact that so many of the participating nations remained mired in incremental, Cold War thinking, seemingly unable to grasp the new risks and opportunities inherent in an interdependent world.

If meager progress in global environmental thinking is indeed an accurate characterization of high-profile conferences like these, then it behooves us to probe beneath the surface of international diplomacy and to examine the fundamental interests, beliefs, and assumptions that underlie the positions of the negotiators and their governments. How they define and rank environmental problems and what kind of causal theory, if any, they employ to explain these problems and to prescribe remedies are critical questions in need of further study. In the chapters that follow, these questions are systematically addressed in order to isolate the key causal factors and problem-solving orientations involved in environmental policy making. Whatever failures can be attributed to the Earth Summit and to the ICPD must be explained in these terms before we can hope to design a system of governance that will overcome them.

Notes

1. The Berlin conference failed to reach consensus on proposals for strict abatement targets and timetables. The delegates agreed, however, that specific targets and timetables for industrialized countries would be part of binding negotiations to be completed by 1997.

2. For a summary of official development assistance and external debt indicators for 152 nations, see *World Resources 1994–95: A Report by The World Resources Institute* (New York: Oxford University Press, 1994), pp. 258–259.

3. The principle, which was introduced in the International Union for the Conservation of Nature's (IUCN) 1980 *World Conservation Strategy*, was later given prominence in the Brundtland Commission's report, *Our Common Future* (World Commission on Environment and Development, 1987).

4. See, for example, Freeman Dyson, *Disturbing the Universe* (New York: Harper & Row, 1979); Louis J. Halle, "A Hopeful Future for Mankind," *Foreign Affairs* Summer 1980, pp. 1129–1136; and Gerard K. O'Neill, *The High Frontier: Human Colonies in Space* (New York: Morrow, 1977).

5. A controversial experiment in a remote area of Arizona, Biosphere II consists of a hermetically sealed, mostly self-regulating, artificial environment in which teams of researchers living for long periods in association with selected plants and animals attempt to maintain in partial equilibrium a microcosm of selected natural ecosystems and renewable resources for food and energy.

6. For a detailed case-study analysis of "complexity of joint action" problems, see Jeffrey L. Pressman and Aaron Wildavsky, *Implementation* (Berkeley: University of California Press, 3d. ed. 1984). For analysis of lowest-common denominator effects, see the literature on international environmental

veto coalitions and bargaining strategies (e.g., Porter and Brown, 1991; Sebenius, 1984; Young, 1989).

7. As a result of agreements reached in Cairo, the United States pledged to triple its funding for population-related programs. The Clinton administration requested $585 million in fiscal 1995 for family-planning and reproductive health programs alone. Germany pledged a total of $2 billion over seven years (averaging about $280 million per year). This represented a six-fold increase over its 1990 spending levels. Japan pledged to spend $8 billion over seven years on a broad package of population programs, representing a ten-fold increase over its preconference level.

CHAPTER 3

Causes of
Environmental Destruction

The initiatives taken at the Earth Summit and at the International Conference on Population and Development represented real progress in focusing global attention on the interactive nature of environmental problems. They did not, however, go very far in exposing the root causes of those problems. For that reason, many of the initiatives offered only superficial or temporary relief from the environmental threats they were meant to contain.

This chapter examines the causal relationships that underlie global environmental threats and the way in which those threats are defined for policy-making purposes. It does this with the aid of a qualitative model of environmental driving forces. The purpose of the model is to identify the human values, consumptive behaviors, growth factors, and institutional structures that result in environmental destruction, and to explain systematically how they interact in the framing of environmental policy issues. Competing environmental perspectives and problem definitions are explored in order to reveal important gaps in the causal theories that underlie many of today's environmental controversies. The objective is to probe perspectives and theories of causation that are influential in the design and development of environmental policy. A better understanding of causation is treated as fundamental to improving environmental governance.

Stepping back from the fray of international negotiation described in the previous chapter, this chapter calls attention to the hidden but powerful assumptions and predispositions that ultimately shape international agreements such as those reached in Rio and Cairo. By constructing an analytical framework for tracing the human causes of environmental destruction, we can better illuminate how attitudes and beliefs about nature, posterity, consumption, reproduction, technology, and wealth have steered and conditioned global environmental thought. We can also better appreciate how fundamental and widespread these attitudes and beliefs really are. Rather than attributing environmental destruction to the actions of a relatively small number of thoughtless and careless individuals, or to some passing phase of industrial recklessness that accompanies an otherwise benign evolutionary process of economic development, the destruction described here is attributed to driving forces that are pervasive, persistent, and deeply ingrained in our values, lifestyles, and institutions.

Framing the Problem

In elevating an environmental condition to the status of a problem, scientists, policy makers, and ordinary citizens typically construct their diagnoses or definitions on a foundation of preconceptions and predispositions that direct their attention to particular factors of causation, change, and response. As Ralph Waldo Emerson noted, we see what our experience has prepared us to see. In the case of environmental science, as Thomas Kuhn (1962) might say, we see what our textbooks have prepared us to see. Thus environmental problems are not just naturally revealed, they are—like conceptions of wealth, knowledge, and politics—socially constructed. For policy makers, the construction typically represents a crude translation of ecology into economics. For deep ecologists, it may represent a conversion of the language of ecology into that of bioethics and philosophy. Human biases influence this process of definition just as surely as words in English add and lose meaning when they are translated into Japanese.

The definition of environmental problems takes place within conceptual frameworks that draw attention to certain features and neglect or exclude others. Like premises that are selected to yield a desired conclusion, the nature and causes of environmental destruction are often defined to yield political advantage for one idea or group over another. To the extent that this is a conscious intent, we can speak of strategic definition or selective interpretation, especially by those who have a favored or "pet" solution and merely need to find the right kind of environmental problem to which it can be attached.[1] Economists, for example, who favor market-based solutions to environmental problems, typically view environmental damage as a result of externalities (unpriced pollution) and other sources of market distortion. By contrast, engineers, who see the damage as a consequence of inadequate systems planning and design; tend to define environmental problems in ways that call for technological fixes. Engineers typically trace the source of the problem to technical design flaws, such as improper sizing, placement, or coupling of waste-processing technology. Other perspectives, such as those of certain religious traditions, regard environmental destruction as indicative of ethical shortcomings or as a symptom of a spiritual malaise that robs human beings of a proper sense of connection with nonhuman nature. Religious conversion or closer observance of religious custom, according to this view, is the most effective response.

The economist, engineer, and religious leader may all observe the same condition; but in defining it as a problem, each tends to approach it differently and to assign it a different root cause. Within each group, a form of consensual knowledge has been achieved that gives direction and purpose to those who share it.[2] Group consensus represents much more than agreement about the basic facts or principles by which the world can be understood; it represents a shared set of core values that influence what count as facts and what count as valid conclusions from those facts (or from *faith*, in the case of religious leaders). Hence, when examining the prospects for global environmental protection, it is helpful to start with an analysis of the different problem definitions and causal models that are employed by major environmental actors and institutions. In this way, the differences that separate key participants in the policy process will become clearer and their grounds for disagreement more understandable.

We shall begin by exploring three overlapping definitions or perspectives of environmental destruction, each focusing on a particular aspect of the problem—contamination (pollution), simplification (lost complexity), and natural resource depletion (consumption). Each definition will then be examined in terms of its implied causal relationships. While it is easy to stretch each of the definitions to in some way encompass major features of the other two, important differences in emphasis remain. Each interpretation or perspective rests on a different notion of human responsibility for environmental changes. Examining them more closely will reveal why such differences matter.

The Contamination Perspective

Many people believe that environmental problems are nothing more than problems of pollution. Pollution, in turn, is usually defined as a process of biochemical contamination. Destruction according to this view arises from a failure to control harmful by-products of human activity. As John Rodman (1983) has observed, there is a popular tendency to divide actions affecting nature into two categories: clean and dirty. Pollution is harmful because it is "dirty"—it represents a defiling of nature. In fact, people from Judeo-Christian backgrounds who build their environmental understanding around this definition often view history as a tragic process in which the Garden of Eden is systematically despoiled. Formerly pristine forests, lakes, and wetlands have slowly been transformed by human activity into repositories for toxic chemicals. From contaminated water, air, or soil to traces of DDT in mother's milk, little in nature remains pure in the face of agricultural and industrial development. The atmospheric experiment introduced in chapter 1 is merely the latest and most globally significant example of this pollution process.

Because images of contamination tend to dominate all other conceptions of environmental deterioration, the most common prescription for improving environmental quality amounts to setting up "poison-control" centers to combat the waste products and invisible impurities of modern civilization. Such diverse problems as acid rain, radiation from nuclear waste, toxic chemicals in groundwater, urban smog, and pesticide residues in food all contribute to the perception that environmental protection is simply a matter of preventing pollution. Where pollution has already occurred, cleanup is the answer. Human responsibility essentially ends with pollution control.

In practice, the prevention and mitigation of pollution is driven primarily by human health concerns. Protecting the integrity of ecosystems is at best a secondary consideration in most pollution-control programs. Habitat protection cannot compete successfully with health and safety concerns for the simple reason that the political legitimacy of pollution-fighting programs is heavily reliant on their perceived role in preventing human cancers and birth defects. Although human health is ultimately dependent on the health of ecological systems, the pollution-fighter mentality stresses the self-destructive aspects of contamination taking place in human communities. "Fouling the nest" is a common metaphor used to describe this process, usually without apparent awareness that the metaphor implies a concern for nonhuman subjects. To the extent that ecosystems do become the subject of pollution-control efforts, it is usually because of their utility as early-warning systems of contamination threats to human health, or at least to human aesthetics. Like the coal miner's canary, their value is largely instrumental.

The Eco-Simplification Perspective

The second effort to define environmental destruction focuses on the process of homogenization and simplification in naturally complex ecosystems. Environmental damage from this perspective is largely a matter of lost biological diversity arising from the expansion of human settlements and development activities, as in the biological experiment introduced in chapter 1. The level of complexity, not contamination, is thus the principal indicator of damage to be employed. Those who base their environmental prescriptions on this definition certainly would not deny that environmental contamination is a problem, but they argue that the prominence it receives in public discussion diverts us from the more important problem of lost diversity in what are necessarily complex ecosystems governed by intricate food webs and energy flows.

For ecologists, an ecosystem requires more than an absence of pollution in order to be "pure" or unspoiled. In their view, the preoccupation with clean versus dirty masks what may be an even more important dichotomy for understanding environmental problems: simple versus complex. The world's natural diversity, they argue, is being rapidly destroyed by a combination of technological, demographic, and economic forces that are eroding complex forms of social and biological community and replacing them with relatively simple, homogenized forms of existence. For ecologists, the loss of natural diversity is a process of biological erosion and impoverishment in much the same way that declining cultural diversity represents for many anthropologists a loss of social wealth and collective human imagination. The leading indicators of biological erosion are the soaring numbers of threatened and endangered species that are being identified by scientists. Anthropogenic extinctions of five hundred thousand to two million species may occur by the end of this century (U.S. Council on Environmental Quality, 1980:37).

The "biodiversity" problem, as it has come to be known, is perhaps better understood as the "habitat" problem. Although trade in endangered species, sport hunting, overfishing and harvesting, and toxic pollution have all played significant roles in increasing the natural extinction rates of various species, it is the destruction of species' habitat by the spread of human development, especially agriculture impinging on forests, that accounts for the most profound losses in biodiversity. Tropical deforestation alone accounts for the loss of up to six thousand species a year—ten thousand times greater than natural extinction rates at the dawn of humankind (Wilson, 1989: 111). Globally, the rate of extinction is likely to be about fifty thousand species a year for the next two decades (Raven, 1994: 6). Although it may be a critical factor in the loss of certain wetlands and aquatic environments, as well as in the damage to forest areas affected by acid deposition, pollution, in the clean-versus-dirty sense, is not the primary cause of habitat destruction. For the most part, it is the spread of human population and large-scale development that poses the greatest threat to the planet's biological wealth. Even where development is accompanied by extensive environmental safeguards, such as in the growth of the ecotourism industry, the consequences for biodiversity can be disastrous (Boo, 1990; Lamb, 1990).

The Natural Resource Consumption Perspective

Environmental damage can also be construed as a resource economics problem in which a combination of availability, accessibility, and renewability of a valuable natural resource determines the degree of environmental protection that is needed. Emphasis here is on the instrumental value of the environment as a source of natural resources for human consumption. Externalities, unsustainable consumption, and a failure to distinguish man-made capital from natural capital are fundamental to the definition of damage employed in this perspective. Those who stress this definition are not blind to the contributions of the contamination and eco-simplification perspectives of environmental change, but their preference is to relate to nature as consumers and to reduce harm to the environment by regulating consumption of scarce natural resources.

The destructive impacts of consumption involve pollution or loss of complexity only indirectly; the key factor is the instrumental value placed on nonrenewable or slowly regenerating natural resources that can be mined, milked, pumped, sawed or uprooted, hunted, fished, collected, or otherwise consumed for human benefit. Whereas environmental pollution and losses in biological diversity are typically unintended consequences or side-effects of growth and development, in the consumption case, natural resources are specifically targeted for consumption or exploitation. They are the intended objects of destructive behavior—forests cleared for timber, oceans overfished for food, and a host of other environmental sacrifices that are typically justified on grounds of human wants and needs. While the end results of all three processes may seem to be identical, it is important to separate these forms of environmental destruction in order to understand the different motivations and behaviors involved at the causal end of the process.

Environmental protection, according to the consumption perspective, requires the calculation of maximum sustainable yields for renewable resources and long-term conservation strategies for the management of nonrenewable resources. In recent years it has also included proposals for what is called "natural resource accounting," in which unpriced ecological services are included in national income accounts based on the amount of expenditures that would be needed to replace them with artificial substitutes or otherwise repair or reclaim them for sustainable use. Without this adjustment, economic growth indicators, such as gross domestic product (GDP), often rise as a direct result of natural resource depletion. The apparent improvement in economic welfare, purchased at the expense of future generations, is of course a cruel illusion.

A country could sell off its timber and minerals, erode its soils, pollute its aquifers, deplete its fisheries, and the national accounts would treat all the proceeds as current income. Mistaking a decline in wealth for a rise in income is a confusion likely to end in bankruptcy. (Repetto, 1990, p.3)

For a new breed of ecological economists, the primary cause of this mistake has been the failure to distinguish between man-made capital, such as machines or buildings, and natural capital, such as topsoil. In their view, the wise use of natural resources requires that we extend our professed economic ideology to encompass the products of earth, wind, and fire in such a way as to acknowledge their immense value prior to or independent of human exploitation. No longer would the labor theory of value—the notion that these resources have zero value until we mix our labor with them—permit growing societies to take for granted the ecological infrastructure on which human wealth ultimately depends.

For those who reject the notion that nature's bounty exists for human benefit—that it is not property and that it cannot morally be appropriated for human purposes—the consumption perspective is not only distorted, but dangerous. Treating two-thousand-year-old redwoods or great blue whales as natural resource stocks is offensive to these people. Identifying with preservationists like the legendary John Muir, many ecological economics reject the emphasis on natural resource conservation. They argue against modern-day Gifford Pinchots, who champion natural resource conservation as a proper compromise between the preservation ideal and the insatiable appetite of human consumers.[3] Some critics have even argued that human population will have to be drastically reduced in order to prolong the illusion of limitless material development through the scientific management of nature (Catton, 1980). The most radical look to AIDS and other medical scourges to solve the problem (Conner, 1987). Others fear that the growing preoccupation with resource scarcity will lead increasingly to relative deprivation conflicts and wars over water, fertile soil, fisheries, and the like. (Homer-Dixon et al., 1993)

Environmental Driving Forces

Given the different ways in which environmental harm is defined, it is difficult to find a single model or causal explanation that encompasses all major forms of environmental destruction. Most approaches reveal something important about the causes of environmental ruin, but no single explanation offers an understanding of the problem that is adequate in scope. It is only by combining approaches, concentrating on the key variables and on the linkages between them, that a satisfactory understanding can be achieved. Achieving this synthesis requires a careful examination of the environmental driving forces and theories of causation employed in model building. Each of these forces and theories can then be assessed for its individual explanatory power as a cause of pollution, lost biodiversity, and natural resource depletion.

A number of factors or variables have been identified as key driving forces in previous models or explanations of global ecological destruction. Meadows et al., the authors of the 1972 bestseller, *Limits to Growth*, developed a systems model of global environmental threats based on the interactions of population growth, industrial technology output, food production, and nonrenewable resource consumption. In a 1992 sequel to their book, entitled *Beyond the Limits*, the authors argue that the same driving forces, though refined in terms of measurable indicators and parameters, continue to operate but with even greater effect on the planet's ecology. Other authors have developed even simpler models of environmental driving forces. Paul and Anne Erhlich (1991) conceive of environmental impacts as the product function of three variables. In its simplest form, their model can be expressed as the equation $I = P \times A \times T$ where I is impact on the environment, P is population growth, A is affluence, and T is technology. Population, according to the Erhlichs's analysis, is by far the most important variable. Barry Commoner, who developed a similar framework in his book *The Closing Circle* (1972), argues that *technology* is the key explanatory variable. The reasons for the different weights assigned to population and technology have been advanced during a long-running debate between Commoner and Paul Erhlich, and will be discussed later in this chapter.

While previous environmental models go a long way in explaining the pollution, loss of diversity, and natural resource depletion that comprise today's environmental threats, they make little allowance for the values and ideologies that shape the human ends for which population growth, affluence, and technology are employed. Taking the $I = P \times A \times T$ equation, for example, we need to know what kind of values are represented in the population, how it uses its wealth, and to what extent its technology is environmentally benign. David Durham (1992) suggests that the $I = PAT$ formula be broadened to $I = PACT$, where C stands for cultural value choices, in order to encompass such normative concerns. Others have argued that the technology variable should be indexed and signed (+ or –) according to the scale, purpose, or managerial requirements of the technology in question.

As a thought exercise, imagine an affluent population of six billion environmentalists who rely heavily on solar energy and hydrogen fuels, electric vehicles and mass transit systems, vegetarian diets, and elaborate waste minimization and recycling technologies. Then imagine a less affluent population of, say, one billion industrial workers—all of them gas-guzzling car enthusiasts who prefer an economy based on cheap oil, an endless array of consumer goods, heavy beef diets, and subsidized land-fills. Which scenario involves greater environmental damage? Clearly, models like those based on the $I = PAT$ formula are of very limited use unless they can incorporate values, lifestyle choices, and divergent technological aims or cultures in their specification of variables.

Critics may counter that the thought exercise, when applied to the real world, is misleading because it assumes an incompatible set of circumstances or conditions. Beyond the obvious problem of assuming homogeneity in human wants and values, there are a number of feasibility issues that critics might raise. For example, they might challenge the assumption that six billion environmentalists could remain wealthy after opting for what are, by today's standards, very expensive alternative energy systems, such as solar hydrogen. A plausible scenario, in their view, would have to incorporate trade-offs between economic wealth and environmental excellence. It would have to deal with matters of political economy that frequently render the aims of affluence and the aims of the ecology movement counteractive.

Other critics would presumably concentrate on the population assumptions, arguing that six billion well-meaning environmentalists would merely slow, not reverse, the inexorable process by which nonhuman species are being squeezed off the planet. Their critique would stress that population size matters, regardless of the values held by the individuals who comprise the population. If the environmentalists were really well meaning, so goes the argument, they would be doing everything in their power—short of war, famine, and the withholding of basic medical care—to reduce humanity's numbers to perhaps a few hundred million individuals. Given modest assumptions about technology, this may be the maximum population size that can be peacefully sustained without significantly diminishing the opportunities for other species to flourish.

Adding Complexity

While there are many other possible objections to the thought exercise and its implications, the exercise is nevertheless useful for illustrating why it takes more than three or four variables to construct a satisfactory model. In order to encompass all of the major causal factors that are involved in the three types of environmental destruction previously outlined, we shall attempt to construct a model of our own. The building blocks needed for this model are independent variables that can be used to explain why environmental destruction around the world occurs and why it has increased. The interaction of these variables is responsible for a wide range of environmental damage.

At least eight such variables or driving forces appear highly relevant to this task of model building: (1) anthropocentrism, (2) contempocentrism, (3) technological advance, (4) human population growth, (5) poverty, (6) affluence, (7) market failure, and (8) failure to have markets. *Anthropocentrism* refers to the preoccupation with human progress and domination at the expense of other species. Derived from the Greek word for "man," *anthropos*, it also encompasses the almost universal domination of women by men and the ecological consequences that such domination produces. *Contempocentrism* involves the human preoccupation with the present, often at the expense of future generations—both human and nonhuman. The *technology* factor represents the enormous impact, for both good and ill, that technological developments have on the environment. Perhaps the most controversial driving force, the *population* factor, involves the neo-Malthusian argument that human numbers are exceeding the ecological carrying capacity. Related to population growth is the role of human *poverty*. It is a major factor in the creation of ecological poverty, a condition in which over one billion individuals living at or near subsistence levels are devouring habitat and natural resources in their search for food, water, energy, and other necessities of life. *Affluence*, in contrast, is a driving force whose "throw-away" consumer lifestyle encourages environmental destruction through overconsumption and through a lack of concern for natural resource depletion. Focusing on the structure of economic incentives, finally, are the market-based explanations of environmental ruin. These can be divided into *market failures*, in the form of environmental externalities and unpriced opportunity costs, and *failure to have markets*, which is due to the absence of assigned property rights or to a failure to recognize economic value in vital ecological resources and services.

Each of the variables identified above is linked in a particular way to one of the other variables. Anthropocentrism and contempocentrism provide much of the normative basis for ecologically destructive behavior; they represent the fundamental belief structures that influence most human attitudes toward nature, and hence can be thought of as *core values*. The growth of human population and technology serves to magnify or extend the destructive consequences of the other six driving forces; hence they can be thought of as *amplifiers*—that is, the instrumental means by which human values, behaviors, and possessions are extended or expanded. Affluence and poverty serve as indexes of basic human consumption patterns. As such, they can be termed *consumptive behavior* variables. Consumptive behavior represents the tension between human needs and wants. The ecological consequences it produces are treated as distribution functions of material wealth. The final two factors, market failure and failure to have markets, represent the inappropriate incentive structures in which consumption takes place. They are treated here under the rubric of *political economy* and will be used to explain the nexus of economics and political ideology as a source of environmental problems. Table 3-1 provides a summary of each category, with examples that illustrate each of the driving forces.

By combining knowledge about human values, consumptive behaviors, the amplifying agents that foster rapid growth, and the political economy that organizes it, we can construct not only a list of key driving forces but a model of their interactions as well. In the belief that a more elaborate model will reveal more than it obscures, we shall attempt to develop a framework that gives greater coherence to the relationships among the eight aforementioned driving forces and the three types of environmental destruction that they produce. The objective will be to integrate these factors and systematically develop them into a single, comprehensive model that is at least heuristically valuable, if not empirically operational.

Figure 3-1 illustrates the basic relationships between the driving forces and the different forms of environmental destruction. To oversimplify just a bit, anthropocentrism and contempocentrism represent pervasive values or behaviors, affecting and in turn affected by each of the other six factors under consideration. Population growth and technology serve

TABLE 3-1. *Environmental Driving Forces*

Core values—The fundamental belief structures that influence human attitudes toward ecology.
  1. Anthropocentrism (e.g., sacrificing species to satisfy human wants)
  2. Contempocentrism (e.g., lack of regard for future generations)

Amplifiers—The instrumental means by which human values, behaviors, and possessions are extended or expanded.
  3. Population growth (e.g., impacts of projected 9–11 billion people)
  4. Technology (e.g., unintended consequences of chlorofluorocarbons)

Consumptive behavior—The tension between human needs and wants, and its ecological consequences as a function of material wealth.
  5. Poverty (e.g., deforestation for fuelwood in developing countries)
  6. Affluence (e.g., high-per-capita consumption of "throw-away" goods)

Political economy—The dominant economic structure and ideology used to explain environmental problems.
  7. Market failure (e.g., unpriced costs of acid rain pollution)
  8. Failure to have markets (e.g., overfishing as a "tragedy of the commons")

---

primarily as amplifying forces for all three types of environmental destruction; they increase environmental impacts exponentially as a result of associated development pressures and advances in the power of organized knowledge and machines to extend the reach of human desires. The final four factors—poverty, affluence, market failure, and failure to have markets—reflect fundamental environmental differences that are manifest in world geography: North versus South, and East versus West. In the South or "Third World," poverty is a major factor in rapid depletion of natural resources and in eco-simplification, just as affluence, in the form of overconsumption, lies behind much of the pollution damage occurring in the more industrialized world. In the exchange economies of the West, environmental threats are often described as market failures, while in the decaying command economies of the East, it has been the absence of market forces that many say explains much of the environmental destruction. This is particularly true in the case of eco-simplification, where the absence of market incentives for protecting habitat or common property appears to have its greatest impact.

While it would be ludicrous to claim that such neat dichotomies faithfully reflect all of the environmental realities shaping international relations today, the categories themselves are useful as a first step toward

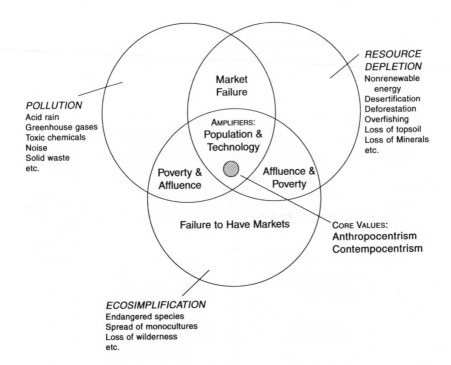

POLLUTION
Acid rain
Greenhouse gases
Toxic chemicals
Noise
Solid waste
etc.

Market
Failure

AMPLIFIERS:
Population &
Technology

RESOURCE
DEPLETION
Nonrenewable
energy
Desertification
Deforestation
Overfishing
Loss of topsoil
Loss of Minerals
etc.

Poverty &
Affluence

Affluence &
Poverty

Failure to Have Markets

CORE VALUES:
Anthropocentrism
Contempocentrism

ECOSIMPLIFICATION
Endangered species
Spread of monocultures
Loss of wilderness
etc.

FIGURE 3-1. *Three types of environmental destruction and their driving
forces.*

conceptual orientation. A more sophisticated approach to modeling
would be to transform the dichotomies into continua and locate individual nations or regions along each continuum, as illustrated in figure
3-2.

Although superimposing the "affluence–poverty" and "market failure–failure to have market" continua on the North–South and West–East
axes of figure 3-2 implies a much stronger relationship between geography and economic conditions than actually exists, it nevertheless may be
useful to characterize part of the world in this way for model-building
purposes. Such representations, however, will not work for the other
four causal factors—anthropocentrism, contempocentrism, population
growth, and technology. The relationship between these factors is neither dichotomous nor continuous. There is no reason to treat them in a
bipolar fashion, since each one represents a distinct category. Their op-
posites or their absences, with the possible exception of technology, are
not implicated in global environmental destruction.

64   Environmental Governance

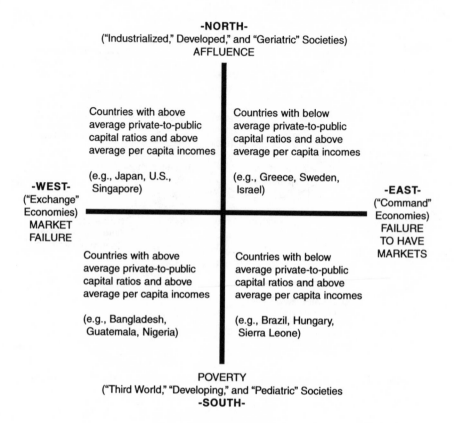

-NORTH-
("Industrialized," Developed," and "Geriatric" Societies)
AFFLUENCE

Countries with above
average private-to-public
capital ratios and above
average per capita incomes

(e.g., Japan, U.S.,
Singapore)

Countries with below
average private-to-public
capital ratios and above
average per capita incomes

(e.g., Greece, Sweden,
Israel)

-WEST-
("Exchange"
Economies)
MARKET
FAILURE

-EAST-
("Command"
Economies)
FAILURE
TO HAVE
MARKETS

Countries with above
average private-to-public
capital ratios and above
average per capita incomes

(e.g., Bangladesh,
Guatemala, Nigeria)

Countries with below
average private-to-public
capital ratios and above
average per capita incomes

(e.g., Brazil, Hungary,
Sierra Leone)

POVERTY
("Third World," "Developing," and "Pediatric" Societies
-SOUTH-

FIGURE 3-2. *Driving forces as geopolitical continua: Relationship
between wealth and type of political economy.*

The principal virtue of the causal model employed here is that it traces
the interaction of major environmental variables across four key sectors
of analysis, consisting of human values, consumptive behaviors, their influence on the structure of political economy, and their amplification
through the agency of human fertility and technology. A crude conceptual equation for the model can be constructed as an alternative to the
popular $I = PAT$ formula:

$$I = (V + C + M) \times A$$

where I is impact, V is value orientation, C is consumptive behavior—an
expression of unmet needs and wants—M is market structure (or absence

thereof), and A stands for amplifying agents, principally growth factors for population and technology.

While important for what it implies about the basic normative and behavioral components of environmental degradation, a more useful rendering of the conceptual equation would incorporate the eight key driving forces by name and differentiate among "green" (ecologically healthy) and "brown" (ecologically destructive) values, behaviors, and technologies. Such a refined equation might be written as follows:

$$IMPACT = [\text{"brown" } VALUES \text{ (anthropocentrism + contempocentrism)}]$$
$$+ [\text{unmet } NEEDS \text{ (poverty)} + \text{"brown" } WANTS \text{ (affluence)}]$$
$$+ [MARKET\ STRUCTURE \text{ (Market Failure } \pm \text{ absence of markets)}]$$
$$\times [AMPLIFIERS \text{ (Population} \times \text{"brown" Technology)}]$$

Running this equation backwards, it is evident that a major and sustainable improvement in the quality of life for both human and nonhuman beings will require some combination of "green" technologies, human population stabilization, the design of efficient markets to allocate resources, full social cost pricing, restrictions on material consumption, the elimination of absolute poverty, and the widespread adoption of ecologically based values and ecologically compatible lifestyles. Implicit in such changes is the need to redesign and strengthen local, regional, and transnational political institutions and policies.

Having outlined the model and its interactions, we can now examine the driving forces one by one, with an eye to their individual explanatory power and relative importance in the overall scheme of environmental problems and response strategies. By exploring each variable separately and in relation to the others, we can better appreciate the difficulties in attempting to design policy responses that will reduce one driving force without enlarging another.

Core Values

Although anthropocentrism and contempocentrism are the principal beliefs affecting human attitudes toward nonhuman nature and ecological sustainability, they are by no means the only ones of significance for those who are concerned about environmental protection. Beliefs about ethnicity, race, and religion also play an important role. Their influence, however, is more difficult to assess. Patriarchal, white, Christian societies have had enormous influence in the design of the world's economic and political structures, which in turn have had an enormously destructive impact on the natural environment. The dominant beliefs of Westernized societies appear to have reinforced and expanded anthropocentrism and contempocentrism, although it can be argued that Christian theology attempts to shift human concerns away from a preoccupation with self and the present to the eternal future.

While a serious and systematic examination of these values and their consequences is beyond the purview of this book, it is nevertheless important to note that anthropocentrism and contempocentrism are derivative from many other values and beliefs, not the least of which are greed and narcissism. To the extent that human aggrandizement for the here and now comes at the expense of nonhuman nature and posterity, it is possible to view self-centered behavior—both individual and as a species—as the ultimate threat to our planet. Ironically, self-centeredness may have had important evolutionary survival value for our species. What makes it such a serious threat today are the ways in which it is amplified through rapid population growth and new technologies.

Anthropocentrism

Copernicus's success in replacing the geocentric universe with a heliocentric one may have helped, strangely enough, to elevate Western man as the measure of that universe. The decline of theocracy in Europe and the rise of science infused Western civilization with a peculiarly self-confident belief in the human ability to dominate nature. No longer merely caretakers of God's creations, people began to imagine themselves, in René Descarte's words, as the "lords and possessors of nature." The global ecological repercussions of this transformation are only now becoming clear.

Anthropocentrism, in its most common form, is related to the concept of hubris in Greek mythology. By conceiving of man as the center of all existence, an overconfident belief in human mastery arises that ends in tragic overreaching. From time to time, a massive volcano, earthquake, hurricane, or other natural disaster reminds us of the limitations of our control over nature. Sometimes an event like the Chernobyl nuclear accident or the Challenger space shuttle disaster reveals the fragility of modern technology and can have the same effect. Most of the time, however, the vast majority of the world's people are focused on ways to extend man's grasp over nature. Their success, exemplified in modern agriculture, weather modification, genetic engineering, and the damming of wild rivers, has not been achieved without significant cost. Today it is extremely difficult to experience anything that is not in some way a by-product or artifact of earlier human activity. As Philip Slater (1970):

We rarely come into contact with a force which is clearly and cleanly Not-Us. Every struggle is a struggle with ourselves, because there is a little piece of ourselves in everything we encounter—houses, clothes, cars, cities, machines, even our foods. There is an uneasy, anesthetized feeling about this kind of life. . . . Even that part of the world which is not man-made impinges upon us through a symbolic network we have created. We encounter primarily our own fantasies: we have a concept and image of a mountain, a lake, or a forest almost before we ever see one. (pp. 18–19)

The consequence of this anthropocentric dilemma is the modern nostalgia for environments that contain something other than human creations or artifacts. It is expressed in the thinly concealed mixture of joy and apprehension that many people experience in the face of an approaching hurricane or massive snowstorm. It is seldom expressed, however, in a desire to reintegrate with nature. Few human beings choose to grant nonhuman nature the status that they reserve for, say, computers, automobiles, or other pervasive products of advanced technology. The sacrifice of live animals in testing products for their safety or crash-worthiness is but one indication of this. It is perhaps the ultimate conceit of anthropocentrism that upwards of ten thousand species may have been extinguished in the last decade due to human development activities, and that only a tiny fraction of humanity will be aware of this destruction or will think it sad.

It must be emphasized that anthropocentric views are not necessarily incompatible with the goals of environmental protection. Preventing pollution and resource depletion can be perfectly consistent with anthropocentric aims where it is clear that a healthy environment serves human interests. Even the protection of other species thought to be without economic value is often justified on the chance that they will be found useful at a later time in medical research or, like the canary in the coal mine, prove useful as an early-warning system for threats to human health or comfort. Nevertheless, anthropocentrism does permit wholesale extinction to occur once humans are satisfied that a particular species is unlikely to yield significant medical, biotechnological, or other forms of economic benefit. Likewise, where immediate benefits to human beings result from actions that cause pollution or resource depletion, environmental constraints will usually be ignored.

There is a second meaning of anthropocentrism, alluded to earlier, that relates to the role that men play vis-à-vis women in the creation of environmental dilemmas. It has to do in part with gender differences that become symbolized in the way nature—"She"—is defined and treated. More concretely, it involves the environmental consequences that gender discrimination fosters with respect to the roles of women in family planning, the socialization of children, the division of labor, property ownership, and access to education (Merchant, 1989; Plumwood, 1988). The gender basis for the problem of soaring population growth has become so pronounced that even the male-governed World Bank has begun calling for the empowerment of women as one of the most important ways to lower birth rates and protect the environment. Andrew Steer, then deputy director of the Bank's environmental division, told delegates attending the Earth Summit in 1992 that efforts in developing countries to educate girls, if only to the same level as their male counterparts, would result in dramatic reductions in birth rates. In Africa, for example, where the population is likely to double in the next twenty years, the average family size declines from about 7.5 to 4.5 children when females are allowed to receive a primary school education. For those obtaining a high school education, the average family size, controlling for other factors, drops to about 3.5. If female literacy programs were combined with changes in the law permitting women to own and inherit property, gain access to credit, and pursue careers outside of childraising, the birth rates would probably fall even further.

The crucial role of women in reducing environmental damage is perhaps one of the most important insights to emerge from the U.N. meetings Rio and in Cairo. At the 1992 Earth Summit, women made up less than 3 percent of the summit's assembled national leaders, but their voices were much stronger than the official numbers suggest. At the Cairo Conference on population and development, women made up nearly 40 percent of the official delegations. Even stronger representation of women took place at the nongovernmental forums that accompanied the official meetings. In both 1992 and 1994, women from all over the world conducted their own summits on sustainable development. There, in the midst of heated debates about abortion, forced sterilization, and gender-based discrimination, the realization spread that while men conduct virtually all of the business and environmental negotiations, it is women who hold most of the keys to future environmental progress, especially women from developing countries. They represent the gender with overwhelming responsibility for socializing children; they are the ones most affected by the growing fuelwood crisis and the scourge of indoor air pollution from cooking fires; they are the principal victims of pronatalist policies and inadequate family-planning services; and they often represent the last remaining cultural repositories of ancient knowledge about nurturing life and living in harmony with nature. Without fundamental changes in the treatment of women in society and without their full participation in environmental reforms, none of the agreements reached in the male-dominated policy arena may do more than briefly delay irreversible ecological losses.

Contempocentrism

The preoccupation with the here and now is both a cultural value and to some extent a genetically programmed survival trait. It appears that humans at both ends of the developmental continuum (i.e., from Paleolithic hunters and gatherers to today's corporate managers) lack the luxury of spending long periods of their lives contemplating history or worrying about the future of their progeny. In Paleolithic times, the needs for food, water, shelter, and protection from hostile beings were presumably great enough to concentrate human attention on the immediate present and impending future, although some anthropologists dispute this claim (e.g., Sahlins, 1968; Clarke and Hindley, 1975). In modern times, the steep investment in demanding careers and in programmed leisure may lead to the same short-term outlook. It appears that both subsistence living and "yuppie" affluence interfere with the development of long-range foresight. But what about the many individuals for whom neither characterization is appropriate? Why is it that people who are free of basic sustenance needs, and free as well of the "rat-race" demands of certain modern lifestyles, still choose to discount the future in ways that may ecologically impoverish or threaten the lives of future generations, including their own progeny?

Our knowledge of human nature permits no easy answers. The preoccupation with the present appears to be, at base, a preoccupation with the self. Unlike anthropocentrism, which is concerned with "self" at the species level, contempocentrism focuses on the selfish individual or generation. It is reinforced and rationalized by a widespread economic ideology that assigns value according to temporal factors that in other respects seem reasonable and necessary. As every student of economics knows, a dollar in the hand today is worth much more than the promise of two dollars twenty-five years from now. In fact, using a conventional long-term discount rate of 10 percent, a dollar today will be worth only about a dime in twenty-five years. Conversely, using the classic net present value (NPV) formula,

$$\text{NPV} = \sum_{t=0}^{n} \frac{B_t - C_t}{(1+r)^t}$$

where B and C are the benefit and cost in year t, and r is the rate of interest, it would require a return on investment of $10.83 in twenty-five years to forego spending one dollar today. While this makes perfectly good sense to an investor operating in a capitalistic society, the environmental implications can be disastrous. By discounting the future in this way, present generations lay claim to all of the planet's natural capital, reserving very little for future generations. A $100 investment today for protecting groundwater or preserving wilderness for enjoyment twenty-five years from now cannot be justified with this formula unless the net benefit afforded by the water or the wilderness experience twenty-five years hence is at least $1,083. In fifty years, it would have to be valued at nearly $12,000 in order to justify a $100 investment today. A century hence, the monetizable net benefit would have to be 13,780 times greater than the initial cost, that is, $1,378,000. For the same reasons, a destructive change in climate that caused $1 million in ecological losses a century from now would warrant no more than a $73 investment today in order to prevent the damage. The magic of discounting is that it can seemingly define problems out of existence when they involve long delays or lag times.

Contempocentrism represents the elevation of individualism over the human community, just as anthropocentrism represents the elevation of the human community over the rest of nature. While a community is in a sense immortal, individual members of the community clearly are not. It is the mortality of individual members, coupled with other forms of uncertainty about the future, that underlies much of contempocentric thought (Daly and Cobb, 1989: 152). Net present value maximization is simply the most widely accepted rationale for placing individual self-interest above that of the collective human and biospheric community.

The irony of contempocentrism is that what was once adaptive, in social and evolutionary terms, is now proving to be dangerously counterproductive. While the survival of human gene pools once required day-to-day attention to basic needs, today it may require long-term foresight about ecological events and trends that do not yet seem significant. In this respect, variants of anthropocentrism that stress long-term survival of the human species are at odds with the short-term thinking that contempocentrism entails. The narrow preoccupation with the welfare of human individuals for the immediate term may end up threatening both long-term human welfare and that of nature as a whole.

Amplifiers

The principal way in which environmental impacts become globally significant is through population growth and technological development. Expanding population and advancing technology serve to extend the reach of anthropocentrism and contempocentrism, while simultaneously reinforcing their hold on human nature. As soaring numbers of people occupy more and more of the planet, it is hard to escape the anthropocentric fantasy that the world is really made by and for people. As technological advances such as microwave cooking or credit cards assist our search for instant gratification, it becomes easier to embrace the contempocentric fantasy that the needs of the present moment are paramount. Ultimately, it is the exponential growth of human populations and technological capacities that separates the relatively trivial environmental threats posed by Early Man from the deadly environmental impacts of his modern counterpart.

Population

Of all the driving forces resulting in ecological destruction, rapid population growth is regarded by most environmental writers to be the most sweeping and powerful (e.g., Mazur, 1994). Since the late 1960s, it has been cited more often than any other factor as the principal source of global ecological stress. Many environmentalists look no further than the demographic history of *Homo sapiens*, with its familiar "J" curves and population doubling times, to explain virtually all forms of pollution, ecosimplification, and overconsumption of natural resources. The 5.6 billion humans who live on the planet today represent a one-thousand-fold increase over the estimated population of ten thousand years ago. Nearly three billion of these people have been added in just the last forty years, largely as a result of declining mortality rates. Another billion will be added during the next eleven years—about three persons per second—making it the fastest increase in human history.

While the average population growth rate has actually decreased slightly in the last two decades, from 2.0 to 1.9 percent per year, the swelling global population base ensures that annual net growth will increase for several more decades. Enormous numbers of today's children will reach childbearing age in the next century, and in the absence of either miracles or far-reaching catastrophes, they will drive world population to somewhere in the 8–11 billion range. The median U.N. population projection for the year 2025 is 8.5 billion, with nearly 95 percent of the projected growth taking place in developing countries. Stabilization, according to U.N. forecasts, will not occur until human population reaches about 10.5 billion (United Nations, 1992). While these numbers represent a slight downward adjustment in projections made two decades earlier, the environmental implications remain staggering for most observers. Not only will population pressures continue to increase in the twenty-first century, but they will do so in extremely uneven ways.

Today, thirty-four developing countries (mostly African) have annual population growth rates of 3 percent or more, compared with an annual average rate of only about 0.5 percent among developed and overdeveloped countries. Kenya's nearly 4 percent annual rate, for example, means that its population may double in as little as eighteen years, potentially fostering both ecological and economic disasters. As Lester Brown (1984: 20) has noted, such growth rates were easier to tolerate when the world economy was growing at 4 percent or more per year, but population growth now leads economic growth in many countries, thus intensifying resource consumption and increasing the gap between the world's rich and poor. Humanity will soon be adding nearly one hundred million individuals each year to its population base, a net increase equivalent to adding another city the size of New York every month.

The chief environmental consequences of overpopulation are usually explained in terms of ecological carrying capacities that have been exceeded for too long. Problems such as overconsumption of natural resources, shrinking land availability, deforestation, urban smog and congestion, and habitat destruction are all partly caused, or at least exacerbated, by the failure to contain human numbers within the carrying capacities and assimilative limits of natural systems. As some writers have observed, Malthus may not have been wrong; only premature. The exponential rate of growth, by which we now add each decade more people than inhabited the earth for the first four hundred thousand years, represents the supreme driving force of the late twentieth century.

Technology

Population growth may provide the ultimate test of human carrying capacity, but technology and its increasingly close companion, science, will determine just how much expansion of that capacity is possible. To that end, technoscientific growth may provide the ultimate test of human foresight capacity. Technology, with its dual capacities for salvation and ruin, is foremost among all of the driving forces the most unpredictable variable affecting future environmental quality. As an amplifier, it exists in a black box that transforms values (e.g., contempocentrism) and behaviors (e.g., affluent consumption) into everything from heart pacemakers to hydrogen bombs.

While human numbers have increased a thousand fold over the past one hundred centuries, the developmental rate of technology has been even greater—*much* greater. The advances of just the past century, whether measured by agricultural productivity, by the destructive capacity of weaponry, or by the healing powers of modern medicine, have so enlarged humanity's sense of what is possible, technologically, that the enlargement of humanity itself (i.e., population growth) almost goes unnoticed. The exploding numbers of new technologies and of human beings, however, are not unrelated. Advances in technology serve both as potent stimuli and indirect responses to population growth. Population growth represents a triumph thus far of agricultural and medical technology over the technology of war. To the extent that reductions in mortality achieved by agriculture and medicine far exceed the increase in mortality attributable to high-tech armaments, it is reasonable to speak of technology as an amplifier of population. Conversely, to the extent that population growth creates demand for new technology and expands the supply of inventive minds, it is plausible to speak of population growth as an amplifier of technoscientific progress. Population and technology thus serve not only as amplifiers for the other six driving forces, but up to a point they also act as *mutual* amplifiers, reinforcing each other's growth and development through positive feedback loops.

The rapid expansion of technology can be traced to a variety of factors, including the growth of technical education, the availability of artificially cheap energy, the industrial organization of labor beginning in the nineteenth century, and the increased economic competition and rising economies of scale that earlier technological revolutions made possible. One indication of the rapidity with which this expansion has occurred is world automobile production, which required only about fifty years to reach the one billion mark. Television sets show an even larger and faster growth trajectory. Pollution control technologies, such as catalytic converters for controlling automotive emissions, have one of the fastest trajectories of the past twenty years.

Technology's impact on the environment is hard to characterize because it is so pervasive and in some cases ambiguous. The same advances that permit uranium to replace dirty coal as a source of energy also tend to replace air-quality concerns with fears about radiation or nuclear proliferation. Although many writers have argued that technology is neutral and that the environmental consequences of its advancement are just as likely to be beneficial as damaging, the net effect of modern technology on the global environment has unquestionably been one of massive destruction. Defenders of technology argue that we must not blame the "tool" for the environmental insensitivity of its users. "Technology merely opens doors, it does not compel us to enter," argues Lynn White. But such notions of technological neutrality ignore what Jerome Ravetz (1971: 56) calls the "intoxicating possibilities" of new technologies, not to mention the conceptual problems that arise when technology is reduced to the status of a tool (Winner, 1986). The doors that open on technology can seldom be closed again, if only because some combination of curiosity, hubris, and the forward momentum of humanity's rising expectations usually makes it unthinkable.

Interestingly, the book that is often credited with launching the modern environmental movement, Rachel Carson's *Silent Spring* (1962), dealt primarily with the environmental consequences of faulty technology. In her examination of the pesticide DDT, Carson argued that the chemical barrage being unleashed on the environment showed that the unintended side-effects of modern science and technology were becoming more important than their intended benefits. Similar arguments were presented in Barry Commoner's influential book *The Closing Circle: Nature, Man and Technology* (1972). Commoner argued that the technologies of agricultural and industrial production, especially those developed after the outbreak of World War II, had forged far ahead of the other two causal factors in his model, population growth and affluence, as the principal cause of environmental destruction. Using indicators such as nitrogen fertilizers, pesticides, phosphates in cleaning solutions, lead and nitrogen oxide emissions from automobiles, and even unrecycled beer bottles, Commoner attempted to quantify the relative contributions of his three driving forces:

> *The increase in population accounts for from 12 to 20 percent of the various increases in total pollutant output since 1946. The affluence factor (i.e., amount of economic good per capita), accounts for from 1 to 5 percent of the total increase in pollutant output, except in the case of passenger travel, where the contribution rises to about 40 percent of the total. . . . The technology factor—that is, the increased output of pollutants per unit of production resulting from the introduction of new productive technologies since 1946—accounts for about 95 percent of the total output of pollutants, except in the case of passenger travel, where it accounts for about 40 percent of the total. (p. 176)*

While the evidence Commoner presented is not very convincing by today's standards, it calls attention to a split between the forces of technology control and population control, which has divided the modern environmental movement from its inception in the late 1960s. The contrast is vividly captured in an exchange that took place between Commoner and Stanford biologist Paul Erhlich in 1972, at the famous Stockholm Conference on the Human Environment. There, in a forum organized for scientists that ran concurrently with the official U.N. conference, Erhlich, the author of the best selling book *The Population Bomb* (1968), engaged in a heated debate with Commoner and his colleagues over the proposition that population growth lay at the heart of the world's most serious environmental dilemmas. Commoner, with his emphasis on reforming technology, had the strong support of representatives from developing countries and groups from the political Left, who perceived population control as a thinly disguised tool of Western imperialism and even genocide. While both Commoner and Erhlich recognized some validity in the other's argument, their different emphases in terms of problem definition and causal mechanisms tended to polarize thinking about which policies should be pursued in the interest of a healthy environment.[4] Twenty years later—a period in which two billion people (and almost half as many motor vehicles) were added to the planet—the debate could still be heard in dozens of fora and hallway conversations taking place at the Earth Summit in Brazil.

Clearly, both demographic and technological driving forces figure prominently in the ecological changes sweeping across the earth. What remains to be seen is whether there is something strongly asymmetrical about their roles as amplifiers. For instance, technology may solve or reduce some of the problems that population growth creates. It is hard to imagine, however, how growing population will contribute to a reduction in environmental problems caused by modern technology.

Consumptive Behavior

The worldwide gap between rich and poor is growing rapidly, producing worsening consequences in the form of environmental destruction, relative deprivation conflicts, and economically induced migration. In a world of over two hundred billionaires and over one billion poor earning less than $200 a month, it is hard to say which end of the economic spectrum poses a bigger threat to the planet's ecological wealth. While middle-class consumers may represent in aggregate terms the largest source of ecological "draw down" damage, it is the tension between poverty and affluence that matters most in driving this consumptive behavior. Moreover, it is this tension that accounts for much of the political paralysis that affects environmental governance.

Poverty

Poverty contributes to all three major types of environmental destruction. For example, it often results in serious contamination of water supplies, due to a lack of sewage treatment facilities. It promotes overexploitation of natural resources, such as fisheries and forests. And it encourages eco-simplification through the destructive effects that poor people in search of land, fodder, and fuel have on habitat and on vulnerable species.

The relationship between poverty and environmental destruction is most striking in sub-Saharan Africa and South Asia, where most of the world's 1.3 billion people who live in absolute poverty can be found, trapped in a downward spiral of deprivation and degradation that is exacerbated by rapid population growth, urban–rural migration flows, and unscrupulous development practices. The principal environmental impacts occur as these individuals attempt to achieve adequate levels of subsistence by desperately exploiting marginal agricultural lands and forest resources for food and fuelwood. Attempting to grow crops on steep hillsides, grazing livestock on land threatened by desertification, and clearing forests for use by shifting cultivators are common examples of what happens when an expanding rural population outgrows its land base or is denied access to productive lands as a consequence of geography, economics, and politics. Other examples can be found in urban areas, where growing concentrations of slum dwellers and homeless urban nomads foul their environment with untreated sewage and disease. Lacking adequate health care and the infrastructure for clean water and sanitation, both the urban and the rural poor are condemned to abbreviated lives that are twenty years shorter on average than those of people with high incomes.

One of the simplest illustrations of the poverty and pollution connection is presented in figure 3-3. Here the inverse relationship between income and the generation of untreated human wastes is captured in a

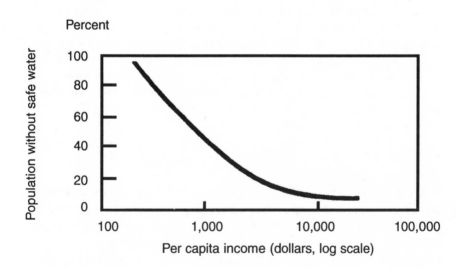

FIGURE 3-3. *Relationship between drinking water quality and country income levels.*

Source: Shafik and Bandypadhyay, 1992.

straightforward depiction of national average per capita income levels and their relationship to adequate sanitation services. Poverty in this case results in an incapacity to control pollution. Amplified by population growth, the untreated human waste stream increasingly overwhelms the assimilative capacities of rivers, lakes, estuaries, and oceans—waste "sinks" that a century or two earlier were adequate for safely absorbing or breaking down the pollution.

Clearly, figure 3-3 is not the only way to represent the poverty and pollution connection. Evidence is growing that some relationships between income and environmental contamination are biradial, that is to say they are expressed graphically by a bell curve. There may be threshold or saturation points at which the direction of the relationship between poverty and certain forms of environmental damage reverses. Figure 3-4 , for example, presents such a relationship between sulfur dioxide emissions and income. It shows that urban concentrations of sulfur dioxide increase rapidly as annual per capita income rises to about $2,000, then decline just as steeply as income continues to rise. The standard explanation for this behavior is that below some threshold for meeting basic needs, people do not invest in environmental protection; but once the bare necessities are provided and discretionary income begins to grow, investments in

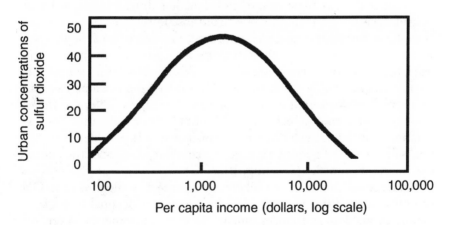

FIGURE 3-4. *Relationship between sulfur dioxide emissions and country income levels.*

Source: Shafik and Bandypadhyay, 1992.

emissions control increase to the point that the per capita emissions of sulfur dioxide by the very rich and by the very poor are virtually identical. It is a little like saying that a little wealth is a dangerous thing—an all-or-nothing approach in such cases seems superior from an environmental viewpoint. The poorest of the poor simply do not have the means to pollute beyond the human wastes they contribute to local water systems. Once the tide of development begins to lift their incomes and expand their consumption, some forms of pollution may rise sharply, only to fall later as quality of life concerns begin to replace concerns about day-to-day survival. Eventually, developing societies place more emphasis on high-value goods and services that are less natural resource intensive, except in the case of energy perhaps.

Affluence

The distribution of wealth in the modern world is in one sense quite equitable. The money is increasingly concentrated in the North, while the remaining biological wealth is largely found in the otherwise impoverished South. Unfortunately, biological wealth is seldom prized by those who live in its midst. It is money and what it purchases, not biological riches, that confer status and influence. While this is not a new phenomenon, the consequences are becoming increasingly ominous as those who live in the South convert their biological endowment into commodities that can be exported to the North for foreign exchange.

People in the top 20 percent of global income distribution have on average fifteen times greater income than those in the bottom 20 percent. If wealth rather than annual income is used, the ratio is much higher. And when the distribution of wealth or income is measured at the nation-state level, the disparity is even more striking. Within Brazil, for example, the income ratio is nearly thirty to one. Nation-to-nation comparisons are also revealing. Measured in terms of 1989 per capita GNP, the richest country, Switzerland ($30,270), is 378 times better off than the poorest, Mozambique ($80). Such disparities explain why it is possible for the annual sales of luxury goods to exceed the combined GNPs of the poorest one hundred countries (Durning, 1992: 22).

Affluence, of course, is not inherently a cause of ecological ruin. One can imagine an affluent society in which wealth is devoted to environmental protection and enhancement. Such an outcome, however, depends on a different definition of affluence than the one employed here. I shall argue that achieving *material* affluence, in the context of industrial society, constitutes an inexorable assault on nature. To be rich, in the conventional sense, means to have inherited or earned by one's labor and investment the fruit obtained from a century-long binge of exploitation and domination of nature.

The relationship between affluence and environmental destruction has often been trivialized by focusing on the omnipresent trappings of conspicuous consumption, such as disposable diapers, plastic litter, and nonreusable aluminum containers. While these are important symbols of affluence and its impact on ecology, they are not the principal means by which the affluence and environment connection should be understood. They divert attention from more damaging forms of consumption. Bad as throwaway containers are for the environment, their impacts are relatively minor when compared to the effects of affluence on the consumption of nonrenewable energy, beef, automobiles, land, and building materials. Figure 3-5 shows one such relationship between affluence, in the form of fossil fuel consumption and carbon dioxide emissions. Note that unlike the previous example of sulfur dioxide emissions, carbon production continues to climb with country income levels.

On a per capita basis, wealthy people of all countries consume far more natural resources than do their fellow citizens who are poor. And they generate much more pollution, with the exception of untreated sewage. For example, the richest decile of Americans generate 11 tons of carbon per capita each year from the burning of fossil fuels, while the world's

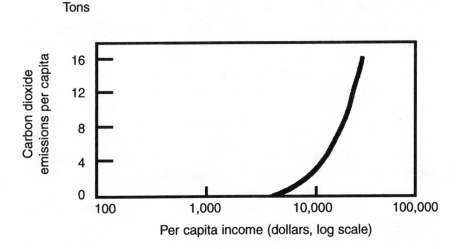

FIGURE 3-5. *Relationship between per capita emissions of carbon dioxide and income levels.*

Source: Shafik and Bandypadhyay, 1992.

poorest decile is responsible for the release of about 0.1 ton per capita (Durning, 1992: 49–50). In poor countries, pockets of affluence are often maintained at the expense of a viable middle class. A few individuals or families often own or control enormous portions of a country's economic resources. Their overconsumption may be flagrant, even by industrial country standards.

In a sense, much of the overconsumption in the world is either cultivated or legislated. For example, mass advertising creates inordinate desires for status and positional goods. Some government policies produce a similar effect. Building a house in wealthy nations requires compliance with planning and zoning regulations, building codes, and local health and safety laws that virtually preclude simple structures that rely on a bare minimum of scarce resources to provide shelter. To maximize safety, size, and comfort in one's home, zones of ecological sacrifice are created elsewhere in order to provide the requisite timber, plastics, metals, and waste depositories. Reinforcing the process is a barrage of beguiling images of fame and fortune that are intended to cultivate additional wants and then to transform them into felt needs. In much of the world, quality is still confused with quantity. More is better. Thus, almost regardless of its diminishing utility and its increasing energy, environmental, and materials costs, the desired square footage (per occupant) of new homes continues to expand, as does the perceived need for additional appliances, home entertainment technology, and the like.

Citizens of affluent societies not only live in oversized houses, they tend to heat and air condition their dwellings even when they are away. Their lives at home and at work are linked by road systems and parking structures that may cover a third or more of the urban landscape. Furthermore, they are sustained by food, water, and energy systems that often require thousands of miles of transport. According to Alan Durning (1992) of the Worldwatch Institute, tracing a typical bite of food in America back to its origins on some farm involves a journey of over twelve hundred miles. The drinking water of choice for many affluent Americans travels even farther—all the way from France. As Durning notes, there is a profound irony in comparing the huge financial success of Perrier, which sells most of America's forty-five million gallons of imported drinking water, with the continuing failure of the United Nations to secure adequate funding for local water supply improvements that would aid the one billion children and adults who currently lack safe drinking water.

Such tenuous connections between affluence and poverty turn out to be the basis for important insights into the causes of environmental damage. The growing global gap in income and wealth between rich and poor results in perverse incentives to close the gap at the expense of the environment. Even if the standard of living for the poorest of the poor begins to improve, the concept of relative deprivation suggests that pressures for unsustainable development will continue to increase. Third World citizens, their appetites for status goods and services whetted by the spread of global communications technology and mass-media advertising, aspire to consume at Western levels that are now almost universally regarded as indicators of personal importance and success. The great wealth of the industrialized countries, and the fact that so much of it was purchased at the expense of nature, is seized on by Third World countries to justify the rapid exploitation of their own natural resources and to excuse as "temporary" the inclination to overlook the environmental costs of conventional development. The self-destructive psychology of the situation is evident in the words of an African observer attending the 1992 Earth Summit: "We'll never catch up to America if we seriously worry about trees and elephants and greenhouse gases."

Unfortunately, "catching up to America" could become the ultimate driving force behind future global environmental destruction. While those who concentrate on birth rates worry about adding a population the size of today's India in the next decade, the world could probably cope ecologically with several more Indias but surely not another United States. The United States alone accounts for a quarter of the world's current fossil-fuel consumption and a third of the world's paper and paperboard consumption. The three biggest economies combined—the United States, Japan, and Germany—currently consume 45 percent of the world's refined aluminum and nickel, 44 percent of the refined copper, 41 percent of the refined tin, 39 percent of the refined lead, and 30 percent of the crude steel (World Resources Institute, 1992: 18). This industrial consumption entails enormous environmental costs, both direct and indirect in the form of air and water pollution, fossil-fuel depletion, and other impacts related to resource extraction, processing, and transportation. Meanwhile, the modernization of agriculture made possible by affluence ends up consuming huge amounts of environmentally costly water, fertilizer, and pesticides, while displacing millions of rural farmers who often turn to ecologically sensitive frontier areas in search of marginally productive land. Although some studies indicate that the world's soil could support fifteen billion vegetarians, they would presumably have to be vegetarians who refused to own cars, spacious houses, or televisions that displayed advertising designed to encourage material consumption.

Political Economy

It is *de rigueur* in environmental-policy analysis to emphasize the roles that externalities, inefficiencies, and unassigned property rights play in the fate of our planet. From the problems of urban smog to the loss of wilderness, debates about how to protect the environment are often reduced to debates about market failure or the absence of markets. Developing and expanding market incentives for environmental protection is typically viewed as the key to effective environmental governance, and reducing government intervention in the marketplace is commonly thought to be necessary for those incentives to work.

Market Failure

In trying to understand the causes of environmental destruction, it is helpful to rely on a favorite axiom of all good detectives, political campaigners, and prosecuting attorneys: "Follow the money!" Economic driving forces are woven into almost every form of environmental degradation caused by human beings. The financial basis of environmental deterioration has attained the status of self-evident truth. At the same time, however, the failure of self-correcting markets to prevent or substantially reduce such deterioration has become a source of nagging doubt among those who seek to reconcile political economy with political ecology.

The leading cause of market failure is simple to express and to understand: The price we pay for goods and services seldom reflects the environmental harm incurred by their provision. The consumption of energy, water, food, clothing, and building materials almost invariably causes environmental damage at one or more points in their development, transport, use, and disposal. The solution, according to students of economics, is to internalize the costs of environmental damage in the purchase price of consumer goods and services. The market will then automatically adjust to bring marginal demand and marginal supply curves into a more harmonious alignment with ecological imperatives. An important theorem of economics, developed by Ronald Coase (1960), is that it does not matter who internalizes environmental externalities—the polluter, for example, or the victim of pollution—so long as property rights to land, air, or water have been allocated in such a way that the parties can bargain either to compensate the polluter for his or her abatement costs or to compensate the pollution sufferer for accepting the damage.[5]

In general, economists are only interested in the pollution and resource-depletion definitions of environmental harm. Eco-simplification becomes important only if the measurable loss of diversity and complexity entails significant opportunity costs for human society *in the near term*. Since future generations are logically denied representation in the market, the relevant problem for the economist is largely one of achieving an efficient allocation of resources for present generations, while correcting pricing distortions that result in either harmful rates of resource depletion and nonsubstitutable exhaustion, or harmful production of "residuals" (i.e., pollution), which must be reduced, treated, or recycled if environmental quality is to be maintained. Most economists believe that a free market is the best way to achieve efficiency in resource allocation as well as reduce or recover negative residuals.

The persistence of environmental problems in market economies is frequently attributed to failures in market operation, which in turn are often attributed to bumbling government intervention in the marketplace. According to most economists, major failures and their negative environmental consequences would be rare in a truly free-market structure. While most grant that some government regulation is necessary— for example, to enforce contracts, prevent monopoly, and promote a more equitable distribution of wealth—the true believers in market sovereignty hold that almost all failures in market operation can be repaired with incentives and inducements provided by the market itself. They do not argue, however, that all environmental harm can or should be repaired in this way. Some environmental damage, in their view, should be accepted as a normal and healthy trade-off between the production of human goods and services and the protection of the environment. Using terms like "optimal pollution," they explain that some environmental damage is actually the result not of market failure, but of a market that is functioning properly. "Acceptable" amounts of environmental damage should, in their view, be determined by an unfettered marketplace, one that is self-correcting so that environmental destruction, while not eliminated, is reduced. This has led some environmental critics to conclude that the real economic driving force behind environmental destruction is neither market failure nor the failure to have markets, but rather the presence of markets that are working *too well*.

Failure to Have Markets

To many economists, the only thing worse than market failures that remain uncorrected is the development of political institutions that prevent markets from operating at all. The contest between exchange and command economies has seemingly ended in complete vindication for the marketeers. For the moment, at least, the market ideal has eclipsed that of its rival—though the victory may be hollow. Beyond the disappearing Aral Sea, from Chernobyl to Silezia, the breakup of the Soviet empire has afforded a disturbing view of the ecological consequences of command economies. The legacy of collective ownership, centralized planning, and Soviet-style administration is as visible in the degradation of nature as it is in the endless stockpiles of rusting tanks, rockets, and warplanes. However troublesome the environmental conditions in the West may be, the festering environmental sores uncovered in the East appear to be worse. The West, of course, is in no position to gloat. Even in countries with strong market economies, there are plenty of so-called "common property" or "common pool" resources that lie outside the market and suffer the consequences of being regarded as free for the taking. From the polluted air of Los Angeles to the waters of Chesapeake Bay—wherever nature's amenities are, in the economists' jargon, jointly supplied and nonexclusive—the potential for ecological ruin exists. The absence of market structures is used to explain everything from the rapid drawdown and contamination of groundwater to the growing quantities of solid waste and rocket debris in outerspace. It is used by most economists to account for ozone depletion, greenhouse warming, deforestation, and desertification. It is also used to explain the growing threat to biodiversity. For example, the decline of local fisheries and coral reefs adjacent to thousands of coastal towns and villages is said to result from an absence of private oceanic property rights.

The classic interpretation of the "missing market" problem was popularized by Garret Hardin in his parable "The Tragedy of the Commons" (1968). According to Hardin, a group of herdsmen raising sheep on a common pasture rationally calculate, as individuals, that adding another sheep in the absence of property or grazing rights inevitably increases wealth. The problem, of course, is that what seems rational on an individual basis becomes ruinous for the collectivity as the added sheep combine to overgraze and destroy the commons. The point of Hardin's lesson is that individual rationality and collective rationality diverge when it comes to the use of common pool resources such as oceans, the atmosphere, groundwater, and even subterranean pools of oil. It is the failure to have markets with clearly assigned property rights and obligations that accounts for most of the major environmental threats, according to this view. Like the other seven driving forces, the "tragedy of the commons" raises profound questions about the kind of world we are making for our children and grandchildren.

Surprisingly, the empirical evidence for Hardin's widely accepted thesis is full of contradictions. Studies in anthropology, human ecology, and political economy clearly show that communal property has often been sustainably managed for centuries on the basis of cultural practices and elaborate community institutions for self-regulation (Feeny et al., 1990). Even the medieval commons of England, from which Hardin takes his metaphor, have been found to be far more stable, ecologically, than the rift between individual and collective rationality would seem to suggest. Indigenous peoples left to their own ways have managed to develop many effective methods for controlling access to a commons and protecting the environmental and other services that it provides. Examples from fisheries, forests, grazing lands, water resources, and wildlife have been thoroughly documented in the growing literature on common property resources. What is also clear, however, is that the cultural practices and community-based institutions that have in the past served to protect these resources are now in decline as a result of cultural homogenization and outside development pressures. Common property is increasingly managed by remote nation-state bureaucracies or, worse yet, left in a state of unrestricted access. Thus Hardin's argument, like Malthus's argument about population, may turn out to be incomplete and premature but ultimately correct.

Another aspect of the missing market problem can be understood as a failure to fight market-created problems with market-based solutions. The slaughter of African elephants for their ivory, for example, is a tragic example of the laws of supply and demand working all too well to the detriment of wildlife protection. While a thriving black market for ivory exists, the elephants themselves are relegated to the status of common property, with the result that their numbers have been reduced by over 50 percent in just the last decade (World Wildlife Fund, 1992: 1). It is clear that government regulation of poaching has been ineffective in protecting the elephant population in many parts of Africa. A poacher can earn in one night what a beginning wildlife ranger makes in a year—which helps explain why some rangers turn to poaching for a living. Responding to the problem, some economists have proposed that a special market be created in which African villagers would share property rights in elephants that were native to their region. The villagers would be allowed to cull the herd up to some allowable harvest limit, based on conservation management principles. Only by increasing the size of the herd would their harvest rights also be permitted to increase. In this way, the indigenous people would acquire a financial stake in the preservation of elephants. In the words of one economist, "preventing poaching would become easier because poachers would become a threat to the local community, not merely a threat to a distant national government that inspires little allegiance" (Tietenberg, 1991: 225).

Similar measures have been proposed for protecting other species of birds and animals, ranging from eagles to whales (e.g., Amacher et al., 1976). One of the most interesting schemes, however, involves an effort on the part of certain Chinese communes to create individual property rights for trees in a communally owned forest.[6] While each member's right to particular trees and associated forest products can be traded or passed down to their children, the decision of when and how much to harvest remains with the collective. The objective is to assign individual property rights in a newly created market, thereby avoiding the "tragedy of the commons" while limiting the operation of that market in keeping with the collective needs of the community.

Both the failure of markets and the failure to *have* markets have developed into powerful explanations for many of the predicaments facing our planet, especially among those trained in economics and among practitioners of Western capitalism. The acceptance of these explanations by noneconomists and by people schooled in non-Western cultures and traditions, however, is far from complete. Amory Lovins (1990), for example, argues:

> *We are making a mistake if we ask markets to do things they are not designed to do. Markets are only meant to allocate resources in the short-term, not to tell you how much is enough, or how to achieve integrity or justice. Markets are meant to be efficient, not sufficient; greedy, not fair. If they do something good for whales or wilderness or God or grandchildren, that's purely coincidental.*

For many of those who question the emphasis placed on market structures or on their absence, a preferred causal explanation for environmental destruction is the failure of modern political institutions and policies to demonstrate ecological wisdom and foresight, that is a failure of human governance. A common view among these critics of market ideology is that markets, along with technology, should function primarily as tools for achieving ends that are largely determined by democratic processes. Such a view merits careful consideration. However, rather than treating failures of governance as yet another driving force in our model, we shall treat it as derivative or symptomatic of the values and behaviors already captured by the model. In subsequent chapters, we will examine the argument in much more detail, particularly as it concerns tensions between market ideologies and environmental politics.

Conclusion

Together, the eight driving forces presented in this chapter account for most of the ecological damage and deterioration that can be attributed to human beings. While it is difficult to rank each factor in terms of its past importance, present explanatory power, or future potential for destruction, some generalizations about the relative contributions of key factors can be offered. First, the centrality of population growth as an amplifier of environmental impacts must be stressed. Regardless of what happens to blunt or reverse the impacts of anthropocentrism, contempocentrism, technology, poverty, affluence, market failure, or the failure to have markets, population growth looms as the ultimate threat to the planet's ecology. As Paul Ehrlich and others have argued, "Whatever your cause, it's a lost cause without population control." Humanity is adding (net) about 260,000 individuals every single day, over 200,000 of them in developing countries. There is no denying the mathematical arguments for limiting exponential growth in human numbers. However, there are good reasons to question whether population control *policies* should be our highest priority.

Rapid population growth, as I have tried to show, is largely a function of poverty, poor education, the low status of women, and technological change. Even more fundamentally, it is a function of basic anthropocentric and cultural values that people use to define their place in nature. How one best attacks the population problem depends largely on one's perspective of human nature. For the deep ecologist, the most promising answer for curbing population growth consists of value changes or new "paradigms" that restore the human sense of connection with nonhuman nature and with posterity. For the economist, the only practical solution lies in the development of incentive structures that appeal to individual self-interest, and at the same time influence family-planning decisions that serve the collective self-interest. For the modern technologist, the answer beckons in the form of cheap, effective, and easily distributed birth-control technology, along with education programs to implement population control and appropriate technologies for energy, food production, and transportation to sustain its benefits. For many humanists, the solution lies in efforts to reduce poverty and eradicate the pernicious influence of racism, sexism, and illiteracy on world fertility rates. The humanists differ appreciably from the deep ecologists primarily in the sense that the value changes they champion seldom include an end to anthropocentrism in its species-defined (as opposed to gender-defined) context.

While deep ecologists, economists, technologists, and humanists differ over where to place the emphasis in responding to environmental threats, they can perhaps agree that solving global environmental problems will require action on many different fronts, using a variety of strategies and approaches. Chief among these must be education. Education is an environmental driving force in its own right, one that has been widely neglected with respect to ecological "literacy" (Orr, 1992), a subject we shall examine in chapter 9. Unfortunately, much of what passes for institutionalized education is concerned with forms of rationality that strengthen and perpetuate the anthropocentrism, contempocentrism, and other values that underlie our looming environmental crisis. Education that aims at genuine ecological learning, starting with young children, is desperately needed.

One of the truly critical insights that ecological education brings is the realization that knowledge based on understanding interdependence and interactivity is superior to knowledge based on reductionism. Classifying the components of environmental destruction is not nearly as helpful as understanding their system interactions. Since each of the driving forces identified in this chapter is both a cause and an effect of one or more of the other driving forces, no single perspective or unicausal theory of problem solving can suffice. Trying to rank driving forces in terms of their environmental importance may lead policy astray. Modeling the dynamic and multidimensional nature of environmental destruction requires circular pathways and feedback mechanisms. A successful modeler will recognize that poverty, for example, can be both a source and a consequence of rapid population growth, which in turn can be both a source and a consequence of environmental decline and the additional poverty that it fosters. In other words, a driving force can trigger changes that affect its own behavior in the future. It is the interactions of the model, not merely the individual components, that policy makers must understand if they are to be effective in protecting the global environment.

If we really wish to comprehend how these interactions work, it will be necessary to bring the model down from the clouds and apply it to current problems in international environmental management. By testing the model's explanatory power for understanding a particular environmental problem, we can better appreciate its uses and limitations. The next chapter presents an application of the model to one of the largest and most contentious of current environmental debates: greenhouse warming. It is a debate, as we shall see, that takes place in a peculiar arena where science and politics come together. While our conceptual model can explain the climate-change issue quite nicely, we shall see that it requires additional frameworks to explain how the melding of science and politics affects the conversion of environmental knowledge into power.

Notes

1. The proverbial man with a hammer, who tends to see everything as a nail that needs pounding, has a number of environmental analogs, ranging

from the vegetarian who focuses on beef consumption as the principal cause of environmental ruin to the nuclear-power advocate who worries out loud about the carbon dioxide emissions produced by coal-fired electricity. Sometimes referred to as the "garbage can" theory of organizational problem solving (Cohen et al., 1972), the notion that desired "solutions" sometimes precede and help to define problems seems at first a dubious claim, but it is in fact no more preposterous than the idea that one person's problem can become another person's opportunity, and vice versa. The conceptual lenses through which problems are viewed remain a powerful aide in perception, even if they *are* self-serving for the person or group using them.

2. Ernst Haas has defined consensual knowledge as "a body of belief about cause and effect and ends–means relationships among variables (activities, aspirations, values, demands) that is widely accepted by the relevant actors, irrespective of the absolute or final 'truth' of these beliefs." For a discussion of this concept, see Haas, *When Knowledge Is Power* (Berkeley: University of California, 1990), and Haas et al., *Scientists and World Order: The Uses of Technical Knowledge in International Organizations* (Berkeley: University of California Press, 1977).

3. Muir, a preservationist, and Pinchot, a conservationist who was appointed to head the U.S. Forestry Division (later renamed the U.S. Forest Service) in 1898, personified the gulf between spiritualist naturalist approaches to nature and those of scientific managers. For an insightful account of the Muir–Pinchot debate and its implications for today, see Bob Pepperman Taylor, *Our Limits Transgressed: Environmental Political Thought in America* (Lawrence: University of Kansas Press, 1992).

4. For a lively account of the debate and its importance, see Wade Rowland, *The Plot to Save the World* (Toronto: Clarke, Irwin & Co., 1973).

5. For a critique of the Coase theorem, see David W. Pearce and R. Kerry Turner, *Economics of Natural Resources and the Environment* (Baltimore: Johns Hopkins University Press, 1990), pp. 73–79.

6. For a review and analysis of this and other community forestry practices, see Changjin Sun, "Community Forestry in Southern China," *Journal of Forestry* 90, 6 (June 1992): 35–40.

CHAPTER 4

Global Warming: The Changing Climate in Science and Politics

In the late 1980s, while political observers discussed the "end of history" (Fukuyama, 1989), atmospheric scientists (e.g., Hansen, 1988; Schneider, 1989b) were sounding alarms about greenhouse warming and stratospheric ozone depletion. Euphoria over the dismantling of the Berlin Wall was juxtaposed with growing concern about global climate change and exposure to deadly ultraviolet radiation. The simultaneous rise of political hope and environmental fear encouraged thousands of scientists and policy makers from around the world to engage in spirited debates about global atmospheric protection. While high levels of scientific uncertainty characterized much of what was debated, lack of certainty did not prevent a large body of scientists from urging policy makers to take prompt action to reduce greenhouse gas emissions and ozone-depleting chemicals. In the case of ozone depletion, where the evidence of damage was stronger and the costs of prevention lower, policy responses were relatively swift and sure (Benedick, 1991). But in the case of greenhouse warming, the conversion of science into policy proved to be more difficult. In fact, a small but influential group of scientists (e.g., Seitz et al., 1989; Singer, 1989; Kerr, 1989; Lindzen, 1990), all greenhouse skeptics, repeatedly advised policy makers to defer action on the climate issue, pending the results of further research. They argued that even if climate risks turned out to be serious, the penalty for another decade of inaction would be small (Schlesinger and Jiang, 1991: 221).

Adding urgency to the debate were the efforts, described in chapter 2, of more than 150 governments to prepare an international climate convention for consideration at the June 1992 Earth Summit. The summit, like the famous Stockholm conference of 1972, was designed to provide a framework for international cooperation in protecting the global environment. The climate convention was expected to serve as the centerpiece of that framework.

During the two-and-one-half years of preparations for the U.N. conference, greenhouse skeptics frequently complained that environmental politics were outracing science in the quest for answers about climate risks. They warned that alarmists and media "hype" were undermining the slow and deliberate process of scientific inquiry and turning it into a race for political influence. Conversely, those alarmed about possible climate changes argued that key policy makers were ignoring the growing scientific evidence and "dragging their feet" behind an emerging consensus for control of greenhouse gas emissions. Some accused prominent policy makers of selecting scientific advice on the basis of its political and economic acceptability rather than on its technical merit.

Almost from the beginning of negotiations, divisions between the United States and its traditional allies over interpretations of greenhouse science threatened to scuttle plans for a climate treaty with binding commitments. Most of the disagreement centered on the control of carbon dioxide (CO_2) emissions, the principal greenhouse gas implicated in global warming. The Bush White House opposed the inclusion of CO_2 emission targets and timetables, arguing that greenhouse science was still in its infancy and that there was too much uncertainty to justify abatement measures that might inhibit growth of the U.S. economy. Although leaders from several other countries apparently shared the economic concerns expressed by President Bush, few were willing to argue publicly that the near-term cost of climate protection was likely to exceed the long-term benefit. Besides, those who represented nations with low carbon emissions may have calculated that since the cost of carbon abatement would be concentrated in major industrial countries, tough international standards might reward their own nation with a comparative economic advantage.

By the time the final preparatory conference for the summit took place, the United States officially stood alone in its opposition to carbon-abatement targets. Nevertheless, U.S. negotiators succeeded in keeping specific language about abatement targets out of the draft convention in exchange for President Bush's pledge of support and his agreement personally to attend the summit. Meeting six weeks later in Brazil with 116 other heads of state, Bush was strongly criticized for his administration's position on carbon abatement and for his refusal to sign a related biodiversity treaty. A common refrain among the nine thousand journalists attending the summit was that the U.S. position represented a triumph of election year politics over environmental science.

Greenhouse Science

The fact that the vast majority of atmospheric scientists and climatologists regard greenhouse warming as a potentially serious long-term threat is not, by itself, sufficient grounds for rejecting the arguments of the greenhouse skeptics. The "tyranny of the majority" can be just as damaging to good science as it is to democratic politics. In the case of climate issues, however, it appears that the minority view in science has sometimes dominated the political debate. [1]

In order to understand more about the controversies in greenhouse science and their political importance, it is necessary to examine briefly the assumptions and methodological problems that underlie the continuing debate. As in many previous environmental controversies, what appears to separate greenhouse science from politics is more a matter of values than of knowledge. The chief source of scientific dissension has been the design and application of quantitative models for predicting climate interactions. Both defenders and critics of greenhouse orthodoxy attribute much of the public confusion and issue distortion to a lack of understanding about the uses and limitations of general circulation models (GCMs), which are the principal tools of climate forecasting. Achieving scientific consensus on the nature and consequences of greenhouse warming has been hampered by continuing disagreement between atmospheric modelers and empiricists over model design and the accuracy of data used in modeling. In general, the models indicate that the earth should have already warmed more than it actually has. Critics argue that despite a 40 percent increase in equivalent CO_2 levels over the past one hundred years, the global mean temperature has increased only half as much as many of the leading GCMs estimate when run retrospectively— about 0.5°C, instead of the predicted 1.0°C (Balling, 1992). Why, they ask, should we trust the model's predictions for the future when they have performed so poorly in "predicting" the past and present?

Those who place their faith in the models, while acknowledging the problem, argue that some combination of counteractive cooling effects from ozone depletion and sulfur dioxide pollution are masking the effects of growing concentrations of greenhouse gases. In 1991, scientists announced that chlorofluorocarbons (CFCs), which are both powerful greenhouse gases and ozone depleters, were probably causing a cooling of the lower stratosphere as a result of ozone destruction—enough cooling perhaps to cancel out most or all of the enhanced greenhouse effect of the CFCs (Ramaswamy, 1992: 811–812). At almost the same time, many scientists concluded that sulfur emissions and smoke, mostly from the burning of coal, forests, and grasslands, were being distributed as aerosols in the atmosphere, and that these aerosols were reducing the solar radiation hitting the surface of the earth over much of the northern hemisphere (Charlson et al., 1992; Kerr, 1992). The combined cooling effects of CFCs and sulfur aerosols are now widely believed to account for much of the disparity between predicted and observed effects of the greenhouse gas buildup in the atmosphere.[2]

Additional factors included gaps in scientific understanding about thermal absorption by the oceans, poor emissions data, inconsistencies in world temperature measurement, external forcing factors (e.g., the cooling effects of dust from volcanic eruptions), and basic design flaws in the models themselves. As modeling ability and computation power improve, many scientists argue that the discrepancies between what the models show and what is actually observed will become smaller. Skeptics reply, however, that improved modeling may raise more questions than it answers.

Despite the important disagreements that make up the present greenhouse debate, there are equally important areas of consensus. For instance, scientists basically agree that the average surface temperature of the earth is warming, albeit more slowly than most models predict, and that it will continue warming due to increasing anthropogenic emissions of greenhouse gases—principally carbon dioxide, CFCs, methane, nitrous oxides, and tropospheric ozone (urban smog). Furthermore, they agree that billions of years of infrared trapping by nature's greenhouse gases—mostly water vapor—has made the earth's surface temperature about 35°C (56–63°F) warmer than it would otherwise be. There is strong agreement that anthropogenic emissions have increased exponentially since the Industrial Revolution and that the resulting warming will be greater at the high latitudes than at the equator. Approximately one-half of this expected warming is attributed to the infrared trapping effects of atmospheric CO_2 emissions from fossil fuel combustion and deforestation. While everyone seems to agree that the principal uncertainties arise from future cloud and oceanic behavior, no one has yet found a convincing way to model the cloud–ocean–atmosphere interactions. The one point on which there is virtually unanimous agreement is that any signals of climate change resulting from these interactions will be embedded in a background of "noisy" atmospheric chemistry and physics. Table 4-1 provides a summary of consensus levels reached among atmospheric scientists regarding claims about climate change.

Among the major sources of uncertainty in predicting changes in climate are the effects of volcanic eruptions, variations in solar output, slight changes in the earth's orbit, and shifts in ocean currents, such as the Pacific Ocean's El Niño phenomenon. The natural variability of solar

TABLE 4-1. *Scientific Consensus Levels for Major Claims about Greenhouse Warming*

Claim	Consensus Level
Claims about Global Changes	
At projected emission rates, concentrations of greenhouse gases will double by the year 2050	Very high
A doubling of atmospheric concentrations will result in a 1–4.5 °C rise in mean global surface temperature	High
Projected temperature increases will cause a slow rise in sea level of up to 2 meters in the next 100–150 years	Medium
Warming of ocean surface water will accelerate evaporation rates that will in turn greatly amplify greenhouse warming ("supergreenhouse" effect)	Low
Claims about Regional Changes	
Warming at the poles will be much higher than at the equator	High
While total precipitation will increase, regional droughts in continental interiors will also increase	Medium
The rapidity of climate-induced regional vegetation changes will severely disrupt ecosystems	Low–medium
The West Antarctic ice sheet will melt within a few centuries	Low

Sources: J. Chahine, Jet Propulsion Laboratory; J. Mahlman, Geophysical Fluid Dynamics Laboratory (NOAA); and I. Mintzer, Stockholm Environment Institute.

output and its effect on the earth's climate may be one of the least understood of these external "forcing" factors. Without carefully analyzing the changes that occur in a normal solar cycle—about twenty-two years—and isolating them from the effects of greenhouse warming, it is almost impossible to tie increases in particular greenhouse gases to changes in climate.

Another key source of uncertainty is the chemical and physical buffering capacity of the oceans. Scientists are in agreement that heat is transferred much more slowly deep in the oceans than in the atmosphere. As a result of the lag in heat transfer, the earth's surface temperature may represent only a portion of the eventual equilibrium temperature that will be realized. Many scientists believe that the surface temperature increase measured after a doubling of CO_2 equivalent gases will be only about half of the "committed" temperature increase realized at equilibrium (U.S. National Academy of Sciences, 1991: 26).

The final, and perhaps most unpredictable, factor in climate prediction involves the creation and behavior of clouds under different atmospheric conditions. It is clear that cloud formations are capable of both accelerating and retarding warming at the earth's surface. Depending on their altitude, size, shape, albedo, and location over land and water, clouds may either reflect or trap solar radiation. Low marine clouds are generally thought to have a cooling effect on the earth's surface, while high, cirrocumulus clouds, for example, may trap heat and add to the rise in mean global temperature.

Tracing the Human Causes

The immediate and predominant causes of greenhouse warming can be traced to energy, transportation, and land-use practices that involve combustion of fossil fuels and the burning or clearing of forests. Fossil energy use alone accounts for over 70 percent of anthropogenic CO_2 emissions, with deforestation accounting for most of the remainder. While other emissions sources, such as landfills, CFC-based refrigerants, and nitrogen fertilizers, emit greenhouse gases that are much more potent than CO_2 (molecule for molecule), their aggregate and cumulative contribution to potential global warming remains significantly less than that of fossil fuel combustion. Hence, the most critical link in the chain of causation for greenhouse problems is the choice of energy sources and the efficiency with which fossil energy is used.

Beyond the direct and immediate causes of climate threats lie what may be called the *ultimate* causes. These are represented by the eight driving forces developed in chapter 3: anthropocentrism, contempocentrism, population growth, technology, poverty, affluence, market failure, and the failure to have markets. Although each factor provides a partial explanation for the rise of greenhouse gas emissions, some are clearly more important than others in terms of their explanatory power. All, however, warrant a brief examination.

Anthropocentrism

The claim that the earth exists principally for human habitation and exploitation is frequently invoked to justify certain types of environmental destruction. Because it has been incorporated in so many religious and economic doctrines, not to mention general conceptions of modernity or progress, the anthropocentric perspective permeates many of the world's cultures and belief systems. It fosters attitudes and behaviors that permit and even encourage rapacious consumption of natural resources, habitat removal, and pollution, so long as human health is not visibly impaired.

In the case of greenhouse warming, anthropocentric values encourage "drawdown" behaviors that consume coal, oil, forests, and other natural resources, producing nearly seven billion tons of greenhouse gases each year. Moreover, they encourage a reckless disregard for the potential climatic impacts of human activities on plants and animals. It is not unusual to hear people at public hearings and cocktail parties argue that if climate change becomes severe, people will just have to turn on more air conditioners or migrate to places with better climates. Attention is seldom given to the limits of climate adaptation in other organisms or, for that matter, to the limits of human adaptation.

Ironically, human beings have successfully developed comfort-controlled microclimates at the expense of nature's macroclimatic stability. Heating and cooling of buildings has been made possible on a global scale by the burning of fossil fuels and trees, contributing massively to greenhouse gas concentrations in the atmosphere. As much as 15 percent of carbon dioxide emissions, for example, are the result of efforts to maintain comfortable room temperatures. While it is hard to begrudge people who live in cold climates from trying to stay warm and those living in hot climates from trying to cool off, it is increasingly apparent that artificial climate control exacts a huge cost in energy and energy-related emissions. In a less anthropocentric world, the indoor temperature and humidity control that human comfort seems to require could be achieved without discomforting the rest of nature. Innovations in building design, solar energy, and thermal insulation make heavy reliance on carbon-rich fuels unnecessary and unwise, especially where the cost of clean and efficient alternatives is competitive.

Contempocentrism

Long-term problems such as greenhouse warming, which unfold over periods of many decades and even centuries, are almost certain to be underestimated or ignored in modern societies because of the powerful incentives that exist to discount the future. According to a 1990 report by the U.S. President's Council of Economic Advisors, a $1 investment in greenhouse gas abatement would have to yield at least $20 of climate benefits in the year 2050 in order to justify the expenditure today (U.S. Council of Economic Advisors, 1990: 215). Over a period of two hundred years, using a time discount rate of 8 percent, the estimated benefit would have to be nearly $5 million to justify the protective investment. While such use of discounting appears to violate fundamental principles of ecological responsibility and intergenerational equity, it is nevertheless central to the greenhouse policy debate. Two cross-cutting, contempocentric questions define the economic margins of that debate:

1. What is the net present value of an avoided climatic catastrophe?

2. What is the opportunity cost of trying to stabilize greenhouse gas emissions now, particularly if emissions from future population growth swamp anticipated gains?

Public officials will calculate the *political* opportunity cost as well, especially if the greenhouse warming threat turns out to be a false alarm or at least a smaller problem than expected. This is because the political rewards and penalties for action versus inaction on greenhouse problems are very uneven. If it turns out that the greenhouse threat is serious, leaders who failed to take prompt action will probably be forgotten by the time unambiguous climate impacts are felt by the general citizenry. Conversely, those who support strong and immediate greenhouse gas–abatement measures may, if they prevail, encounter high "front-end" costs, both politically and economically, while finding few or no tangible climatic benefits in the short term to claim in justification. Hence the politics of greenhouse warming seem to follow the classic pattern of "pay now and benefit later" (i.e., immediate costs and deferred benefits)—a prospect that usually erodes political courage, especially in representative forms of government with relatively short election cycles.

Perhaps the most telling evidence of contempocentrism's influence on the formation of greenhouse policy can be seen in the way in which the climate issue first came to public attention. It took a series of record heat waves, storms, and droughts during the summer of 1988 to arouse public concern about a plausible linkage between certain atmospheric emissions and so-called "bad weather." Although most scientists were quick to point out that no unambiguous links could be drawn, it was the perceived immediacy of the threat, enlarged by extensive media coverage, that thrust the issue of greenhouse-induced climate change into prominence. Many atmospheric scientists, although pleased that the public was starting to pay attention, feared that a few years of "normal" weather patterns would send their issue back into obscurity again, all because of the public's preoccupation with the conditions of the moment.

Population

Human population growth increases the aggregate consumption of carbon-based fuels, nitrogen fertilizers, trees, and consumer products that use CFCs. It also adds to the demand for rice and cattle production, which are major sources of methane gas. Given current projections of a doubling of world population within forty years, it follows that average per capita greenhouse emissions will have to decline by 50 percent in the same period just to remain at current aggregate levels. Thus, efficiency improvements in fossil energy use and major reductions in consumption of greenhouse gas–emitting products, manufacturing processes, and services would have to be accomplished very rapidly in order to offset the effects of population growth. These improvements and reductions, however, would not be equally feasible or affordable across different countries. Developing countries, where 84 percent of the world's population growth is forecast to take place, will be especially hard pressed to reduce per capita emissions. Given existing poverty levels and the high energy and manufacturing requirements associated with establishing an industrial infrastructure, there is little hope in these countries of significantly offsetting future population growth with reductions in per capita consumption. Vaclav Smil (1993) estimates that China, which is expected to add 125 million people during the 1990s alone, will become the number-one emitter of carbon dioxide by the year 2020—accounting for approximately 20 percent of global carbon emissions from fossil fuels.

Technology

The contribution of modern technology to greenhouse problems is seen most vividly in the carbon emissions from internal combustion engines and power plants, and the CFC emissions from air conditioners, refrigerators, and solvents used to clean computer chips. By far the biggest culprit is the technology used to extract, process, transport, and utilize fossil fuels. The world's 600 million gasoline-powered motor vehicles represent an enormous source of carbon emissions—about 800 million tons annually. In the United States the operation of cars and trucks accounts for about 25 percent (323 million tons annually) of the nation's anthropogenic carbon emissions to the atmosphere (U.S. Congress OTA, 1991b). If emissions from auto manufacturing, fuel processing, and infrastructure development and maintenance (e.g., road building) are included, vehicular technologies account for about one-third of the national total.

The degree to which coal and oil have shaped industrial forms of technology is most striking perhaps in the transportation sector, but almost as important is the role they have played in electrification and in modern agriculture. U.S. electric utilities account for 7.5 percent of global carbon emissions from fossil fuel combustion (Cogan, 1992: 350). Emissions associated with fossil fuels used in the application of agricultural technology, while harder to quantify, are also very important. Mechanized farming, petroleum-based fertilizers, and pesticides have made it possible to alter vast areas of the earth's land mass, resulting in large net reductions in carbon sequestration by forests and wetlands, and major increases in nitrogen dioxide and methane emissions from rice paddies and cattle.

On the brighter side, it is important to remember that technological innovation may also be one of humanity's best hopes for reducing greenhouse gas emissions and climate impacts. Photovoltaic cells, CFC substitutes, and other new products may soon provide affordable alternatives to many of the conventional technologies that now contribute to greenhouse warming. New technologies are also being designed to intervene in the greenhouse warming process, although many scientists are concerned about unintended side-effects. Examples include space mirrors to reflect part of the sun's radiation, lasers to blast CFC molecules in the atmosphere, and iron supplements in the ocean to induce the growth of carbon-absorbing phytoplankton.

Poverty

Despite the strong relationship between population growth and poverty, it is important to remember that poverty is in many ways a relative measure of deprivation, one that will continue to operate with or without rapid population growth. For this reason, poverty can be assessed in its own right as an important environmental driving force. The single greatest source of greenhouse impacts attributed to this factor is deforestation caused by subsistence-level villagers seeking fuelwood and by landless peasants in search of public lands to clear for crops or to use for grazing livestock. Since trees "scrub" or sequester carbon dioxide from the air and release large amounts of carbon when they are burned, the wholesale destruction of forests contributes up to 25 percent of the excess carbon in the atmosphere. Poverty is also a major factor in the decisions by China, India, and other developing countries to accelerate sharply their burning of coal and oil for industrial development.

In a more subtle way, widespread poverty also prevents many potential solutions to the greenhouse problem from coming to fruition, because the proposed measures would disproportionately hurt those who are already poor. For example, highly regressive tax solutions, such as a steep carbon tax or a gasoline sales tax indexed to pollution, may be politically infeasible in many countries because of their distributional impacts on the poor and because inadequate programs exist to compensate those in poverty in other ways. Despite the large environmental benefits that such taxes could bring in the form of greenhouse gas abatement, even environmentalists often oppose tax options on these grounds.

Affluence

The flip side of the poverty explanation is the role that material affluence may play in future climate change. Because of the consumption patterns that it affords, and the "throwaway" lifestyle that it makes possible, affluence is indirectly a major contributor of greenhouse gas emissions. Affluence does not always express itself in material acquisitions, but that is clearly its most common manifestation. Even the traditional asceticism of many Asian cultures has been threatened with a growing preference for conspicuous consumption among many of the youth. Granted that affluent societies usually have better health care, educational opportunities, and environmental regulation; but that is not the same as saying that they have better health, education, and environmental quality. Envying the rich, many developing countries seem resigned to trading ecological wealth for material wealth. Consider the Chinese goal of acquiring CFC-based refrigerators for each family by the end of this century or Brazil's long-standing development program to replace large portions of Amazon rainforest with cattle ranches. Affluence allows owners of gas-guzzling luxury cars and yachts to ignore the fossil fuel costs of operating them and by extension the higher carbon emissions they produce per mile of travel. It can also encourage planned obsolescence and undermine economic incentives for recycling, which means additional aggregate emissions coming from new products and product lines.

Market Failure

Assessing the role of market failure as a cause of greenhouse problems is complicated by the need to distinguish structural failures in market design from failures that can be attributed to the people who manipulate or regulate the market. In theory, the problem of environmental externalities, in the form of greenhouse gas emissions, can be solved by correctly pricing the costs of pollution and including them in the consumer price of the products and services that account for the emissions. In practice, of course, it is almost impossible to find agreement on what the external costs should include and how they should be priced. Should the estimated costs of CO_2-induced climate change be limited to those cases that can be shown to affect human health directly, or should other costs, such as lost forest productivity, be counted as well? What should the cost of gasoline be, given that each gallon that is burned releases nearly twenty pounds of CO_2? And what about the dilemmas that contempocentrism raises for market design? How should the future costs of climate change (i.e., costs to future generations) be calculated?

Economists have attempted to answer these questions by employing elaborate econometric models to determine appropriate levels of environmental taxation, fiscal incentives, and subsidy removal. William Cline (1992), author of one of the most thorough analyses to date, has proposed that market distortions be corrected by the gradual imposition of a carbon tax, beginning with an annual increment of $5 per ton of carbon emitted (in constant 1991 dollars, which is equivalent to about a $0.66 tax on the carbon emissions from burning a barrel of oil). At the beginning, proactive nations would voluntarily tax themselves, based on the principle of "emulative initiative." Other nations would be invited to emulate their actions, encouraged perhaps by pressure from NGOs and the world press. After eight years (i.e., $40 per ton), the tax plan would be reassessed based on the degree to which scientific findings confirmed previous estimates of climate risk. If further tax increases appeared to be justified, a second phase of market corrections would begin, using larger tax increments and efforts to develop international carbon emissions quotas. These additional measures, in the eyes of most economists, would require strong evidence of substantial, near-term climate risks. And even then, the justification for further taxes and quotas would be argued less on the grounds of market failure than as compensation for a political failure to establish a market for climate services.

Failure To Have Markets

Because there are no property rights to the atmosphere and no market for the climate services that it provides, it is widely believed by economists that the greenhouse problem should be viewed as a global commons problem. The potential tragedy of this atmospheric commons is that individual greenhouse gas emitters from all over the world, rationally calculating that their emissions are insignificant and easily justified by the benefits the emitting activity creates, may collectively and unwittingly bring about climatic ruin.

According to the dominant economic theory, by establishing a market for climate stability (i.e., greenhouse gas–abatement measures), this tragedy of the commons can be avoided. To this end, the U.N. Conference on Trade and Development (UNCTAD) published a major study in 1992 calling for the development of an international market for carbon entitlements. Establishing such a market would require an international agreement that set emissions ceilings or reduction targets for each of the participating nations. Marketable permits and allocation rules would then be developed, probably based on some combination of each nation's historical and projected future emissions. Emission permits would be allotted to low-emitting firms or countries, who would have the choice of increasing emissions up to the standard or selling their carbon entitlements to finance measures, such as energy efficiency improvements or reforestation programs, that would prevent the increases from occurring in the first place. High-level emitters (those emitting in excess of quotas) would either have to reduce emissions or buy permits. In economic terms, both permit buyers and sellers would have an incentive to reduce carbon emissions until the marginal cost of further reduction equaled the permit price. Practical applications of this idea are discussed in chapter 7.

Converting Science into Policy

Identifying the probable causes of climate risk, and some promising risk-reduction strategies, is only the beginning of a difficult political process. The scientific investigation of driving forces, and of measures to prevent or mitigate their impacts, is likely to be much more orderly and in many ways easier than the political and economic examination that is needed to weigh scientific findings for the making of public policy. As tables 4-2 and 4-3 indicate, the professional goals of scientists and policy makers appear to be very different.

TABLE 4-2. *Climate Change: Scientists' Goals and Considerations*

1. Develop and test plausible explanations
2. Determine causes of uncertainty. Possible causes:
   - insufficient or poor data
   - lack of basic knowledge about processes and relationships
   - lack of tools (e.g., computing power) or skills to operate them
   - fundamental limits to prediction (e.g., chaotic behavior)
3. Reduce levels of uncertainty and complexity. Approaches:
   - modeling (GCMs): identify process interactions; identify feedback loops
   - empirical investigation: improve quality of the paleoclimate data (e.g., ice core and fossil pollen studies); strengthen data interpretation (e.g., clarify signal-to-noise ratio, natural variability)
4. Peer review, publication, and replication of results
5. Professional status and influence
6. Service to science and society (e.g., information, advice, and education)

Adapted from J. Chahine, Jet Propulsion Laboratory.

TABLE 4-3. *Climate Change: Policy Makers' Goals and Considerations*

1. Interpret scientific findings in terms of public needs, personal political ambitions, and present government agendas. Key issues:
   - level of scientific consensus achieved
   - credibility of scientists and scientific methods
   - apparent need for action
   - ability of policy maker to influence outcome
2. Assess constituents' interests and political implications for policy maker. Key issues:
   - range and intensity of public opinion
   - political will of leaders, interest groups, and advocacy coalitions
   - availability of financial resources (i.e., budget priorities)
   - administrative capacity for action
   - policy maker's integrity and normative values
   - opportunities for linkage to other important policy issues
3. Determine acceptable risks and prudent response strategies. Key issues:
   - costs of overreaction versus costs of underreaction
   - short-term versus long-term risks and costs
   - power of stakeholders to shape policy
4. Retention of power (e.g., reelection!)

In 1863, when Tyndall introduced the greenhouse metaphor and 1908, when Svante Arrhenius published the first estimates of CO_2-induced warming, atmospheric science was in its infancy and policy makers were blissfully ignorant about the implications of greenhouse gas buildup. Since then, scientific investigation of the greenhouse effect and its potential impacts has developed into a multibillion-dollar research activity. Moreover, policy makers from around the world have become unusually attentive to developments in greenhouse science, particularly since 1988, when a series of disastrous weather events led to widespread speculation about the connection between changes in weather patterns and increasing atmospheric concentrations of greenhouse gases. With six of the ten warmest years ever recorded occurring during the past decade, many observers concluded that the link between observed changes and emissions was far from coincidental. Although most climatologists remained skeptical about these connections, they welcomed the increased government support for atmospheric research that such speculation stimulated. Less welcomed were the sometimes vitriolic disputes over greenhouse science that arose among and between groups of scientists and policy makers.

As research has become more closely tied to policy questions about if, when, and how nations should respond to potential climate threats, scientists have become increasingly embroiled in political debates about which course of action or delay is the most prudent. Most have argued for a proactive approach. In January 1990, for example, more than seven hundred scientists, including forty-nine Nobel laureates, petitioned President George Bush to take prompt action on global warming so that "future generations will not be put at risk" (*Science News*, 1990: 95). More recently, many scientists have favored a comprehensive strategy in which climate protection measures are integrated with biodiversity, population, and natural resource policies. An example of this approach can be seen in the 1993 "World Scientists' Warning to Humanity," which was signed by more than seventeen hundred scientists, including over one hundred Nobel laureates (Union of Concerned Scientists, 1992). Development of alternative energy sources, a halt to deforestation, and population stabilization were among the key policy measures endorsed by the signatories.

Few public concerns are as science-driven as those of global environmental protection. Not only is the public dependent on science for monitoring and explanation of global environmental changes, but it must also rely on science for risk assessments and evaluations of impact mitigation and prevention strategies. As a consequence, the way in which scientists reach consensus and attempt to influence policy is of tremendous importance for understanding today's agenda-setting process for global environmental issues.

In order to determine where (or if) climate issues belong on today's policy agenda, a number of critical questions about consensual knowledge must first be answered. Attempts to answer these questions sometimes divide scientists and policy makers into opposing factions, though the answers themselves remain elusive. The differences between science and politics undoubtedly influence the way in which questions are formulated and addressed. Four questions, along with several ancillary questions, appear to be at the center of present disputes about global warming:

1. Is the threat real?

    a. What counts as proof?

    b. Who counts as an expert?

2. Is the threat significant in the short term?

    a. What is the rate and magnitude of risk exposure?

    b. What is the comparative risk?

3. Is the threat cumulative?

    a. Are there threshold effects?

    b. Are there irreversible outcomes?

4. Is prevention better (i.e. cheaper) than adaptation to change?

    a. What are the limits of ecological carrying capacity?

    b. What are the limits of human adaptability?

    c. What is the cost of delayed action?

The divergent ways in which participants in the greenhouse debate address these questions can be partially traced to their views about the credibility of scientific knowledge and practice; the methods and values they use to compare risks; their ideological predispositions; and their national, institutional, and professional loyalties. Of particular importance are the disparate ways in which they define the problem in the first place. For some (e.g., Mathews, 1989; McKibben, 1989; Gribbin, 1990; Kemp, 1990; Oppenheimer and Boyle, 1990; Weiner, 1990), the greenhouse problem is a metaphor—a symbolic basket containing a vast, interactive set of environmental crises that will require sweeping changes in the way nations define security and economic progress. Others (e.g., Singer, 1989; Seitz et al., 1989; Lindzen, 1990) see the problem as a singular and relatively discrete issue of atmospheric modification, one that may eventually result in climatic improvements for large regions of the world. A few dismiss the entire greenhouse debate as nothing more than "a policy in search of a problem" (Solow and Broadus, 1990) or a radical environmental ploy "to stop unfettered market-based economic expansion" (Brookes, 1989).

Granting that science alone is incapable of persuading all participants in the debate to accept a particular interpretation of the greenhouse problem and its risks, the fact remains that scientists have the upper hand in legitimizing policy choices on issues of this complexity. The history of modern environmental policy making, from the preservation programs of Victorian naturalists to the latest standards for radon exposure, can be understood largely as a science-driven process. Without a scientific basis or justification for moving beyond common law and natural law traditions, environmental policy making must be confined to obvious and immediate threats to human health and property.

Although scientists have played a major role in past environmental policy making, they have never influenced the environmental agenda more rapidly or forcefully than in the contemporary case of global atmospheric protection. Even the 1960s' wave of scientific concern about DDT, captured in Rachel Carson's landmark book *Silent Spring* (1962), cannot match the international anxiety that followed the discovery by British scientist Joe Farman of the ozone hole over Antarctica, or the intense public debate that followed the U.S. Senate testimony of NASA scientist James Hansen (1988), who argued that the "signal" of greenhouse warming had been detected. Although neither claim of discovery had much immediate effect on policy formation (the Montreal Protocol had already been drafted by the time the link between CFCs and the ozone hole became firmly established), both had a galvanizing effect on public opinion. Much earlier discoveries had been reported of causal connections between CFCs and ozone destruction (Molina and Rowland, 1974; Stolarski and Cicerone, 1974), and between greenhouse gas emissions and atmospheric warming (Arrhenius, 1896), but it was not until the occurrence of these "triggering" (Cobb and Elder, 1983) or focusing events, which are described in the next chapter, in the mid to late 1980s that genuine prospects for international action became palpable.

In the brief aftermath of these events, thousands of scientists have produced a state of knowledge in which consensus reigns on the basic theory and direction of atmospheric changes; but as we have seen, disagreement remains rife on the critical questions of rate and magnitude—questions that are central to virtually all policy discussions. Many scientists, convinced that conclusive evidence of atmospheric destruction will arrive too late for preventive measures to be effective, have decided to act on the basis of incomplete information.

Because scientists are often loath to be identified as environmentalists—a label that some interpret to mean irrational seekers of zero-risk, pollution-free societies—the historic alliance between science and environmentalism has tended to be an uneasy one. Within the environmental community, scientific meddling in nature is often viewed as a major cause of environmental destruction. Many green activists blame scientific hubris and detachment for encouraging, or at least allowing, the ultimate "geophysical experiment" with greenhouse warming to proceed. Others criticize science for its strong reductionist tendencies and for its compartmentalized approach to global environmental change. The most significant criticism of science, however, pertains to its perceived authority, not to its methods or approaches. Greenhouse science, in particular, has political implications that seem to rival in significance its implications for planetary ecology. Its complexity calls into question the capacity of ordinary citizens to understand global warming and to determine how much climate risk is acceptable. As a consequence, the twenty-first century may not only provide scientists with answers to key questions about climate change, it may also reveal whether modern science and politics can be reconciled in democratic governance. An increasing number of citizens may lose faith in the ability of democratic institutions to decide issues involving enormous scientific and technological complexity. Is this, critics ask, the kind of Hobson's choice that global action on greenhouse warming entails?

Thus far in the international greenhouse debate, it is difficult to find evidence that such a choice is either necessary or likely to develop. Politics has dominated scientific inquiry on greenhouse issues for a long time and probably will continue to do so in the foreseeable future. Far from being a monolithic force, scientists are openly divided on many issues—including many aspects of greenhouse warming. They cannot be counted on to unite in the presence of anxious policy makers. Exploiting this fact, policy makers have occasionally indulged in self-serving efforts, aided by the news media, to exacerbate or amplify differences of opinion among scientific experts. There is a disquieting tendency extending from the congressional hearing room to television newsrooms to give equal time to "round earth" and "flat earth" scientists. While the minority view in greenhouse science must not be dismissed as flat earth fantasy, there is no question that on many occasions it has gained disproportionate access and influence in key policy deliberations. The ease with which legitimate scientific disagreements can be turned into prime-time battles of the experts appears to ensure that the divide-and-conquer tactics of politicians will continue to serve, for good or ill, as potent means for maintaining political control over science.

Policy Response Options

For most policy makers and some scientists, costly greenhouse gas–abatement efforts cannot be justified unless further study reveals new and alarming linkages between emissions and damaging changes in climate. Their position is that this is a time for scientific pondering rather than policy intervention. Many others, however, view the probability of deleterious climate change as being sufficiently high to warrant near-term governmental action. Most favor a mixed set of policy responses, ranging from incremental improvements in the energy efficiency of vehicles, appliances, and lighting to sweeping transformations of global trade and development practices. While most of the measures target carbon dioxide emissions, strategies for controlling methane and other greenhouse gases are also being developed.

In general, there are four basic and progressively demanding choices for policy makers to consider in responding to concerns about climate change:

1. Inaction—await the results of further study

2. Adaptation to any future climate changes through the use of regional contingency plans, countermeasures (e.g., sea walls to hold back a rising sea), and migration policies

3. Sequestration ("absorption") of existing greenhouse gases through sustained afforestation (i.e., tree growth sequesters carbon dioxide) and other geoengineering and biochemical "scrubbing" processes

4. Prevention of additional greenhouse gas emissions by, for example, switching to carbon-free fuels or increasing automotive fuel efficiency (each gallon of gasoline burned releases nearly twenty pounds of CO_2).

Each of these options carries its own set of risks and rewards.

While inaction may turn out to be the most costly option of all, well-intended but unnecessary tinkering with people's lifestyles, with nature's buffering mechanisms, or with a $13 trillion energy infrastructure could also prove to be exceedingly costly. To the extent that there is a consensus among greenhouse scientists on this issue, it is that the risks of premature and economically wasteful action, while potentially high, appear significantly lower than the risks of inaction or postponed action. Because of atmospheric commitment—the idea that temperature effects of some of today's emissions will not show up for twenty years or more—the margin for error in current greenhouse policy deliberations may be uncomfortably low. Hence a majority of scientists appear to regard stepped-up prevention as prudent policy.

Figure 4-1 depicts a policy option "tree" in which the various branches represent strategic choices and pathways for responding to carbon dioxide emissions. Each pathway involves trade-offs in potential costs, complexity, speed, effectiveness, political feasibility, and distributional consequences. If following an adaptation strategy, for example, weather modification and other local countermeasures for reducing greenhouse gas–induced drought and storm impacts are likely to be expensive, hard to control, fast but fleeting, ineffective on a regional basis, politically controversial, and inequitable in terms of cost burdens and benefits. One has only to examine recent controversies over cloud seeding to understand why one community's solution can become another community's problem (e.g., unintended flooding). On the other hand, there may be net benefits to a community from cloud seeding that can be achieved at lower cost than the local benefits derived from prevention strategies. This suggests how the geographical scope of policy-making jurisdictions will affect the choice of strategy employed. While those who think in global terms are likely to favor transnational prevention strategies, those with a predominantly regional, national, or local community orientation may calculate that climate impact mitigation and countermeasures are the best policies to advance their interests.

The leading carbon-abatement strategy among prevention-minded environmentalists is to improve energy efficiency, thus cutting demand for carbon-based fuels. More efficient cars, planes, manufacturing processes, and electricity uses are seen as the most feasible ways to curtail carbon emissions. For example, increasing the fuel efficiency of cars driven ten thousand miles per year from twenty to fifty miles per gallon will reduce automotive CO_2 emissions by a factor of five—from five tons of CO_2 per vehicle per year to one ton. Similarly, replacing one-hundred-watt tungsten lightbulbs with efficient, compact fluorescent bulbs of the same luminescence will achieve a fourfold reduction in CO_2 emissions, all other things being equal. Even greater reductions may be possible with a new sulfur quartz lamp being developed in the United States.

Another popular strategy with environmental groups is to plant trees and preserve existing forests. Trees sequester carbon as part of the process of photosynthesis. Scientists estimate that it would take an area of 1.25 to 2.5 billion acres to sequester the excess carbon that human activities introduce into the atmosphere (Intergovernmental Panel on Cli-

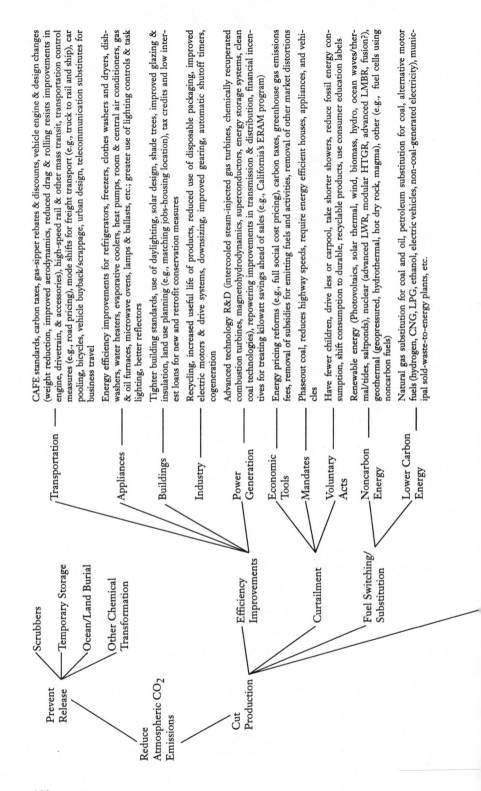

Reduce Atmospheric CO₂ Emissions

- **Prevent Release**
  - Scrubbers
  - Temporary Storage
  - Ocean/Land Burial
  - Other Chemical Transformation

- **Cut Production**
  - **Efficiency Improvements**
    - Transportation — CAFE standards, carbon taxes, gas-sipper rebates & discounts, vehicle engine & design changes (weight reduction, improved aerodynamics, reduced drag & rolling resists improvements in engine, drivetrain, & accessories), high-speed rail & other mass transit, transportation control measures (e.g., road pricing), mode shifts for freight transport (e.g., truck to rail and ship), car pooling, bicycles, vehicle buyback/scrappage, urban design, telecommunication substitutes for business travel
    - Appliances — Energy efficiency improvements for refrigerators, freezers, clothes washers and dryers, dishwashers, water heaters, evaporative coolers, heat pumps, room & central air conditioners, gas & oil furnaces, microwave ovens, lamps & ballasts, etc.; greater use of lighting controls & task lighting, better reflectors
    - Buildings — Tighter building standards, use of daylighting, solar design, shade trees, improved glazing & insulation, land use planning (e.g., matching jobs-housing location), tax credits and low interest loans for new and retrofit conservation measures
    - Industry — Recycling, increased useful life of products, reduced use of disposable packaging, improved electric motors & drive systems, downsizing, improved gearing, automatic shutoff timers, cogeneration
    - Power Generation — Advanced technology R&D (intercooled steam-injected gas turbines, chemically recuperated combustion turbines, magnetohydrodynamics, superconductors, energy storage systems, clean coal technologies), repowering improvements in transmission & distribution, financial incentives for treating kilowatt savings ahead of sales (e.g., California's ERAM program)
  - **Curtailment**
    - Economic Tools — Energy pricing reforms (e.g., full social cost pricing), carbon taxes, greenhouse gas emissions fees, removal of subsidies for emitting fuels and activities, removal of other market distortions
    - Mandates — Phaseout coal, reduces highway speeds, require energy efficient houses, appliances, and vehicles
    - Voluntary Acts — Have fewer children, drive less or carpool, take shorter showers, reduce fossil energy consumption, shift consumption to durable, recyclable products, use consumer education labels
  - **Fuel Switching/Substitution**
    - Noncarbon Energy — Renewable energy (Photovoltaics, solar thermal, wind, biomass, hydro, ocean waves/thermal/tides, saltponds), nuclear (advanced LWR, modular HTGR, advanced LMBR, fusion?), geothermal (geopressured, hydrothermal, hot dry rock, magma), other (e.g., fuel cells using noncarbon fuels)
    - Lower Carbon Energy — Natural gas substitution for coal and oil, petroleum substitution for coal, alternative motor fuels (hydrogen, CNG, LPG, ethanol, electric vehicles, non-coal-generated electricity), municipal solid-waste-to-energy plants, etc.

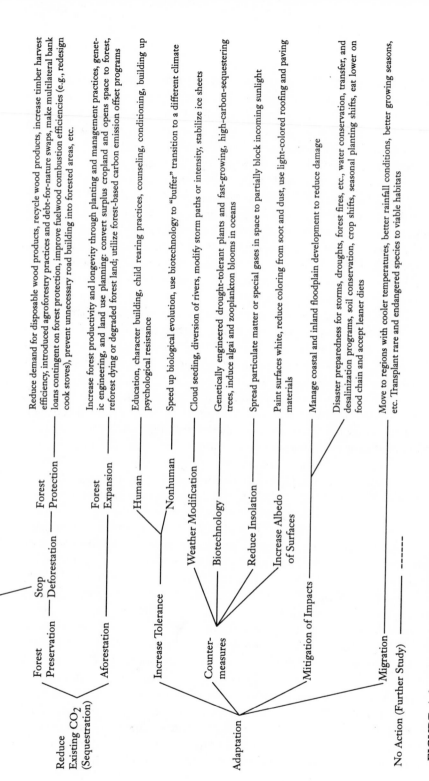

FIGURE 4-1. CO_2 abatement options.

mate Change, 1990). Although some experts estimate the cost of the forest-sequestration option at less than $0.25 per ton of carbon, under best-case conditions, the cost is typically much higher.[3] Besides, sequestration is at best a temporary solution, since the trees will give back their stored carbon to the atmosphere when they die and decay (Marland, 1988). A detailed discussion of this option is presented in chapter 7.

The most uncertain, and perhaps the most controversial, options under consideration involve proposed geoengineering strategies in which scientists would actively intervene in global atmospheric processes to counter the effects of greenhouse gases. A good example is the proposal cited earlier to permit aerial spraying of iron compounds over large expanses of ocean for the purpose of inducing the growth of organisms that would aid in carbon sequestration. Critics of such "ocean fertilization" schemes argue that measures that increase carbon uptake in this way would have many unintended and unwanted side effects. Similar controversy surrounds proposals to shoot dust particles into orbit in order to screen out incoming solar radiation. On the questions of feasibility and advisability of these geoengineering options, most scientists are extremely cautious, urging only further study.

Among those who perceive the threat of climate change to be small, the most prudent option is to facilitate adaptation. Successful adaptation to future changes in climate can involve everything from lifestyle changes and hazard response planning to learning to live with the negative impacts and agreeing to share losses caused by greenhouse warming. Due to a combination of psychological denial, widespread discounting of future costs, and confidence in technological fixes, adaptive responses often look easier and cheaper than preventive ones. Turning up the air conditioner sounds more cost-effective to many people than converting the world's coal-fired power plants to natural gas or, better yet, solar energy. As we have seen, however, facilitating adaptation for nonhuman organisms is a far more daunting challenge. The adaptive capacities of people, plants, and animals vary significantly, both within and between species. Many species may be doomed by their inability to ride on the coattails of human advancements. They cannot develop and maintain comfortable, artificially controlled environments, long-distance water delivery, protective clothing and cremes, and a global trade network for food and energy. Even within human societies, the adaptation demanded by some climate scenarios may exceed the capacities for change in certain regions, sectors, and age groups. Agriculture and water resources in some regions could be severely affected by climate change, making timely adaptation very difficult. Public health, which few scientists expect to deteriorate overall due to climate changes in the next century, could nevertheless decline among senior citizens and other vulnerable segments of the population if temperatures were to increase sharply in some regions. The most severely affected of all human enterprises may be coastal cities and irrigated agricultural regions. The costs of adaptation facing people in some of these areas could prove to be prohibitive.

International Cooperation

Greenhouse response strategies vary significantly across nations and regions, reflecting different economic and political considerations. Most developing countries see global warming as a problem that rich nations caused and that rich nations must solve. While sometimes accepting responsibility for past emissions, leaders of the industrial world counter that developing nations will become the principal emitters of greenhouse gases in the twenty-first century. Today, the North alone appears to have the combination of culpability and capability to initiate large-scale action on the climate front; but it is the fast-growing populations of the South that will ultimately determine whether such action is futile or not. Unfortunately, each side can point to the lack of resolve by the other in order to justify its own lack of progress.

In the absence of a strong, binding greenhouse-abatement treaty, action on climate risk has been limited to a number of small but impressive initiatives undertaken on a unilateral basis by the Nordic countries and by a small number of their allies. Few national governments have developed the foresight capacity, political will, and public support—or, at least, acquiescence—that is required for bold leadership in this area. And even where conditions are favorable and a nation has decided voluntarily to reduce its greenhouse emissions, the efficacy of unilateral action remains in doubt.

Nations that unilaterally pursue climate-protection programs face the disturbing possibility that their actions will not be emulated and, worse yet, may even be counterproductive for controlling greenhouse gas emissions. Unilateral greenhouse gas–abatement measures have the obvious problem of shifting production activities that generate large emissions to other places, without necessarily achieving any net improvements in atmospheric concentrations. For example, if Germany unilaterally adopted a stiff carbon tax, the resulting tendency would be for the Germans to import more energy-intensive products, providing an incentive for nations without carbon taxes to export more energy-intensive products to Germany, thus raising their carbon emissions to perhaps equal or surpass the amounts reduced in Germany. Because atmospheric pollution of this type is essentially a transboundary phenomenon, the emission changes produced by such a policy are likely to be negative, since the average carbon intensity of the exporting nation's energy production and manufacturing processes in most cases will be greater than that of Germany. From a German perspective, this would make any real or perceived sacrifice of lost jobs and manufacturing at home not only painful and unnecessary but counterproductive.

Because of fears that they will be placed at a competitive disadvantage by aggressive climate-protection policies, many nations understandably make their policy preferences contingent on what other nations choose to do or not do. In classic game theory terms, they follow globally strategic rather than narrowly rational bargaining processes. Recalling William Cline's principle of "emulative initiative," we can see that agreement among nations on climate protection may require both unilateral action, to break the ice, and faithful imitation by other nations in order to overcome the initial barriers to cooperation. Clearly, postponing environmental actions until 189 nations can agree on the level, direction, and timing of their efforts is a recipe for inaction.

Cooperation on climate protection remains one of the greatest and most uncertain of the political challenges facing the world today. The essence of this challenge is to design an effective climate insurance policy that encourages broad international participation, while limiting claims of national sovereignty. This must be accomplished within an international policy process that is constrained by vast differences in wealth, power, and resources; severe population pressures; absence of hegemonic leaders; and a lack of permanent fora and institutions that are scaled to the global requirements of the problem. Further complicating the task are fundamental disagreements about the burdens and standards of proof to be used in assessing climate risks and, as previously noted, about the political interpretation of what counts as proof and who counts as an expert.

Like actors deliberating behind John Rawl's (1971) "veil of ignorance," nations confronting the greenhouse dilemma are asked to act in advance of reliable knowledge about how they will fare in a changing climate. Unable to tell who the relative (if not absolute) winners and losers will be, they are asked to place global considerations above those of national self-interest. And owing to the lag effects of atmospheric change, they are told that they must act soon, perhaps at substantial cost, in order to remove a potential threat that may take a half-century or more to materialize.

Despite the mobilizing rhetoric expressed in the 1992 Climate Convention signed in Rio de Janeiro, many nations still perceive cooperation as a greater risk than damages from climate change. Their reasons are not hard to fathom. Most political leaders and business interests prefer inaction to potentially costly climate insurance policies. Among the explanations already touched on is the fact that scientific uncertainty levels remain high with regard to the timing and extent of climate change, thus inhibiting all preventive actions that are deemed expensive. More important, perhaps, some governments fear that cooperation on climate issues will provide additional channels for erosion of their sovereignty.

Noncooperation may also be explained by the daunting belief that many countries will attempt a "free ride" on climate stabilization measures, and others will oppose stabilization measures on the grounds that their economy might benefit from climatic changes, at least in relative terms. Another familiar explanation, while granting that all nations may be at risk and that cooperation without loss of sovereignty may be possible, holds that long-term, incremental adaptation to climate change will be easier and perhaps cheaper than international efforts to prevent it. Those who hold this view favor a wait-and-see approach to one of crisis-driven policy formation. Still others eschew near-term mitigation actions in favor of distant technological fixes, based on the conviction that technoscientific progress will enable future generations to cope effectively with whatever climate changes are in store. Since international competition is typically viewed as a healthy and stimulating condition for technological innovation, cooperation tends to be downplayed, except for an occasional technology transfer program offered in the name of humane assistance.

A final reason for noncooperation or inaction stems from the process of underdevelopment in the Third World and from the feared rise of civil violence and relative deprivation conflicts that may prevent many of the poorest and most populous countries from even worrying about, let alone helping to reverse, global environmental deterioration. Because some of these countries are among the fastest-growing emitters of greenhouse gases, critics argue that international attempts to protect the atmosphere will ultimately prove futile. Third World population growth, increasing poverty, and declining scientific literacy, in their view, will sap the political will and technical understanding needed for effective global action.

Weighing all of these obstacles and arguments has provided world leaders with ample political justification to pursue unilateral policies of inaction, or at least deferred action. However, the political mobilization and media coverage surrounding the weather disasters of the late 1980s and the preparations for the 1992 Earth Summit have made it desirable for most governments, at the very least, to appear interested in joint action. The result of this confluence of circumstances is the 1992 Climate

Convention, which was signed at the Earth Summit. While clearly a step in the right direction, the climate treaty signed in Rio is an example of a framework convention with very demanding objectives and very weak instruments to achieve them. Article 2 of the convention states that the objective will be to achieve

> *stabilization of greenhouse gas concentrations in the atmosphere at a level that would prevent dangerous anthropogenic interference with the climate system. Such a level should be achieved within a time frame sufficient to allow ecosystems to adapt naturally to climate change, to ensure that food production is not threatened and to enable economic development to proceed in a sustainable manner.*

Unfortunately, the commitments set forth to achieve this objective were largely exhortative in nature. Developed country parties to the convention agreed to recognize the *desirability* of returning carbon and other greenhouse gas emissions to their 1990 levels by the year 2000. They agreed to adopt unspecified national policies to mitigate climate change and prepare inventories of their emissions and abatement activities. All the parties agreed to cooperate in research, planning, and in the sharing of relevant information and appropriate technology. As explained at the beginning of this chapter, however, no binding emissions targets or timetables were included, reflecting the insistence of the Bush administration that the state of scientific knowledge could not justify the economic sacrifices associated with such measures.

Conclusion

The politics of climate protection are embedded in a set of larger concerns involving technoscientific progress, demographic change, redistribution of wealth, an ethic of ecological responsibility, and the building of transnational law and institutions. The deeper currents of this politics raise questions about the ability of scientific rationality to overcome ecological limits to growth or, failing that, to stave off a confrontation between North and South that would prevent effective responses to those limits.

The rapid growth of literature about greenhouse warming reflects both the hope and the fear that the risk of major changes in global climate will necessitate new political, economic, and institutional arrangements. Among hopeful observers, the changing atmosphere is viewed as a global commons that offers an unusual opportunity to redirect world

politics and economic policy along the lines of energy-efficient and ecologically sustainable development. Their hope is that the long strides already taken in protecting the ozone layer may, with enough forward momentum, carry over to protection of the global climate. In contrast,
fearful observers view the changing atmosphere as an insurmountable
challenge for international cooperation and democratic governance.
Their fear is that the steps needed to avert additional global warming will
be almost impossible to foster democratically and far more complicated
to coordinate than the steps required to protect the ozone layer.

Fortunately, most who agree that the risks of ecological destruction are
high enough to warrant action are also convinced that many of the measures needed to reduce these risks are politically feasible and economically affordable. Some argue that democratic and cooperative approaches
to climate risk reduction will be not only prudent but also profitable for
societies that manage to combine governmental foresight with a sense of
ecological responsibility. Almost all agree that organizing cooperation to
combat changes in the physical climate may have appreciable benefits for
the international political climate.

Clearly, there is much that warrants closer attention by the international community. The stakes are high, the facts are uncertain, the potential for conflict is great, basic political and economic values are in dispute, and the need for action may be urgent. Accordingly, much more
must be learned about the obstacles to international regime formation,
about the incentives for cooperation and coalition building, and about
the nature of large-scale policy making and implementation in a transnational context. That is the subject to which we shall now turn.

Notes

1. A good example of how a minority view in science briefly dominated
U.S. debate on greenhouse policy can be seen in the influence of the Marshall Institute (Seitz et al., 1989) on the Bush administration's position with
regard to the 1992 climate convention. Marshall Institute scientists attributed much of the earth's mean temperature variations to sunspot activity.
John Sununu, President Bush's chief of staff until shortly before the Earth
Summit, played a major role in elevating the controversial views of Marshall
Institute scientists above those of much larger and more respected atmospheric science organizations, presumably to buttress the White House's
argument for a "go slow" policy on greenhouse gas abatement.

2. It is unclear how the uneven cooling influence of ozone depletion and
aerosols will affect greenhouse dynamics in the long run. When modelers

take these offsetting factors into account, some forecasts of future warming have to be revised downward by as much as 30 percent. Conversely, the masking effect of aerosols and ozone depletion indicates that climate sensitivity to atmospheric carbon may be much greater than earlier modeling indicated. Moreover, recent paleoclimate findings suggest that the earth's climate system is capable of much more rapid change than was assumed in previous modeling. Hence, the dynamic nature of the problem makes it very difficult to sort out exactly what the positive and negative implications of counter-cooling effects may be. For a discussion of some of these implications, see T. Wigley and S. Raper, "Implications for Climate and Sea Level of Revised IPCC Emissions Scenarios," *Nature* 357, 6376 (1992): 299–300.

3. The Intergovernmental Panel on Climate Change, in the *1992 IPCC Supplement* (Geneva, Switzerland: World Meteorological Organization and United Nations Environment Program, February, 1992), estimates that sequestration through afforestation will cost about $10–$30 per ton of carbon in tropical regions and as much as $60 per ton in boreal forest zones.

CHAPTER 5

The Environmental
Policy-Making Process

For champions of scientific rationality, the ideal environmental policy-making process would be one in which science replaced politics in shaping all but the ceremonial functions of governance. Debates over environmental policy would presumably be much more fruitful if contending ideas and arguments were judged solely on their technical merits. If policy makers could agree on what the facts were and what they meant, then the focus of their debates could shift from questions about whether to act, and in what direction, to matters of timing and prudent response levels. Policy formation would rely much more than it does today on the authority of science for legitimacy. Science would guide policy with a steady hand, while politicians argued at the margins over who should pay for needed policy reforms and how much environmental risk was acceptable.

Unfortunately, at least for the apostles of scientific rationality, policy arguments seldom win on their merits. Even if merit were the accepted standard, there would be very little agreement, even among scientists, on what constitutes merit. Politics dominates when science equivocates. In fact, about the only useful way to predict most policy outcomes in pluralistic societies is to apply the physicist's notion of vector sums or resultants to the dynamic interaction of competing interests, assigning each interest group a political influence level based on its commitment of available resources and its image status—for example, staff, money, access to information and expertise, prestige and legitimacy in the eyes of the public, and ability to mobilize membership.

Most policy making is a process of incremental distribution or redistribution of wealth and power. It steers benefits disproportionately to groups that are politically organized and viewed positively by policy elites, while spreading costs across the citizenry as a whole or more narrowly across groups burdened with negative social constructions (Schneider and Ingram, 1993). At the international level, policy making is far more complicated due to the sovereign status of each participating policy maker and the immense diversity of cultural influences represented. The process, however, is conceptually similar to what takes place within deliberative bodies at all levels of government, at least within democratic societies. Whether adopting local environmental standards for the disposal of motor oil or developing international safety standards for oil tankers, the fundamental steps of policy making apply, albeit seldom in a linear fashion. The purpose of this chapter is to examine these steps, show how they affect policy content, and indicate where they lead with respect to international environmental agreements.

A Policy Process Heuristic

The content of public policy almost invariably reflects the process by which it is made. Form influences content to such an extent that few policies end up looking like what their proposers intended. Because of the many procedural steps or "clearances" involved in policy making, it may be more accurate to think in terms of policy evolution than policy choice. The policy-making process works on the principle of "survival of the fittest," but fitness is defined and evaluated largely in political terms. If judged by the criteria of ecological well-being, efficiency, social justice, and efficacy, many of today's surviving policies would have been stillborn. Conversely, the most promising policies (in terms of net social benefits) often perish in the fires of political feasibility.

Despite all of these haphazard qualities, however, there is a certain degree of logic and elegant design involved in the making and execution of many public policies. Figure 5-1 presents a highly simplified lifecycle model of policy making with seven distinct stages. The model depicts a far more rational and linear process than can be found in the real world (Stone, 1988), but one that is nevertheless of heuristic value. In practice, policy-making stages overlap and repeat in dizzying combinations. Policies must be constantly adjusted and retooled as new information and

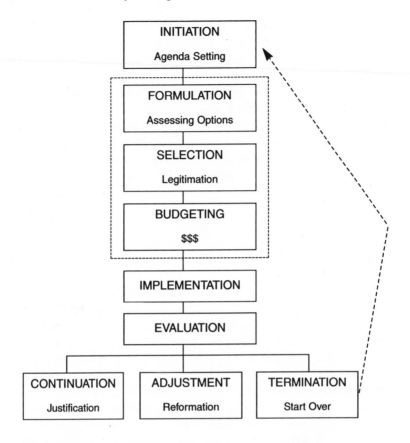

FIGURE 5-1. *Model of "rational" policy making.*

new public perceptions of need or risk arise. Moreover, procedures for implementation frequently alter a policy's content in order to meet the changing demands of target groups and the desires of implementing agencies. Sometimes, policy agreements evolve into something very different from what was first envisioned. Many policies, in fact, are reformulated during the process of implementation. Sometimes, good policies get transformed into measures with bad outcomes (and vice versa), but more often they are merely adjusted in an incremental fashion that is consistent with budgetary priorities of the moment and the cautionary lessons of past political learning.

Because policy is seldom assembled systematically in production stages, the compartmentalized "conveyor belt" model is unreliable as a means of prediction and analysis. As a heuristic device, however, it provides a useful starting point from which to organize thinking about policy making at the local, national, and international level. It captures the procedural logic of policy making in a clear, albeit idealistic, fashion. And because it depicts the various phases and venues in which policy can be altered, the model illuminates how the process can influence policy content. Viewed as a rational ideal (i.e., how scientists think policy should be made), it can even be used to explore the tension between science and politics that often arises in the greenhouse debate and other environmental policy-making controversies. Its principal application in this book, however, is as a partial foundation on which to construct a more specialized and realistic model of international environmental policy making.

No one who understands politics is surprised that the day-to-day practice of policy making differs from the assembly line models touted in many textbooks. Most observers, however, fail to grasp the significant differences between policy making in the environmental arena and policy making in, say, the arenas of education, housing, or defense. Environmental policy has a number of characteristics that set it apart. For example, it alone treats nonhuman beneficiaries of policy as prominent target groups, as in the 1992 global convention on biodiversity. It not only regulates human activity to benefit plants and animals, but it also intentionally redistributes environmental benefits to future generations of people. In that sense, it gives an added dimension to Theodore Lowi's (1972) classic typology of "distributive," "regulatory," and "redistributive" policy.[1] Furthermore, unlike many of the other issue areas, environmental policy making typically grants science a strong voice in agenda setting, formulation, and evaluation. It is more often science-driven or led than are other policy domains, even highly technical ones such as health care or defense policy. It must be noted, however, that many environmental policy makers rely selectively on science to justify or legitimate their preexisting preferences rather than to determine what their preferences should be. Finally, contrary to most patterns of policy development, the environmental policy-formation process tends to be less incremental than processes for other issues (although implementation tends to follow an incremental pattern). This is largely because environmental goals are often presented not only as crisis driven, but as threshold bound.

Environmental quality is often not obtainable with incremental approaches. The goals of ecological restoration and sustainability require large-scale systemic responses rather than piecemeal actions. As Paul Schulman (1980: 10) argues, "These objectives entail the provision of indivisible payoffs by indivisible means. That is to say, policy benefits cannot be derived in amounts proportionate to resource expenditures. They are, instead, derived in 'lumps'." Although there are exceptions (e.g., recycling of paper and plastic), many environmental goals and challenges, such as maintaining biological carrying capacity or stabilizing atmospheric concentrations of greenhouse gases, are essentially all-or-nothing propositions. Achieving 99 percent of what is necessary to avoid collapse of a system still counts as failure to those concerned about good outcomes rather than good intentions.

International Policy Making

In the international arena, environmental policy making involves many of the same blends of science and politics found in domestic settings, but usually without binding institutional mechanisms to force compliance once policies have been agreed on. Most of the nearly 180 international environmental agreements that have been adopted thus far are enforced only to the extent that the parties perceive cooperation to be in their interest. Compliance without enforcement has been the tendency (Chayes and Chayes, 1991). Instead of tough sanctions, the principal tools of international implementation are gentle persuasion and embarrassment caused by media exposure of noncompliance. The majority of these agreements address pollution that threatens a shared water resource. Many focus on transnational polluting activities that cause damage to neighbors. Most have a regional purpose, such as protecting river basins, regional seas, or fragile land areas like the Arctic. Increasingly, however, initiatives with global scope have arisen and forced their way on to both national and international agendas.

There are basically two major ways to achieve binding international environmental agreements. The first, exemplified by the Law of the Seas negotiation, attempts to craft omnibus conventions and comprehensive regimes that spell out the rights and responsibilities of the parties. The second route, exemplified by the ozone, biodiversity, and climate negotiations, follows the two-step approach introduced in the previous chapter: a framework convention establishing general objectives and obligations, and perhaps nonbinding action plans, followed by protocols that mandate specific actions. The term *framework* is used to imply that substantive measures—protocols—are needed to complete the structure of the agreement. In symbolic terms, parties to a framework convention are moving into a house whose walls have not yet been constructed. The advantage—and disadvantage—of the two-step approach over the "all-or-nothing" comprehensive convention is that it makes agreement easier to obtain by bracketing off the hard decisions about precise obligations and

actions. Although there is nothing to prevent protocols from being negotiated simultaneously with framework conventions, many international
political strategists favor a clean separation of the two over a period of
months or even years.[2]

Over the past decade, most environmental diplomacy of a global nature has followed the framework model. Although various proposals have
surfaced for a comprehensive "Law of the Atmosphere" to complement
the still unratified Law of the Sea convention, most observers have argued that the path of least resistance lies in the direction of the framework–protocol instrument. The strategy is to get political leaders talking
about shared principles before asking their nations to adopt the kind of
behavior that is implied by the principles.

Constructing a Model

Figure 5-2 presents a model of international environmental policy making based on the framework–protocol approach. It represents the process
followed or likely to be followed in a number of major environmental
issue areas, including ozone depletion and greenhouse warming, biodiversity, transboundary movement of acid rain, and pollution from ships.
Portrayed as a linear, sequential process, the model can be justly criticized on the same grounds as the previous policy process model. While
being mindful of these limitations, there is much that is useful about the
model as designed. Not only does it suggest the importance of policy
learning and coalition behavior in an iterative fashion, but it also reveals
the shifting importance of scientists, policy "entrepreneurs," advocacy
coalitions, the media, interest groups, policy analysts, national leaders,
international organizations, and environmental ministries in shaping the
content of the process. While it is true that substantial overlap of roles is
common (e.g., scientists, media personalities, national opinion leaders,
and representatives of international organizations may all serve from
time-to-time as policy entrepreneurs), it is appropriate to indicate which
roles are most influential at each stage of the process.

Problem Identification and Definition

Causal Connections and Epistemic Communities
Policy process models usually begin with formal agenda setting and the
identification of policy options. In matters of global environmental
change, however, it is important to include steps that precede formal

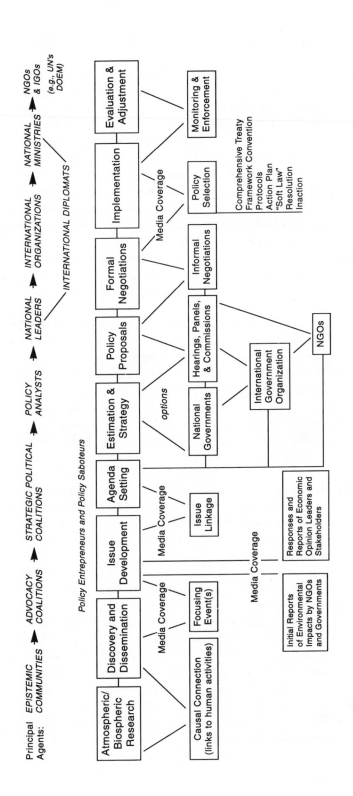

FIGURE 5-2. *The international environmental policy-making process.*

agenda setting—steps that often take place before a policy issue is identified and defined, let alone placed on the agenda. These steps often begin in the mind of a scientist who is investigating a phenomenon or condition that involves unexplained changes in one or more environmental variables or health indicators. Monitoring sharp declines in the population of frogs or sampling acidity levels in Scandinavian lakes are examples of how environmental monitoring has led to the definition of new public policy problems. Another way in which scientists contribute—however inadvertently—to agenda building occurs when their laboratory experiments raise questions about environmental conditions outside the laboratory. A classic example of this can be seen in tests of laboratory animals that reveal environmental cancer risks, or the discovery of ozone-depletion effects associated with CFCs—a discovery that took place in a laboratory, not through atmospheric sampling (Molina and Rowland, 1974).

The pursuit of scientific learning has often led to discoveries that end up inviting widespread policy attention, as the cases of ozone depletion, global warming, and conservation biology amply demonstrate. Lynton Caldwell (1990: 8–9, 14) has described the international movement for environmental protection as a historical process of social learning, assisted by science, and characterized by efforts to reconcile human behavior with knowledge about the biosphere. This notion of social learning appears to be a useful one for conceptualizing the agenda-building and policy-formation stages involved in international environmental protection. Not only does it capture the tentative nature of knowledge about environmental change, but it directs attention to the pivotal role of environmental scientists—more broadly, what Peter Haas (1989) and others have labeled "epistemic communities"—in converting that knowledge into power through the identification and framing of international environmental policy issues.

The role of scientists in the development of policy to protect the ozone layer offers one of the most dramatic examples of how epistemic communities operate. The process began in the early 1970s with research conducted in California by Sherwood Rowland and Mario Molina. Their discovery in the laboratory of a causal connection between CFCs and ozone destruction was reported in the journal *Nature* (Molina and Rowland,1974) and then discussed and analyzed, along with related research by Stolarski and Cicerone (1974), in a decade-long series of meetings, reports, and hearings arranged by scientists, the chemical industry, and the U.S. Congress (Roan, 1989). Although hotly disputed at times, Rowland and Molina's findings were deemed sufficiently compelling by U.S. policy makers to warrant a ban in 1978 on nonessential uses of CFC aerosols. Although Canada and a number of northern European nations followed suit, the influence of Rowland and Molina's discovery on international policy making was not keenly felt until scientists from the British Antarctic Survey discovered the ozone hole in 1984. That discovery, which represents the "focusing event" in the model, greatly accelerated efforts that had begun in Stockholm two years earlier to construct a global convention on ozone protection.

Shifting to the greenhouse issue, the role of epistemic communities is harder to define, but no less important. Scientific claims about global warming due to human activities go back at least 130 years, but the most important research contributions are usually traced to the work of Svante Arrhenius in the 1890s.[3] In more recent years, major reports by the U.N.'s Intergovernmental Panel on Climate Change (Houghton et al., 1990), the U.S. National Academy of Sciences (1991), the World Meteorological Organization (Intergovernmental Panel, 1992), and other prominent scientific bodies have stimulated wide discussion and additional research on the subject. International meetings of scientists in Villach, Bellagio, Toronto, Cairo, Geneva, and elsewhere have resulted in important declarations and recommendations for stepped-up research, not to mention increased calls for international cooperation.[4] As noted in the previous chapter, scientists have organized repeatedly to apply political pressure in the form of petitions, press conferences, and public forums.

The contribution of scientists in the biodiversity debate is in some instances even more influential than in the case of atmospheric issues. The regime to protect polar bears, for example, came about in response to concerns expressed by a small group of Arctic wildlife specialists convened by the International Union for the Conservation of Nature and Natural Resources (Fikkan et al., 1993). Similar efforts have been made by marine biologists concerned about human threats to whales, dolphins, seals, sea otters, and many species of fish. Focusing on terrestrial species, prominent biologists, such as Edward Wilson, Peter Raven, and Edward Wolf, have argued persuasively that the rapid decimation of prime habitat in much of the world's tropical forests and wetlands has created a biodiversity crisis that is unprecedented in the last seventy-five million years. The popular symbols of this crisis have tended to be large, exotic animals like panda bears, blue whales, and elephants; but scientists have continued to point out that the most precipitous declines are occurring in the plant and insect worlds. Although television documentaries and children's shows about unusual animals and fish continue to serve as a major impetus for biodiversity protection, it is the worldwide science community that provides most of the informational content of such programming and that must be credited with bringing to light the desperate situation facing hundreds of thousands and perhaps millions of species.

Focusing Events

The creation of public issues, according to many political scientists, really begins with the occurrence of "triggering" or "focusing" events (Cobb and Elder, 1983), which help to shape issues that are then defined in action terms by "initiators" or "policy entrepreneurs" (Kingdon, 1984). The focusing event is usually a sudden and unexpected change, ranging from some deadly disaster to some miraculous medical discovery. Its dramatic appearance invites news media coverage and public concern, excitement, or curiosity.

The term *policy entrepreneur* refers to a person or small group that facilitates and coordinates the strategic growth of political coalitions around a particular policy problem and proposed response. Policy entrepreneurs typically exploit focusing events to create a problem definition or policy image that is conducive to their interests. Framing of issues is critical to policy success (Schon, 1994). While laboratory discoveries can serve as trigger devices for issue creation, the more probable route in the case of international environmental issues is for dramatic events that occur in nature to be interpreted by the media and the public as confirmations of earlier claims by scientists about impending threats to the biosphere. The discovery of the ozone hole over Antarctic had this confirming effect on the claims of Rowland and Molina. In a less direct way, the revelation that eight of the warmest years on record occurred in the 1980–1992 period has arguably had this effect on public perceptions of the greenhouse issue. With respect to biodiversity, focusing events amplified by the media have been used effectively by environmental policy entrepreneurs to dramatize the dire warnings of biologists about species vulnerability. Examples include the spotted owl controversy in the United States and the public spectacle created in 1989 by Kenyan authorities igniting a giant bonfire of over $3 million worth of ivory that had been confiscated from elephant poachers (Mdlongwa, 1989).

In the case of climate change, the evidence creating the focusing event was highly dubious, but it was public perceptions that counted, once the issue achieved visibility in the popular media. The common perception among nonscientists that the droughts, intense hurricanes, heat waves, and bitter cold spells of the 1980s were signs of climate change, together with scientist James Hansen's Senate testimony, may have provided a series of focusing events comparable in significance to the Antarctic ozone hole. Even more plausible is the possibility that the discovery of a rapidly growing ozone hole became in some sense a surrogate trigger for global-warming concerns. A focusing event in one atmospheric arena seemed to spill inevitably into the other. Similarly, scientific investigations into the plight of China's panda population or African elephants helped stimulate public concern about habitat destruction in faraway places like the Amazon.

The bitter contest to save the Tennessee snail darter had the same kind of effect on efforts to save the California condor and later the spotted owl. In each of these cases it should be noted that the role of scientists in helping to frame the issue and in drawing attention to possibly irreversible environmental changes was critical to the popular debate that followed. It must be noted, however, that in other cases, the international scientific community has remained quiescent, reluctant to express concern without more data, while politically active environmental organizations, and in some cases zealous government leaders, have mounted campaigns to give an issue heightened public visibility. This has often led to friction between scientists and environmental activists over the proper use of science-based arguments in policy development (Ludwig, 1994; Brown, 1993).

Policy Entrepreneurs and Saboteurs

Serving to connect the worlds of scientific discovery and policy action are the individuals and groups who function as catalysts and facilitators for change. Sometimes the entrepreneurs are themselves scientists who personally lobby political leaders and invite media attention for the purpose of influencing policy. In the case of ozone protection, Sherwood Rowland played this role in a protracted debate with DuPont Chemical Corporation as part of an effort to win federal restrictions on CFC use. With regard to global-warming questions, Stephen Schneider of the National Center for Atmospheric Research and James Hansen are examples of researchers whose statements to the media and testimony before Congress earned them a mixture of respect and notoriety that is often reserved for scientists who take their controversial views outside the laboratory and use them to press for specific policy changes.[5] Prominent policy entrepreneurs of conservation biology have included Martin Holdgate, director general of the World Conservation Union; Harvard's Edward Wilson; British author Norman Myers; and Peter Raven, director of the Missouri Botanical Garden.

Another type of policy entrepreneur is the international diplomat who performs the "cross-pollinating" function of getting scientists and policy makers together in dialogue and exploration of the issues and options. In the ozone and greenhouse cases, Mostafa Tolba, former director of the U.N. Environmental Program (UNEP), acted as a key figure in this role. Combining his experience as an Egyptian scientist and as a U.N. diplomat, Tolba persuaded many national leaders to participate in UNEP-sponsored science and policy forums on ozone and greenhouse issues. Nonscientists such as Canada's Maurice Strong and Singapore's Tommy Koh have played crucial roles in suggesting policy frameworks, alternatives, and compromises in key international environmental negotiations. Strong, whose entrepreneurial credentials began as a teenage businessman, has facilitated dozens of international environmental negotiations—most prominently as secretary general of both the Stockholm (1974) and Rio de Janeiro (1992) world conferences on the environment. Koh's efforts to bring opposing parties together on divisive issues at the Rio conference earned him a reputation as one of the most skillful international environmental policy entrepreneurs.

A related type of policy entrepreneur is the national political leader, such as Vice President Al Gore, or a symbolic political leader, such as Britain's Prince Philip, who establishes his or her policy agenda near the center of power and is instrumental in bringing together diplomats, scientists, and ordinary citizens in a variety of forums intended to foster greater understanding of the issues. Perhaps the most effective of all such entrepreneurial politicians in recent years has been Gro Harlem Brundtland, prime minister of Norway and former head of the World Commission on Environment and Development. Brundtland's initiatives on behalf of sustainable development and population stabilization had a great deal of influence on agenda preparations for the 1992 Earth Summit and the 1994 world conference on population.

The final and most diverse category of policy entrepreneur belongs to nongovernmental activists who skillfully build political coalitions and influence public opinion on behalf of specific policy initiatives. Included in this category, for example, are Malaysia's Martin Khor, France's Jacque Cousteau, Kenya's Wangari Maathai, India's Ashok Koshla, Switzerland's Stephan Schmidheiny, Brazil's Jose Goldemberg, the late Petra Kelly of Germany, and America's Jonathan Lash and Lester Brown. Drawing popular attention and visibility to the work of these often invisible entrepreneurs are a number of internationally recognized celebrities in the music and entertainment industry. Such varied personalities as film stars Roger Moore, Jane Fonda, Robert Redford, and Shirley MacLaine; singers Paul McCartney, Sting (Gordon Matthew Sumner), and John Denver; and even a few celebrity athletes, such as former Brazilian soccer star Pele, have lent their names to environmental causes for use by policy entrepreneurs in enlisting public support for environmental action.

Working to counter the efforts of policy entrepreneurs are individuals and small groups who specialize in the formation of blocking coalitions. Their aim is to discourage and sometimes sabotage policy proposals that they deem detrimental to their interests or to those of society in general. At the Rio conference, certain representatives of Middle Eastern oil interests and representatives of the Vatican were accused of playing this role in efforts to amplify dissensus about various energy-conservation and implied population-stabilization measures included in the conference's action plan, Agenda 21. Granting that one policy's entrepreneur is often another's saboteur, the fact is that international politics generally favors the activities of the policy saboteur. As is typically the case in domestic politics, it is usually easier to stop something in the policy process than to make it go forward. As we shall see, however, sabotage is more difficult in the early stages of policy formation, when the entrepreneur's images of crisis and bold solutions are more likely to invite public support for major policy changes. It is during implementation of an "infant" policy that saboteurs often have their greatest influence.

Advocacy Coalitions

Mention has already been made of the struggle among interest groups for political and economic advantage. Interest group competition clearly plays an energizing role in policy formation; however, it is not the only activity driving the policy process. Interest groups come and go with each new proposal or initiative, but some group struggles take place at a deeper level than that of simple interest articulation and aggregation. Many groups owe their continued existence to a public philosophy that transcends the particular interests of its members. Political scientist Paul Sabatier (Sabatier and Jenkins-Smith, 1993) has termed such groups "advocacy coalitions." Advocacy coalitions consist of people with deeply shared belief systems and long-term political interests, as well as members of government, the press, and research organizations who support their interests but do not necessarily share their belief systems. More than an instrumental assemblage of interest groups or "coalitions of convenience," the advocacy coalition is organized to fight protracted wars, not just immediate battles. It engages in policy-oriented learning to bring about long-term change and to buttress its core beliefs. Because its continued existence rarely depends on the outcome of a particular issue or policy debate, a coalition of this type often appears stable over periods of a decade or more. In a sense, advocacy coalitions are the "engines" of the environmental policy-making process. They are the principal means of interest articulation by which the process derives its impetus.

Environmental Advocacy

Active environmentalists constitute one of the world's most significant advocacy coalitions of the past twenty-five years. Technically, it is more accurate to classify environmentalists as members of a social movement made up of numerous advocacy coalitions, each organized around a particular issue or goal, such as clean air, clean water, or the protection of forests, birds, and wildlife. Internationally, the environmental movement is a collection of over six thousand organizations that coalesce into relatively stable clusters of advocacy coalitions and temporary clusters of issue networks and interest groups. These coalitions and issue networks can be further classified into five major groupings on the basis of their members' priorities with respect to environmental protection. Because of overlapping objectives among the members of different clusters, and because many environmentalists maintain active roles in two or more of the clusters, the classification scheme is best used to represent differences in *emphasis* rather than in substance. The five major clusters consist of:

1. Coalitions based on human health concerns (e.g., public and occupational health effects of toxic agents transmitted by air, food, and drinking water)

2. Coalitions that emphasize ecological health and diversity (e.g., wilderness preservation and wildlife protection)

3. Coalitions focused on global geochemical change (e.g., climate and atmospheric protection)

4. Coalitions concerned primarily with sustainable resource consumption and end-use efficiency (e.g., energy and water conservation)

5. Coalitions formed for the purpose of spiritual and ethical development (e.g., certain "new age" philosophies, such as those derived from the "Gaia hypothesis" of James Lovelock).

Together, these advocacy coalitions constitute a formidable force for change in national and international environmental politics.

Arrayed against these environmental advocates has been a powerful set of business- and industry-led advocacy coalitions, which have drawn much of their popular support and legitimacy from the ideal of a market economy based on individual freedom. These coalitions have been organized historically around seven major enterprises: (1) the energy industries—coal, oil, gas, and nuclear power interests; (2) forestry and wood products industries; (3) food and agricultural enterprises; (4) real estate developers and marketers; (5) automotive manufacturers, sellers, repairers, and associated industries; (6) the chemical industry; and last, but not least, (7) government. While it may seem odd to classify government—or, more precisely, a subgovernmental unit—as an advocacy coalition, the fact is that government agencies seldom play a neutral role in the development and implementation of environmental or any other kind of policy. In much of the world, government's role in facilitating unsustainable development and blocking or deferring environmental protection appears to be much more consequential than its attempts to prevent environmental destruction.[6] For this reason, I have included it with coalitions that are often viewed as ardent defenders of the status quo.

The tension between development interests and those seeking to regulate development activities on behalf of environmental protection has often been portrayed with the use of powerful stereotypes. The labels "anti-environment" and "pro-growth" attest to the dichotomous character of environmental conflict. While significant variations exist between countries and between coalitions—some are more consensual, others more confrontational or litigious—most coalitions that are engaged in debates over environmental policy accept the us-versus-them characterizations of developers and regulators. This is particularly the case in Western industrial nations.

Staffed by political activists who generally distrust big business more than big government, environmental coalitions have for the most part followed an adversarial model of public advocacy, urging more regulation of land use and economic development, stronger enforcement of existing regulations, and tougher penalties for violators, based on the "polluter pays" principle (see chapter 7). The economic development coalitions, by contrast, have focused most of their efforts on reducing what they see as government overregulation of business and industry—regulation that they believe is based on exaggerated fears of environmental impacts. Declaring themselves the champions of economic growth, the advocates of free-market progress have skillfully argued that gains in wealth and technology will provide more environmental protection than can be obtained from all the well-intended regulatory maneuvers of environmentalists (see, for example, Simon, 1987; Ray, 1990; Anderson and Leal, 1991). The more dogmatic among them dismiss most environmentalists as pastoral idealists, misanthropic animal lovers, or health fanatics with a penchant for self-denial. Environmental leaders, for their part, have argued that what passes today for economic growth is often, in reality, a tragic episode of ecological plunder carried out by myopic profiteers acting in concert with insatiable consumers, whose preferences have been woefully distorted by mass advertising (see, for example, Commoner, 1990; Goldsmith, 1993).

In retracing the major contours of environmental policy making, it is customary to portray environmental advocacy in terms of binary choices and bipolar politics. To the political analyst, knowing the coalition players in a two-sided contest (e.g., environmentalists versus industry), and their positions, allows one to predict policy outcomes or resultants from the relative amounts of power and resources each advocacy coalition has at its disposal. Unfortunately, those who understand environmental policy making in this dualistic fashion are in a poor position to appreciate the complexity and uncertainty that characterize contemporary environmental politics. The problem with such an understanding is that it treats the policy-making process as a black box in which the demands of opposing forces are reconciled into viable compromise through the exercise of power or persuasion. Such a view leaves too much to imagination and the force of personality, and ignores the enormous momentum of history, culture, symbolic politics, and reliance on standard operating procedures in helping to shape the content and style of policy. What is largely missing from the regulation versus development debate is an appreciation of the degree to which the policy process influences policy outcomes. International environmental policy making, along with that of national governments, cannot be adequately examined by analyzing the opposing views and values of advocacy coalitions alone. A multivariate process orientation is needed—one that gives due consideration to the influence of history, institutional design, and cultural traditions in formulating and implementing policy.

Agenda Setting

Issue Development and Linkage

Once an issue has been defined and brought to the attention of advocacy coalitions and opinion leaders, there is typically a call for authoritative analyses by government and nongovernmental organizations of the policy implications raised by prior scientific reports. These analyses, in turn, are often the subject of critical reports published by skeptics and by stakeholder organizations who fear the costs of environmental regulation that new policies may create. An early example of this process in greenhouse issue development can be seen in the response to reports of the Intergovernmental Panel on Climate Change and the U.S. Environmental

Protection Agency's draft report to Congress, "Policy Options for Stabilizing Global Climate." These reports led to critical studies by the George Marshall Institute arguing that many of the policies under consideration would be "unnecessary or even harmful" (Seitz et al. 1989). Other studies sponsored by the American Coal Association, the Electric Power Research Institute, and various business groups reached similar conclusions. On the other hand, some stakeholder organizations, such as the nuclear power industry, supported the findings of early science and government reports, hoping perhaps that their industry would benefit from changes in energy policy dictated by those findings.

A key factor in agenda building has to do with the addition or subtraction of issues that can be linked to the lead issue(s) under discussion. In international negotiations, the role of issue linkage may be even more important than it is in domestic settings. Unfortunately, research on this subject has been slow to develop. James K. Sebenius's (1983, 1984, 1991) analysis of the Law of the Sea negotiating process is one of the best treatments of issue linkage in the international relations literature. He shows that seemingly unrelated policy issues can be strategically tied together in order to form coalitions and invite compound agreements that would be much more difficult, if not impossible, if the issues had remained separated. He also demonstrates that some compound negotiating problems are better tackled by subtracting issues from the negotiations. It is the sequencing of the process and its promise for mutual advantage that matters most (Susskind, 1994: 82–98).

Unlike much of international relations research that treats issues and actors as constants, research on international agenda building using linkage strategies treats both issues and actors as variables. Both aspects, of course, involve the question of power. Some actors may be able to force issue linkage during negotiations in favor of their interests. The question of who participates in negotiations will also reflect the existing power structure. The most important question raised by Sebenius is whether issue linkage can enhance or reduce a zone of possible agreement among nations.

Basically there are four broad possibilities (Sebenius, 1983). The first type of issue linkage involves the addition of differentially valued, unrelated issues. In the greenhouse case, for example, this could involve linking proposals for a carbon tax, and the revenue it would generate, to proposals for the development of a global environmental trust fund. A second type of issue linkage focuses on overcoming distributional impediments to jointly beneficial agreements by adding side payments. The provision of technology transfers (e.g., CFC substitutes) or direct monetary assistance would constitute a side payment that could facilitate Third

World compliance with possible agreements for ozone and climate protection. A third approach emphasizes the addition of issues to exploit their dependencies. Linking the rainforest-protection issue and industrial CO_2 emissions, for example, would exploit the existing dependencies between these issues (e.g., trees can absorb some of the CO_2 emissions from power plants). Finally, issue linkage can also lead to a reduction in a zone of possible agreement, for example, by adding issues that have no possibility for consensus or by linking issues that have individual zones of possible agreement but a smaller combined zone for concurrence. Proposals to reduce CO_2 emissions by adding nuclear power development to energy conservation strategies have had this effect on the environmental community.

Coalition Building

Setting the formal policy agenda for national governments, international organizations, and multilateral negotiations is largely a function of coalition building, facilitated by issue linkage, successful media coverage, the organizing efforts of policy entrepreneurs, and the pressure of environmental NGOs. Coalition building starts with interest groups that seek to enlarge their political influence by joining with other interest groups to form a strategic political coalition. The term *strategic* is used to indicate that the resulting assemblage is a coalition of convenience or short-term political advantage, rather than an expression of fundamental agreement and deeply shared beliefs. Advocacy coalitions also enter into temporary alliances with interest groups and other coalitions in recognition of common interests and the mutual benefit of acting in concert to realize them. At the same time, however, they are likely to encounter a gulf in core values and belief systems that separates the strategic coalition members, making the arrangement unstable in the long term. These problems are magnified in the mobilization of transnational coalitions, where cultural and other differences may result in conflicting policy preferences and problem definitions. While constantly exploiting ambiguities or nuances in the primary issue and in the response options being raised, policy entrepreneurs add and subtract side issues in order to overcome the reluctance of advocacy coalitions to join temporarily with groups who represent a competing philosophy or approach, or who oppose them on other issues. Most of the time, however, the real or imagined differences in interests and values cannot be sharply drawn on the basis of membership rosters.

   In the cases of ozone and climate protection, the strategic coalitions overlap to a very large degree. They include members from general-purpose environmental organizations, energy-efficiency advocates, the rainforest action coalition, minor political parties such as the Greens, segments of the nuclear power industry, many atmospheric scientists, and numerous public affairs, religious, and professional organizations with an interest in improving international understanding, trade, and cooperation. Biodiversity coalitions include some of the same organizations as the atmospheric coalitions, especially those member organizations with interests in forest protection. Groups such as the World Wildlife Fund, the World Conservation Society (IUCN), and Greenpeace represent international memberships that lend added weight to the agenda demands of national environmental coalitions.

A major difference thus far between biodiversity, ozone, and greenhouse politics is the role of industry in coalition building. In the case of biodiversity, key industries, such as forest products and pharmaceuticals, are at odds over the importance of preservation. Pharmaceutical firms have begun to play a significant role in conservation biology by funding programs in Costa Rica and other countries for the purpose of preserving potential plant species that may contain profitable medical secrets.[7] But timber and agricultural interests clearly have the stronger hand in most debates about the fate of biologically rich forests. In the case of ozone protection, the role of industry has changed dramatically in the past decade. After years of opposition to CFC controls, DuPont and nearly five hundred other CFC manufacturers in 1986 announced a reversal of their position on ozone risks from CFCs, thus removing the largest economic barrier to government action. No corresponding move by carbon-based energy industries, timber extractors, or methane emitters has occurred in the case of greenhouse gases. Ending CFC production is expensive—DuPont pegs the cost of its voluntary phase-out program at $750 million—but it is doubtlessly cheaper than the electric utility industry's cost of phasing out coal, which is estimated in the hundreds of billions of dollars.[8] Partly for this reason, the political coalitions forming around greenhouse issues tend to be more polarized along the traditional lines of environmentalists versus industry. As a result, the domestic and international politics of controlling greenhouse gases will probably continue to be more conflictual than those that brought the CFC issue to the table in Vienna and Montreal.

Policy Formation

Government Estimation and Strategy

Once advocacy coalitions or strategic political coalitions have succeeded in placing an international environmental issue before a national governing body, political attention shifts to encompass domestic political considerations that will help shape and, in some cases, fully determine the nation's negotiating posture at the international level. The most important considerations for government strategists involve how various proposed policy responses might affect their nation's leading economic and political stakeholders, and how such responses could change the comparative advantage or disadvantage of their nation—vis-à-vis other nations—in trade, productivity, military power, and political leverage.

When the policy issues under consideration have a clear transnational character, national governments usually agree to prepare environmental self-assessments that can be deposited with an international agency or preparatory committee and used as a formal starting point for future international negotiations. Past assessments, while often informative, have been prepared, not surprisingly, in self-serving ways. They have typically concentrated on environmental policy issues, definitions, and responses that required little disruption of domestic political agendas and minimal commitment of national funds and government resources on behalf of the global environment. More often than not, the self-assessments have provided a platform for each nation's environmental success stories, the exceptions being certain developing countries that are seeking an infusion of foreign aid and therefore have no desire to minimize the severity of the problems they face.

The most influential forms of national estimation and assessment are performed by environmental ministries, task forces, science and professional academies, and interagency working groups. The dominant voices on strategy, however, are usually reserved for the finance ministries and the government's economic advisors. If a nation-state chooses, or is compelled, to include an international environmental issue on its institutional agenda, financial and budgetary analysts invariably take the lead in identifying ways in which the nation and its leaders might be helped or hurt by possible international agreements. These analysts, while sometimes supportive of environmental goals, may nevertheless attempt to recast the environmental policy issue into one of unemployment, trade, income distribution, or market interference and thereby influence the policy choices open to decision makers.

In theory, nations developing a strategy on a particular international environmental issue can aspire to the role of international leader, supportive follower, "swing voter," or member of a blocking coalition. Practically speaking, strategic positioning is usually a more subtle or ambiguous process. Government leaders may wish to send conflicting signals or to embrace a different policy image when they are talking to environmental groups than when they are addressing, for instance, the business community. At the risk of sounding deeply cynical, the objectives of most governments in environmental estimation and strategy formation are to find scientific validation for the views of the leadership, to appear responsive to powerful domestic political coalitions, and to avoid being stampeded into unwanted action by the mobilizing efforts of domestic NGOs, other nations, or transnational coalitions.

Formal Negotiations

Once political leaders have assessed the implications of their government's analyses, and perhaps reshaped strategy to comport better with personal political ambitions, the process becomes one of defining participation in international preparatory meetings and empowering representatives to negotiate agreements and collective action strategies. As Robert Putnam (1988) argues, this part of the process can be thought of as a "two-level game" in which domestic and international politics interact in ways that often require strategic bargaining at each level to be reconciled by some central decision maker:

> At the national level, domestic groups pursue their interests by pressuring the government to adopt favorable policies, and politicians seek power by constructing coalitions among those groups. At the international level, national governments seek to maximize their own ability to satisfy domestic pressures, while minimizing the adverse consequences of foreign developments. Neither of the two games can be ignored by central decision makers, so long as their countries remain interdependent, yet sovereign. (p. 434)

In Putnam's view, domestic political concerns about what is in the "national interest" will inevitably influence international diplomacy in ways that usually limit and sometimes expand the opportunities for negotiation and agreement. "Winning" basically means getting agreements that can be ratified or legitimized in domestic politics. National negotiating strategies, accordingly, seek to define and link issues, expand coalitions, target threats, distribute side payments, and exploit domestic cleavages or uncertainties in such a way that the national leadership's bargaining positions in domestic and international arenas are simultaneously strengthened.

Although the negotiators for a chief of government may be allowed very little discretion or flexibility in representing their nation at the bargaining table, in environmental issue areas, the rapidly changing scientific knowledge base and the growing pressure of NGO observers in negotiations suggest that governments may have to design their negotiating strategies in the future with greater flexibility and more room for genuine deliberation. The strategic use of experimentation and ambiguity are very inviting in the midst of swiftly changing coalition behavior, government learning, problem framing, and evidence. As a result, it is becoming much more difficult in international environmental negotiations to regard each participant's interests as given and fixed. Increasingly, it appears that the realism approach long vaunted in the study and practice of international politics may be based on a false premise—that nations always know their major interests. National self-interest is becoming harder to calculate in a world of transboundary environmental risks and expanding transnational networks of economic trade and political communication. In response, some scholars (e.g., Feldman, 1990) have proposed an alternative incremental and interactive learning model in which national interests and positions emerge from the bargaining process itself, rather than from preexisting power and interest structures that are etched deeply into the realist models. In this view, static notions of stakeholder interests and influence, left over from the Cold War era, will almost inevitably become maladaptive in future global environmental negotiations.

Policy Selection and Legitimation

Adoption and Ratification

There are at least three broad categories of policy options from which international environmental diplomats routinely select their preferred courses of action: "hard" law (i.e., binding agreements), "soft" law (i.e., nonbinding codes of conduct and guidelines), and *voluntary* action plans.

Hard Law. The formal adoption of binding international environmental policies usually involves a three-stage operation. It begins in prominent cases with a preparatory committee ("PrepCom") agreement or draft treaty that lays out the major terms of a desired final agreement. The political importance of PrepCom agreements is that they reduce uncertainty about whether the negotiating parties will have anything to show for their troubles when the final negotiating conference takes place. Because of the media exposure and public visibility that often surrounds the main conference, governments usually want assurance that the capstone proceedings will be portrayed as productive and successful, from their point of view, before committing the prestige of their high-level representatives or delegates. Most diplomats want to reduce the risk of unpleasant surprises in the final negotiations. As a result, the final meeting of the parties to form an agreement is often a ceremonial affair—most of the hard work having been completed at the PrepCom stage. The process is designed to culminate in the formal signing of an agreement by most of the assembled parties. Once this has taken place, the remaining operation becomes ratification—at least for those governments that require further review and endorsement before the agreement can enter into force.

Soft Law. Most of the time, officials and diplomats charged with the task of policy selection are not interested in strong, binding agreements. In fact, the most popular metaphor used to describe international environmental policy selection is one of softening or dilution—attempts to "water down" proposals. Rather than opposing strong environmental policies outright, governments often attempt to preserve flexibility by softening proposed policies into non-binding principles, standards, and guidelines. Examples of these soft laws include the international drinking-water guidelines established by the World Health Organization, a variety of nuclear power safety guidelines established by the International Atomic Energy Agency, and the ill-fated attempt by the U.N. Food and Agricultural Organization to extend the narrowly defined principle of "common heritage" to the ownership of genetic resources (e.g., seeds derived from wild plants). Some soft laws harden over time into binding agreements, an example being the 1987 Cairo guidelines on hazardous-waste disposal and transport, which blossomed into the Basel Convention on Control of Transboundary Movements of Hazardous Wastes.

Action Plans. Another popular strategy, first employed in preparations for the Stockholm Conference, is to develop a comprehensive action plan for environmental management. Here the emphasis is on creating a consensus document to guide national development policies with respect to environmental protection. Action plans, like soft law, are not legally binding, but they often presuppose international movement, eventually, toward binding policies. Agenda 21 (United Nations, 1992), the best-known action plan, contains hundreds of pages of environmental objectives and proposed policy measures to achieve them. Like the 1975 Mediterranean Action Plan or the 1985 Tropical Forestry Action Plan, Agenda 21 represents an agreement among nations to act on environmental problems, but without the force of binding deadlines or the fear of sanctions for failing to act.

Implementation

International Ends and National Means

The implementation of international environmental agreements is an exercise in international coordination and national interpretation, bureaucratic persuasion, and sometimes outright intimidation. Cooperation is needed both within and between national governments, as well as between international organizations like the World Bank, business and development interests, and environmental NGOs. Because each participating government is responsible for implementing provisions within its territory, the greater the number of state actors or signatories, the greater will tend to be the challenges of cooperation and coordination. In the policy implementation literature, this is know as the "complexity of joint action" problem (Pressman and Wildavsky, 1973). Such collective action problems are particularly difficult when claims of sovereignty confer on all participants political equality in veto power, making their control over state-level implementation absolute. When dozens of sovereign states are involved in executing an agreement, the chances are great that there will be large differences in policy interpretation and implementation strategy, and that these differences will be perpetuated as part of each state's demand for self-determination.

The principal barriers to implementation of international policies arise in the lack of compulsory jurisdictions for overseeing implementation and compliance. In domestic policy settings, implementation is usually made easier by the credible threat of punishment or sanctions for noncompliance. About the best that the world community can do in cases of noncompliance or improper implementation by a treaty member is to accuse the offending party publicly of nonperformance of duty. Censure, trade sanctions, and revocation of certain international memberships and privileges enjoyed by the member are all possible responses, but for the most part, environmental advances at the global level are pushed more by the desire of most state participants to be seen as responsible and cooperative—or alternatively by their fear of embarrassing media coverage—than by any external threat of punishment or retaliation by the international community.

Institutional Coordination and Enforcement

In order to implement international policies in a timely fashion, institutional impediments must be carefully avoided. Since opponents of a policy can often do more damage at the implementation stage than at the adoption stage, lining up institutional support for rapid and coordinated implementation is often the only way to ensure that the policy being implemented will bear a strong resemblance to the policy originally adopted. Unfortunately, however, institutional coordination at the international level is severely hampered by the fact that the institutions in question have little if any role in enforcement and therefore lack the authority to manage implementation. According to Peter Haas et al. (1993: 398), international environmental institutions are basically designed to perform three limited functions:

> *They enhance the ability to make and keep agreements, they promote concern among governments, and they build national political and administrative capacity. We find little evidence that international organizations enforce rules; indeed, in our case studies, monitoring of environmental quality and national policy measures was a far more important institutional activity than direct enforcement.*

Enforcement of international environmental conventions would be much easier if the International Court of Justice (ICJ) at The Hague was given binding authority to review and adjudicate claims of noncompliance with international law. The implied surrender of national sovereignty, however, makes such judicial empowerment politically untenable, at least for now. The ICJ was created in 1945 for the purpose of adjudicating disputes among nations so that the parties to the disputes would not resort to force in order to settle their claims and grievances. Sadly, in the eyes of reformers, the ICJ has not been permitted to play a strong role in either dispute resolution or treaty compliance. The court lacks the authority and power to impose its jurisdiction and its rulings on nonconsenting parties. Only one environmental treaty dispute has been reviewed by the ICJ—the 1974 suit by Australia and New Zealand to enjoin France from testing nuclear weapons in the waters of French Polynesia—but even this case (*Australia* v. *France*, 57 ILR 350-600, *ICJ Reports* 1974: 253) was dropped after France unilaterally decided to confine its testing to underground areas.

In the absence of wide support for supranational dispute resolution and treaty enforcement mechanisms, the international community has had to settle for what amounts to a custom of voluntary compliance. To be sure, voluntary compliance is the preferred outcome in all environmental policy making, but it is important to note that most international environmental treaties today require relatively little sacrifice on the part of signatory nations. As the costs of compliance rise in the future—assuming environmental standards have to be strengthened—voluntary efforts may decline. If this happens, the role of NGOs in calling attention to noncompliance, and in enlisting the help of the mass media to publicize egregious cases, will take on added importance.

With the help of an environmental "shame index," NGOs can help to balance rising compliance costs by increasing the political costs of defiance (i.e., the costs of exercising national sovereignty). Beyond that, however, they can actively help to reduce compliance costs by assisting governments with the monitoring and coordination tasks that efficient policy making requires. Today, international environmental NGOs are often better equipped than governments to carry out programs and studies of environmental protection. In the future, a much more active and responsible role in the policy process is envisioned for NGOs, but winning official recognition of that role is likely to be very difficult.

Within the U.N. system, more than twenty international organizations have major responsibilities for environmental planning and policy coordination (Kimball and Boyd, 1992: 41). Few actively seek partnerships with nongovernmental environmental groups. Table 5-1 provides a summary of these organizations and some of their areas of environmental responsibility. Although calls for "new institutional authority" in global environmental policy making have increased (Sand, 1990: 21), the prevailing sentiment seems to be that the old institutions of the nation-state system will be adequate to usher in a new environmental world order, if indeed one is needed.

To improve environmental coordination at the international level, a number of joint planning and implementation mechanisms have been created for ensuring communication and information flows across institutions and programs. At the center of this activity is a steering committee with the ponderous name Designated Officials on Environmental Matters (DOEM). The DOEM was created by the U.N. Administrative Committee on Coordination (ACC) in 1978, replacing a smaller-scale environmental coordination board within UNEP. The DOEM, while still chaired by UNEP, includes representatives from all U.N. organizations with significant environmental responsibilities and interests. Together, the designated officials oversee what is called the System-Wide Medium-Term Environment Program (SWMTEP)—a synthesis of programs, policies, and action plans aimed at the general goal of sustainable development. In theory, the UNEP–DOEM–SWMTEP linkage provides a strong capability for joint action and coordination; in practice, however, the arrangement is largely an international forum for "show-and-tell." Little in the way of priority setting, program steering, or implementation design is accomplished at this level.

Evaluation and Adjustment

Periodic Review

One of the most significant changes in the international policy process in recent years has been the formal adoption of procedures for the periodic

TABLE 5-1. *U.N. Organizations with Major Environmental Responsibilities*

Organization	Environmental Focus
Food and Agricultural Organization (FAO)	sustainable agriculture and forestry
Intergovernmental Oceanographic Commission	marine pollution and species loss
International Atomic Energy Agency	nuclear power safety and waste
International Fund for Agricultural Development	sustainable agriculture
International Labor Organization	environmental health and safety
International Maritime Organization	marine pollution and oil spills
International Telecommunications Union	earth monitoring by satellite
United Nations Center for Science & Technology Development	environmental technology transfer
United Nations Center on Transnational Corporations	sustainable development
United Nations Childrens Fund (UNICEF)	environment—poverty linkages
United Nations Commission for Human Settlements	ecological refugees
United Nations Commission for Sustainable Development	implementation of Agenda 21
United Nations Development Program	sustainable development
United Nations Education, Scientific, and Cultural Organization	environmental monitoring— Man in the Biosphere Program
United Nations Environment Program	environmental policy coordination
United Nations Industrial Development Organization	industrial pollution control
United Nations Population Fund (UNFPA)	population stabilization
United Nations Sudano-Sahelian Office	desertification
World Food Program	sustainable agriculture
World Health Organization	drinking water quality
World Meteorological Organization	global climate change

review and evaluation of new policies, following their initial implementation. The 1987 Montreal Protocol, for example, stipulates that the policy should be evaluated after three years, and then at least every four years thereafter. The 1989 Basel Convention calls for a similar cycle of evaluation beginning three years from the treaty's effective starting date and then repeated at least every six years.

Given the rapidly changing state of scientific knowledge on which many international environmental agreements rest, the need for periodic review and adjustment can be seen as a requirement of political and scientific legitimacy. Basically, two forms of evaluation are employed in the periodic review of policy: evaluation of the continuing suitability or correctness of the causal theory on which the policy is based, and evaluation of the policy's impacts and outcomes, whether intended or not. For the most part, parties to international agreements seem more concerned about gathering feedback to justify a particular policy or its adjustment, than in finding out about whether the policy was implemented properly and whether it resulted in net benefits to society. "Evaluation as justification" is a common theme in the domestic policy studies literature (Wildavsky, 1979: 212–237), and international organizations appear to be no more immune to its self-serving appeal than are national and subnational organizations.

Monitoring Effectiveness and Compliance

Because most international policies impose more burdens on some states than on others, and because some states have a much smaller capacity than others to absorb policy burdens, the definitions of policy effectiveness and compliance tend to vary among affected states. Few international agreements need flawless implementation and compliance to be successful. In fact, the appropriate goals are usually "good faith" implementation and "substantial" compliance. Evaluation under such circumstances must take account of the differential circumstances under which policy performance and enforcement is to be measured.

Another important consideration is to allow for lag effects in monitoring the progress of policies moving through the process. Lester Lave (1991: 843), an economist, has identified three types of delays in policy development that appear especially significant. The first, recognition lag, refers to the delay that occurs in constructing scientific consensus necessary for policy recommendations. Peer review processes and the desire for replication of controversial findings ensure that consensus will seldom be achieved overnight. The second lag effect, which separates agenda setting from policy adoption, involves the decision-making ("ne-

gotiation–agreement") delay in moving from scientific consensus to social or political consensus. Here the concern is with selective use of
analysis by policy makers seeking to avoid or defer politically costly decisions. The final impediment, implementation lag, reflects the inordinate
amount of time that is often required to carry out the political agreements that are reached. To these, I would add an evaluation lag, which reflects the need to be patient with a policy's implementation and to avoid
drawing conclusions about its success or failure until an appropriate
amount of time has passed to measure its impact and outcomes.

Monitoring and evaluation of international environmental policy remains one of the most difficult and frustrating tasks set forth in the
process model. Some national leaders find it expedient to sign international agreements that they oppose, knowing full well that any evaluation
of their lackluster implementation and compliance records is likely to be
carried out by government agencies under their own control. The nation-state is the ultimate self-evaluating organization, with all that implies about self-serving results. Fortunately, however, the rise of international NGOs, with their own monitoring programs and media access, is
making it harder for such nations to gloss over poor environmental
records.

Conclusion

The domestic and international policy process is obviously intertwined
with structural conditions of international relations. This chapter has
tried to combine perspectives from domestic public policy research and
international relations to illuminate the reciprocal influence and dynamic
relationships between these levels of analysis. This examination clearly
suggests that multidimensional and interdisciplinary research can be
helpful in understanding agenda building, policy formation, and implementation in international environmental politics. A process orientation
is important for understanding the constraints that arise in policy design,
but additional research is needed to determine how the relationships between policy process and content are influenced by international political institutions, cultural practices, and the growing influence of the news
and entertainment media.

To understand the international environmental policy process as a procedural pattern of learning, action, and reaction does not go far enough
in explaining the powerful forces that operate to shape our present system of environmental governance. The "stages heuristic" model developed in this chapter is meant to provide only a starting point for such at-

tempts at explanation. In the next two chapters, issues of process and content are combined within frameworks of political ecology and political economy for purposes of exploring alternative policy ideas, institutions, and processes.

The need for aggressive reform of the present international policy process ought to be obvious to all but those who are most favored by its outcomes. Unfortunately, there is very little consensus about the direction reforms should take. Today's international negotiators must overcome substantial structural impediments to forge major agreements. Given the size of these barriers, they may feel that the process is designed to facilitate the survival of a state-centric system, rather than effective environmental governance. Like many domestic versions of policy-making processes, the political advantage goes to the policy saboteur. Blocking serious environmental proposals is much easier than winning their adoption.

Despite these obstacles, however, some important policies *are* being adopted and implemented. Today's international policy process is neither wholly unworkable nor incapable of improvement. It is, however, inadequate to perform the supranational tasks of peacekeeping and "earthkeeping" in the twenty-first century. The question is whether sufficient increases in policy-making capacity are possible within the existing system, and whether the needed proliferation of green policy proposals can survive the gauntlet-like process set up for their consideration. The answer to this question will not take long to discern, since global environmental issues are likely to remain high on government agendas, if only because the capacity of epistemic communities to detect and measure damage to the environment is expanding at a phenomenal rate. The increasing influence of environmental scientists, NGO advocacy coalitions, and the persistence of green policy entrepreneurs will make it very difficult to maintain the business-as-usual perspective of past years. By the same token, the increased environmental policy "traffic" through the process may make it increasingly difficult to achieve efficient responses and to sort out which policies are working, and for whom. It is appropriate, therefore, to examine the prospects for a different approach to environmental governance.

Notes

1. According to Lowi and many of his colleagues, redistributive policies are the most likely to invite large-scale political conflict because they alter existing allocations of wealth, property, services, or rights within society under perceived conditions of zero-sum costs and benefits.

2. See, for example, Mostafa Tolba, "A Step-by-Step Approach to Protection of the Atmosphere," *International Environmental Affairs* 1: 4 (Fall 1989): 304–308. Tolba, former head of the United Nations Environment Program, repeatedly urged climate policy negotiators to avoid the mistake of seeking a comprehensive convention or "Law of the Atmosphere" that attempted to obtain a "universal solution in one quantum leap." Effective prevention strategies, in his view, occurred incrementally as a result of framework or "umbrella" conventions that provided a basis for specific protocols to follow.

3. See, for example, S. Arrhenius, "On the Influence of Carbonic Acid in the Air upon the Temperature on the Ground," *Philosophy Magazine* 41: 237 (1896).

4. One of the most important of these international meetings was the World Conference on the Changing Atmosphere, which took place in Toronto, June 27–30, 1988. In a concluding statement, participants called for the creation of a World Atmosphere Fund and proposed a CO_2-reduction target of 20 percent by the year 2005.

5. See, for example, Stephen H. Schneider, "The Greenhouse Effect: Science and Policy," *Science* 246 (10 February 1989): 771–781, and Richard Kerr, "Greenhouse Skeptics Out in the Cold," *Science* 246 (1 December 1989): 1118–1119.

6. When the government is both a major developer and an environmental regulator, the role of advocacy coalitions becomes more complicated. In highly authoritarian regimes, environmental advocates are more likely to view government as the principal agent of ecological destruction, or at least as an illegitimate, controlling partner in private development schemes that foster such destruction. In cases where government is viewed as the chief villain, however, environmental advocacy coalitions are less likely to organize, and if they do, they are more likely to operate "underground" or outside of the formal institutions and processes of politics and policy.

7. The best known of these programs, INBIO, was developed in Costa Rica by the Merck pharmaceutical company in 1991.

8. Supply-side alternatives to a coal phase-out, such as installation of smokestack scrubbers for carbon emissions, do not appear economically feasible. The Electric Power Research Institute (Torrens, 1988) estimates that the capital costs of scrubbing CO_2 from existing U.S. power plants would be approximately $584 billion, or $1,230/kWh of installed capacity.

CHAPTER 6

Political Ecology

In the last chapter, we surveyed the international environmental policy-making process as it exists today. In this present chapter, we will examine the institutional design questions that arise in changing that process in order to construct more effective environmental policies and regimes. Two basic approaches for understanding governance issues are introduced in this and the following chapter: political ecology and political economy. The ecology approach is a relatively new and untested field of inquiry, while the political economy perspective arises from a massive and systematic flowering of literature and analysis. Its origins can be traced to Adam Smith's *Wealth of Nations* (1776) and perhaps even earlier. Not surprisingly, the dominant framework for understanding global environmental governance is that of international political economy (IPE) rather than ecology. The former focuses on the competitive relationships of nation-states; the latter focuses on the interdependence of communities.

While the study of political economy offers an indispensable line of inquiry for our purposes, it is by no means the only approach needed for understanding the ebb and flow of global environmental protection. Another and perhaps deeper basis for understanding can be found in the application of ecology to the art of governing. In the broadest sense, political ecology may be defined as the study of interdependence among political units and of interrelationships between political units and their environment. It is fundamentally concerned with the political consequences of environmental change—in both a physical and a symbolic sense. A second and more restrictive definition renders political ecology as "an inquiry into the political sources, conditions, and ramifications of environmental change" (Bryant, 1991: 165). Here, the direction of inquiry is reversed and the emphasis is placed on the physical environmental consequences of political decision-making. In this second definition, the goal of political ecology can be construed as the management of ecological scarcity. Ecological scarcity may be defined, following Ophuls and Boyan (1992: 175), as the limits to growth and associated costs that appear when human development, amplified by expanding population and technology, reaches diminishing returns from exploitation of the biosphere's living and nonliving resources. To a large extent, political units are created to direct this exploitation and to manage its economic, social, and environmental consequences.

Today, the only political units considered important in this regard are the 189 or so nations that declare a sovereign right to transform that portion of nature that lies within their territories into resources for consumption or trade. In political economy terms, these nations ultimately determine the property rights in natural capital (e.g., forests) and, through their control over the domestic use or exchange of this natural capital in international trade they help to manage the production of man-made capital (e.g., paper). While the worst environmental impacts of this arrangement are becoming visible in one ecological disaster after another, the political momentum behind almost four centuries of nation-state dominance makes it very hard to imagine an alternative system of governance by which to ensure global environmental protection.

In conventional political economy terms, a nation's power and wealth are positively related to its "factor endowments"—labor supply, natural resources, favorable climate, availability of man-made capital, and so forth. When combined with information about cultural factors, intellectual capital, innovation rates, and political or military capacity, these endowment characteristics can reveal a great deal about a particular nation's policy preferences and political behavior. Since the standard unit of analysis for comparing endowments remains the nation-state, political economists tend to regard nationalism as one of the principal driving forces in world politics. Many view the pursuit of national competitive advantage as the principal source of both progress and conflict in international affairs. In their estimation, any collective action on the global environmental front will have to be achieved with little or no net loss in a participating nation's economic competitiveness.

Political ecologists start with a different view of endowment characteristics and a different unit of analysis. Endowment is measured as a function of ecological wealth—for example, the availability of clean drinking
water or, more generally, a healthy biosphere (and, by extension, climate).
Such ecological assets are deemed to be far more valuable, ultimately,
than all the factories, farms, and productive workers that can be concentrated within a nation's boundaries. Rather than focusing on nation-
states, students of political ecology pay greater attention to the interaction of smaller units of political organization, particularly those that serve
as the constituent parts and mediating institutions of grassroots political
action. It is people's primary group affiliation or community identity that
matters most in determining their attitudes toward the environment.
The nation-state is viewed predominantly as an aggregation device for
power and security. What makes politics personal and at the same time
transcendent is the link to community. "All politics is local," noted the
late Tip O'Neill, former Speaker of the U.S. House of Representatives.
In keeping with this thought, many political ecologists attempt to combine a global perspective with a local community focus, leaving others to
scrutinize national politics. In contrast, political economists, by focusing
on state-sponsored or state-managed trade and development issues, leave
it to political ecologists to worry about the repercussions of national policies at the global and primary community levels.

Glocalization

This dual concern with global and local politics is derived from the "glocal" perspective introduced in chapter 1.[1] Political ecologists argue that
we must think "glocally" in order to develop the environmental understanding and response measures needed to avert widespread ecological
disaster. Although political ecology runs the risk of being construed as an
ideology of glocalism, it is in fact no more ideologically driven than are
conventional schools of political thought, which uncritically accept the
nation-state system as the baseline from which all major political ideas
are to be measured and interpreted. Taking a glocal perspective does not
mean ignoring the nation-state, but merely downgrading its importance
in addressing the ecological challenges of this planet.

One need not be an environmentalist to see that glocalism is gaining
on nationalism. In fact, one need only be a modern consumer to appreciate that it is economic and technological factors, more than environmental ones, that lie behind its accelerating pace. A provocative examination of the economic and technological driving forces behind glocalism
is provided by Kanichi Ohmae in his book *The Borderless World* (1990).

Ohmae argues that the development of an interlinked economy is simultaneously elevating the importance of global, regional, and community affairs, while at the same time undermining the ability of national governments to serve the interests of their citizens. According to Ohmae, the need for strategic alliances among nations is being rapidly diminished by the rise of global strategic alliances among corporations and local consumer groups. Global markets and the phenomenon of "nationality-less" young consumers are combining to challenge and mock traditional notions of state sovereignty. And the rise of the global marketplace is influencing regional and local political economies to a greater degree than the actions of national economic planners. Addressing the next generation of consumers, Ohmae describes a world economy that is already subverting the principles on which nationalism rests:

> *At the cash register, you don't care about country of origin or country of residence. . . . It does not matter to you that a "British" sneaker by Reebok (now an American-owned company) was made in Korea, a German sneaker by Adidas in Taiwan, or a French ski by Rossignol in Spain. (1990: 3)*

While such views may underestimate the potency of parochial thinking and the influence of nationalistic pride on future economic development, the latest sales and distribution figures from companies such as Reebok, Adidas, and Rosignol suggest that many of today's youthful consumers behave as if they already live in a borderless world. It is their parents and grandparents who have not yet fully discovered how the logic of consumption is rapidly erasing the geographic boundaries of citizenship. Critical theorists understand this as the inevitable result of world capitalism flourishing in an age of instant communication.

For the political ecologist, the implications of economic glocalization, or what Sony's Akio Morita terms "global localization," are perhaps most apparent in the development of fledgling periodicals such as the *Journal of Municipal Foreign Policy* and the creation of foreign trade offices and bilateral international initiatives by large city governments (Shuman, 1992). Given the increasing need for glocal policies and institutions, political ecologists might do well to focus on how to shift the revenue and spending streams of national governments to support greater involvment of local and supranational entities. Those who have recommended sweeping reallocations argue that we should begin with the revenue side. Ohmae, for example, offers an appealingly simple, if simplistic, formula for government taxation:

> *If I had my way, I'd pay a third of all my taxes to an international fund dedicated to solving world problems, such as the environment and famine. A third*

to my community, where my children are educated and my family lives. And then a last third to my country, which each year does less and less for me in terms of security or well-being and instead subsidizes special interests. (1990: 215)

The Political Ecosystem

In order to maintain a sense of both global and local political relationships, students of political ecology employ the concept of an ecosystem to describe and explain the interplay of various political entities.[2] They portray the global political order as an ecosystem consisting of ten thousand human societies spread across more than fourteen major biomes (ecological regions) and eight zoogeographical realms (Lean and Hinrichsen, 1992: 12–13). Organized within this political ecosystem can be found more than 180 nation-states, approximately two thousand intergovernmental organizations, the United Nations system, and nearly eighteen thousand transnational NGOs operating at the intersections of state power (Boulding, 1993: 167). These interstitial organizations attempt to provide improved communication, interest-group representation, conflict resolution, and greater economic opportunity both within and across nation-state boundaries. Providing legal authority and rules for the exchanges and relationships between state actors are approximately sixty-two thousand international treaties, most of them bilateral or regional. Although the nation-state remains the dominant "species" within today's political ecosystem, political ecologists would say it is undergoing an evolutionary transformation toward glocal forms of governance that portend greater interdependence between local, national, and supranational forms of authority.

The essence of political ecology can be found in this concept of interdependence and its relationship with diversity. To ecologists, interdependence is the fundamental basis for community. Its meaning is perhaps best captured in the poet Francis Thompson's expression, "thou canst not stir a flower without troubling a star," or in John Muir's simple observation, "when we try to pick out anything by itself, we find it hitched to everything else in the universe." Ecological diversity refers to the variations in genes, niches, food supplies, and adaptive traits that facilitate species survival (and, by extension, biodiversity) in the face of pathogens or epidemics, increased predator populations, and sudden climate change. It is expressed in the law of heterogeneity—that there is safety in numbers of species and subspecies traits, or for that matter, in numbers of democratic interests (e.g., pluralism). It is also evident in the postmaterialist idea of progress, with its emphasis on qualitative growth through differentiation (e.g., the acorn's future as an oak tree, as contrasted with the undifferentiated growth of cancer cells).[3]

The organizing principle on which the political ecosystem rests is *asymmetric interdependence*. All political units are interdependent to some extent. What is striking about the new era we are entering is that interdependence is growing as a result of advances in information technology and global communication, rapid growth in population and migration, heightened global risks of terrorism and nuclear proliferation, and accelerating rates of transboundary pollution and nonrenewable resource consumption. Meanwhile, the asymmetrical properties of the relationships are growing stronger in some ways (e.g., gaps between rich and poor) and weaker in others (e.g., greater parity in access to weapons technology that can disrupt or destroy societies). The asymmetry arises from the fact that almost all interdependency relationships tend to be stronger in one direction than another. Moreover, those in the stronger position often fail to recognize their own forms of dependency. These differences in dependency—real or falsely perceived—greatly influence the basic power and interest structures that govern competing political units. Some scholars, in fact, define power as a function of asymmetrical interdependence (e.g., Knorr, 1977: 102). These asymmetries also account for the basic inequities in the allocation rules that govern international trade, development, and the use of the global commons. Most important for our purposes, they inhibit the cooperation needed for coordinated responses to global environmental change.

As a complement to the international political economy focus on competition, political ecology's emphasis on asymmetrical interdependence aids in understanding why the state-centric world of today is so poorly equipped to foster the cooperation that is needed for genuine human progress. It reveals the inadequacy of territorial governance in an increasingly borderless world. With nearly two hundred primary territories and several thousand subsidiary jurisdictions, the earth's political geography bears no resemblance to its appearance from space—a solitary blue planet, with a single ocean and seven large land masses. To point out the obvious, however, does little to change people's comfort levels with the political systems under which they are governed. Many still profess a willingness to defend their nation's sovereignty with their lives. Clearly, the political ecology view is unlikely to engage the attention of large numbers of people in the near future unless opinion leaders recognize, and begin to admit publicly, that the fundamental environmental and economic security interests of citizens have transcended the political boundaries of the nation-state. Eventually, of course, the interactive media being developed as part of the information technology revolution will make this fact obvious to all but those who are unable to gain access to computers and to the global networks of digital technology. In the meantime, visionary leadership is called for.

The most ambitious, if short-lived, development in this direction occurred in 1989 with the signing of the Hague Declaration, which called for bold new international environmental institutions and an expansion of U.N. authority to deal with global environmental problems. Led by the prime ministers of France, the Netherlands, and Norway, heads of twenty-four nations agreed to support proposals for international environmental enforcement based on "nonunanimous decisions of supranational entities" (French, 1992b: 35). Other provisions called for new legislative mechanisms and new powers for the International Court of Justice to impose its jurisdiction over the implementation of U.N. environmental treaties. Although nearly forty nations eventually signed the declaration, the impact was small. The conference in March 1989 that created the declaration was marked by the conspicuous absence of the United States, China, Britain, and the former Soviet Union, ensuring that little momentum would develop for a power transition. The implied rebuke by key members of the U.N. Security Council seemed to suggest that the only environmental reforms that were likely to emerge were those they supported or acquiesced in as part of a state-centric system of governance.

Whither the Nation-State?

If the nation-state in its present form is the only viable basis for governance, then the prospects for sustained environmental improvement appear to be very poor. The reasons have less to do with leadership and administrative capacity than with structural design flaws. As we have seen, the modern state is a product of territorial thinking. It is by definition an autonomous part of the earth wherein citizens openly declare their independence from other parts and from the planetary whole. Although it is ecologically untenable to conceive of sovereign parts in an interdependent world, the concept has managed to flourish in its secular form since at least the Treaty of Westphalia in 1648. The need to manage and coordinate large populations, economic trade, and technological innovation has seemingly cemented the nation-state as the ultimate successor to tribal, feudal, and city-state forms of political organization. Because of its amazing capacity for organized power and geopolitical differentiation, the state has become the most widely accepted instrument of group identity outside of the family.

The state derives its power ultimately from the struggle to control land and other resources through the bureaucratic imposition of law and political will, backed by the threat of force. As the supreme power within a territory, modern states perform at least three key functions (Clark and Dear, 1984: 43): (1) forging social consensus and integration, (2) securing the means or conditions of production through social investment practices and the regulation of consumption, and (3) protecting the accumulation of wealth (i.e., ensuring property rights), while providing for the welfare of those at the bottom of the income distribution. Although the effort expended on each of these functions differs markedly from democratic to authoritarian states, and from capitalist to socialist states, the rationale for their inclusion is almost always the same: to manage foreign and domestic conflict arising from differences in ideology, race, ethnicity, territorial ambition, class, and economic competitiveness. Management of conflict in this case means everything from prevention to outright encouragement of violence, depending upon the shifting interests and capabilities of a particular state.

In the past, the legitimacy of a state has depended largely on its ability to provide military and domestic security, enforce contracts, and represent the interests of its citizens in foreign affairs. For the most part, environmental threats that transcended state boundaries became the subject of international attention only insofar as they affected the perceived economic, health, or security interests of powerful nations or their leaders. Since neither domestic nor supranational costs of environmental destruction have been effectively accounted for in national development budgets, international environmental protection today is dependent on the ability of a nation, or coalition of nations, to prove that their territory or citizens have been harmed by the environmentally unsound practices of one or more nations with whom they share a common physical or biological medium (e.g., air, water, migratory wildlife). Where the scope of environmental risk becomes truly global, as in the case of atmospheric change, the nation-state system is put to the severest test. In most cases, it presents member states with an unsavory choice between unilateral action to protect the environment, which often places the eager nation at a competitive disadvantage, or large-scale collective action, which is usually subject to the "slow boat" rule (the rate of progress is set by the least enthusiastic party) and therefore too cumbersome in many instances to permit timely international responses.

According to Mische (1993), and many other environmentalists, the nation-state has become the principal obstacle in securing global environmental protection:

When we try to approach a resolution of today's ecological crises, we soon run into a central dilemma: The Earth does not recognize sovereignty as we now know it. Existing concepts of state sovereignty are incongruent, even antithetical, to the prerequisites for global ecological security. (p. 105)

Critics of the state argue that whatever authority and legitimacy it may have once had, a tide of globalism is eroding away its hold on power. Some want to see the state wither away completely. For example, Edward Goldsmith (1994) editor of *The Ecologist*, asserts:

The state is foreign to society. It is a gesellschaft—a single-purpose association concerned almost exclusively with its own short-term interests and almost invariably oblivious to the real needs of those it has been called upon to govern. There is no place for the state or its specialized institutions in a society that seeks to recreate for itself a sustainable existence on a sustainable planet. (p. 341)

Another British environmental author, R. J. Johnston, argues that because the modern state promotes accumulation and environmentally destructive modes of production, it has precipitated a potential crisis of legitimacy and rationality, brought on by increasing scientific evidence that the accumulation and production it sponsors are irreversibly destroying the earth. In Johnston's view (1989), the dilemma is not likely to be resolved by appealing for international cooperation:

[T]he creation of environmental problems is a product of the dominant mode of production in the world today, and the solution of those problems is difficult because the only institutions within which the necessary collective action could be mobilized exist to promote the interests of that mode of production.

Defenders of the nation-state are apt to apply Churchill's sentiments about democracy to the modern state system: the worst form of government except for all the rest. They acknowledge many of the flaws and limitations of the present system but doubt the promise claimed for alternative forms of political organization. Most reject the notion that a global, regional, or other supranational system of governance is feasible and desirable. Among scholars who study the issue, the prevailing concern is not so much with the state-centric structure of political life as with the way in which state power is concentrated or dispersed within the system.[4] Many students of international relations believe that power convergence is needed for the international system to maintain stability. So-called "hegemonic stability" theorists (e.g., Gilpin, 1981; Keohane, 1984) posit that the system is only orderly when there is a clearly recognized

leading state (or in some variants a bipolar power distribution) to encourage orderly alignment of other state actors. According to those who
hold this view, global environmental cooperation has a better chance of
developing and surviving if a hegemon exists whose perceived interests
are served by collective action. Without a hegemonic leader, wide-open
military competition may ensue, resulting in reduced investment in cooperative activities, such as environmental diplomacy.

Because of the sweeping changes in world power and interests triggered by the end of the Cold War, hegemony has become, like (revision-
ist) history, "not what it used to be." Superpower bipolarity has been pronounced dead and condominium appears to be the order of the day.
Given the strong tendency in contemporary world affairs to assume a
tripolar regional structure—North America, Europe, and East Asia—the
role of hegemonic states and their influence on environmental diplomacy
are likely to become increasingly difficult to define and assess. As the unexpected and unprecedented events of world politics continue to unfold
in the final years of this century, some political ecologists are beginning
to ask whether a viable alternative to state-centric governance may yet
emerge.

Prospects for Supranational Governance

Whatever the flaws of the nation-state system, most political observers
argue that it is here to stay. Only a small group of planetary thinkers seriously entertain the possibility that the world is undergoing a transition
to some form of world government, "global constitutionalism," or world
federalism (e.g., Falk and Kim, 1982). Those in the middle of the spectrum, the "practical internationalists" as Richard Gardner (1992b) calls
them, are prone to argue that a larger *con*federal system of national and
supranational governance is the most likely outcome of present trends.
They imagine an increasing number of interstate regimes that can somehow complement the environmental programs of individual states without threatening their sovereign claims.

These three visions of future environmental governance—continuation of the status quo, world government, and some mixed form of nationalism and nascent supranationalism—are frequently presented as the
leading options available for the twenty-first century. Other authors have
labeled these approaches "incrementalism," "global governance," and
"global partnership" (Porter and Brown, 1991: chapter 5), but the basic
distinctions between content remain the same. So do the rank-order
preferences of many international relations specialists who have evalu-

ated the three options. Maintenance of the state-centric status quo appears doubtful in the face of globalizing and regionalizing forces, such as transboundary environmental protection, the growth of free-trade zones, and European political integration. Even less promising, however, is the hope that nation-states will somehow voluntarily surrender their sovereignty to a central world authority in exchange for untested assurances of collective security. Not surprisingly, many scholars conclude that a hybrid variety or compromise between the other two options remains the best bet, although most expect the outcome to be much closer to the status quo than to a unitary world government. The order in which these analysts present their evaluations and their framework for choosing among options resembles what might be called the "Goldilocks principle" of world politics: The first approach is too "cold," the second too "hot," but the third seems "just right."

For the planetary thinkers who like their porridge hot, the conventional wisdom about future governance structures is just another expression of postmodern pessimism. It serves as a self-fulfilling prophecy, promoting a future of incremental change and timid politics—a future of "the bland leading the bland." Critics of the conventional wisdom argue that a global transformation of political institutions is overdue and likely to occur sometime in the next century, whether we plan it or not. For example, Saul Mendlovitz (1975: xvi), director of the World Order Models Project, argues that the key question about global level governance is not *if* but *how* it will develop—"by cataclysm, drift, more or less rational design"—and what form it will take—"totalitarian, benignly elitist, or participatory (the probabilities being in that order)." While not advocating world government per se, Mendlovitz and many of his colleagues favor a transformation to a constitutional form of world order, one that makes possible the collective realization of five basic goals or values: peace, ecological balance, social justice, economic well-being, and positive personal identity.[5] Some one-world thinkers argue that such goals and values are best realized in a political system that strategically redistributes increments of power from the state to the global and the local levels of human community. In that respect, they think like political ecologists.

Advocates of "postinternational politics" (e.g., Rosenau, 1990) have argued repeatedly that there are at least two policy domains—environment and security—in which glocal or supranational forms of governance are needed to augment national ones. They call for a selective relaxation of national sovereignty in the interest of protecting the biosphere and strengthening global peacekeeping. Ervin Laszlo, a prominent futurist, uses the term "cooperative governance" to describe this two-pronged approach to changing the state-centric system. Central to his political vision is the argument that traditional notions of sovereignty are obsolete:

> *In the last analysis, decision-making can grow to the international dimension if, and only if, the sacrosanct nature of national sovereignty is surrendered. A full recognition of the historical obsolescence of that principle is the single greatest precondition of recovering the governability of contemporary societies in regard to the two most pressing issues of our times: world security, and biospheric sustainability.(Laszlo, 1991: 221)*

Laszlo proposes that cooperative governance, which is similar to the concept of glocalism, be applied solely to international security and environmental issues, at least initially. Nation-states would retain their sovereign powers in all other areas of social and economic life. By carefully delineating what Robert Keohane (Haas et al., 1993) calls "formal" sovereignty (legal independence) from "operational" sovereignty (degrees of freedom under international law), what was previously a dichotomous variable (i.e., sovereign or not) can be turned into a continuous one (i.e., degree of sovereignty). The problem with such apportionments, of course, is that many types of social and economic intervention could theoretically be justified on grounds of security and environmental protection. Perhaps the most sensitive grounds for such intervention involves the protection of basic human rights, which more than any other issue, has been repeatedly invoked to justify proposals for international intervention.

The movement to develop a supranational authority to protect basic human rights has accelerated in the wake of so-called "crimes against humanity" that have taken place in the past five to ten years in South Africa, Tianamin Square, Bosnia, Somalia, Haiti, and parts of the Middle East. Rather than focusing on the security of states and regions, human-rights advocates have sought to protect individuals through the establishment of certain universal rights (e.g., protections against torture and slavery) that are enforceable across territorial and cultural boundaries. Organizations such as Amnesty International have played an influential role in uncovering the systematic abuses that have been committed in the name of state security and economic development. Only recently, however, have environmental quality issues become interwoven with human-rights campaigns. Increasingly, access to safe food and drinking water have appeared on the lists of demands by human-rights activists. Authoritarian national governments that have been accused of gross abuses are vilified as enemies of the people by these activists, but the cloak of sovereignty ultimately protects the governments from meaningful censure. As a result, some activists are pushing for a binding universal declaration of basic rights, backed by an agreement among nations to permit supranational intervention whenever gross abuses of those rights are documented.

Leaving aside the obvious difficulties in arriving at a universal definition of rights in the midst of ethnic, cultural, and national diversity, the prospect of supranational intervention in what is widely perceived to be the internal affairs of nations invariably provokes strong opposition. The key challenge in any architectural design for a new global politics is how to devise safeguards that will induce individual states to relinquish a portion of their sovereignty in return for the collective benefits of enhanced international security and quality of life (Myers, 1993a). To the political ecologist, this is the dilemma of preserving autonomy in the midst of interdependence.

The Federal Option

Throughout much of modern history, the response to such dilemmas has been to design a federal system of governance—a constitutionally guaranteed balance of power between a political center and its peripheral units. For many observers, the greatest challenge of global environmental governance will be to accomplish a peaceful transition from statism to world federalism, relying on regional and global confederations along the way. Federalism applied on a global basis offers, in their view, the most promising way of limiting national sovereignty while still preserving the modern state's unrivaled capability for extracting collective action out of the competing primary group affiliations of its citizens.

The essential feature of federalism is the division of formal authority over people or territory into two levels of governance—central and constituent—with the sharing of power between the two specified in such a way that neither may legally dominate the other in an overall sense (Watts, 1981). Federalism is thus a compromise between autonomy and interdependence; between primary group identity and national or supranational identity. In the past, federalism has invariably functioned as a form of territorial political organization in which power or sovereignty was constitutionally distributed between center and periphery in hopes of achieving some optimal level of national political integration. Federal arrangements were usually the result of a trade-off between statist demands for central authority to manage or coordinate large-scale business and defense enterprises, and community demands for smaller political units that would foster participation and permit self-expression by subnational ethnic, religious, and other interest groups. Regardless of the balance struck between centralized and decentralized authority, the units of political organization were defined territorially. In a global experiment, however, the chief function of federalism would be to allocate power between territorial and nonterritorial instruments of governance, with the constituent units in this case being nation-states, and the central or nonterritorial institution being some form of constitutionally limited world legislature or governing council.

In the debate about global environmental governance, world federalism remains a troubling concept for many participants. Some fear that progress on the environmental front would be achieved at the expense of democratic reform. As nations reluctantly transferred authority for the management of the global commons and transboundary pollution, they would be establishing a "slippery slope" precedent for transfers in other areas. The ultimate test of federal power—the control of military forces—would arise when the questions of enforcement and intervention were addressed. At that point, critics argue, world federalism could become a dangerous end in itself, rather than a means for combating global environmental destruction.

For James Madison, ironically, national federalism was not an end but a means by which to extend democracy for purposes of large-scale governance. It was, in a sense, an inventive political response to the consequences of population growth and technological innovation. Federalism made possible the retention of decentralized political power in the midst of driving forces that constantly increased the scale of economic and social interaction. The question today is whether federalism can (or should) facilitate the transition already underway from a national to a global scale of interaction and interdependence.

Declaring in the 1930s that federalism was obsolete, the political scientist Harold Laski (1939: 367) argued that rather than a means to create large-scale democracies, as Madison had hoped, federalism had become the lackey of large-scale capitalism. "Giant capitalism," as he termed it, was showing signs of incompatibility with democracy, and federalism was no longer able "to keep pace" with its growth and its demands on the political system. Imagine Laski's astonishment were he alive to witness today's influence of global capital. The critique he made of American federalism could easily apply to present proposals for world federalism; one has only to substitute the term nation-state for Laski's references to a subnational state in order to appreciate the potential limitations of federalism in a global system of capitalism, particularly one that is characterized by strong asymmetries in wealth:

> *The poor state is parasitic on the body politic. It offers privileges to giant capitalism to obtain its taxable capacity, offers escape from the impositions of rich states, in order to wrest from the wealthy some poor meed of compensation for its backwardness. It dare not risk offending the great industrial empires—cotton, coal, iron and steel, tobacco—lest it lose the benefits of their patronage. Their vested interests thus begin to define the limits within which the units of the federation may venture to move. And since the division of powers limits, in its turn, the authority of the federal government to intervene—the latter being a government of limited powers—it follows that the great industrial empires can, in fact, prevent the legislation necessary to implement the purposes of a democratic society. (Laski, 1939: 368)*

Clearly an adequate system of governance for the twenty-first century would address both the power and the interests of nationalism and transnational corporations (TNCs)—a subject that is addressed in the next chapter. Federalism, according to Laski's logic, might merely speed the global rise of corporate capitalism, making it for all practical purposes the new hegemon, while subjecting previously sovereign states and their central governing institutions to a debilitating struggle for what is left of the political power. World federalists might object that the power of TNCs has already grown enormously under the state-centric system, and they would argue that a federal system would offer significant advantages in regulating the activities of TNCs; but the fact remains that federal structures could be used to frustrate control of TNC power just as easily as to enhance it.[6]

Today, only about 20 percent of the world's people live in national federations or in nations claiming to be federalist.[7] Even among this 20 percent or so, few citizens appear to be strong advocates of federal arrangements. Perhaps they are convinced that too many clumsy, competing layers of government bureaucracy result. Or perhaps they doubt that federalism can survive the asymmetries of power that typically exist between the center and the periphery. In India, for example, the central government has invoked emergency powers more than ninety times in the past fifty years in order to disband state governments, raising the question of whether India is truly a federal entity. Because of perceptions and experiences like this one, there is little reason to believe that most citizens would prefer supranational federalism over nationalism, even in the interest of global environmental protection. Given the vigor with which national pride is exhibited in many parts of the world, about the most that can be hoped for in the short term—or tolerated, according to today's neorealists—is a stronger confederation of nation-states organized around the existing U.N. system. While supranational federalism appears to offer a very attractive model for building glocal forms of governance, a strengthened U.N. system may well provide the intermediate step needed to facilitate its development.

United Nations Reform

The United Nations represents a half-century experiment with a weak form of world confederation. Although its record of achievements in security and environmental affairs is decidedly mixed, the U.N. system has become, almost by default, the last, best hope of many green globalists. Many have regarded its fragile institutions as potential stepping stones to world federalism or some other kind of constitutional world order. Others, seeing little prospect for effective world government, have opted for a more pragmatic and incremental course of action. They have argued that the U.N. represents the promise of world governance without the risks of world government.[8] Through selective reform and strengthening, the U.N. is capable in their view, of becoming a strong and effective confederation—one that can live with the continuing paradox of state sovereignty in an era of interdependence.

As the scale and significance of supranational problems and opportunities have grown, the limits of cooperation between U.N. member states have become more pronounced. Frustrated diplomats guardedly admit that the environmental and peacekeeping benefits that could flow from stronger U.N. interventions are potentially enormous, but so are the risks of tyranny. Global fascism is the fear lurking behind almost every futuristic image of a powerful United Nations. Meanwhile, progressive states are being confronted as never before with the painful trade-offs that arise when respect for national sovereignty conflicts with respect for human dignity, ecological integrity, and economic efficiency. The peacekeeping challenges encountered in 1994–95 in Bosnia, Cambodia, Somalia, and Haiti, like Western Europe's encounter in 1986 with the fallout from Chernobyl, demonstrated that neither self-reliant unilateralism nor weak collectivism on the part of the U.N. is adequate to contain today's sources of political and ecological danger. The U.N. remains a "paper tiger" when it comes to enforcement. Despite undertaking the three largest peacekeeping missions in its history, all since 1991, the U.N. has gained little respect for its efforts.[9] It may, in fact, have managed only to strengthen the conviction of its critics that a return to hegemonic state intervention offers the surest way to suppress violent nationalistic and ethnic conflict. And when it comes to enforcement of environmental accords, the U.N.'s capability in this area appears even weaker than its peacekeeping powers.

If supranational governance is unlikely and we wish to avoid a return to the risky practice of unilateralism, the U.N.'s authority and capacity for peacekeeping and "earthkeeping" must be strengthened to the point where its agencies can effectively intervene in trouble spots on behalf of the community of nations. Within the environmental movement, reformers have urged that the U.N.'s policy-making apparatus be fundamentally restructured in order to treat ecological security on a par with military and economic security. Among their most ambitious proposals have been plans to create an ecological security council to mirror the existing Security Council or, failing that, to redesign the present council to incorporate transboundary environmental risks as a major part of its purview. Others, perhaps forgetting why supranational governance is so difficult to achieve, have suggested the creation of a standing U.N. peacekeeping force that would also be empowered to enforce trade sanctions or other penalties against those who violate international environmental treaties. Appeals by states accused of violating major treaty provisions would be reviewed under the mandatory jurisdiction of a strengthened International Court of Justice. Some reformers have even proposed that the interests of future generations be given official U.N. representation. For example, one of the more ambitious proposals, suggested that members of the General Assembly be elected and then assigned by lottery so that two-thirds of those elected represent current generations and one-third explicitly align themselves with the interests of future generations, assuming that those interests can be foreseen. Celebrating the fiftieth anniversary of the U.N. in 1995, many of these reformers called for a global summit to consider these and other proposed changes.

The most prominent reform effort to date was launched in late 1992 with the creation of the Commission on Global Governance, an independent study group composed of twenty-eight international diplomats, scholars, and NGO leaders who were asked "to explore opportunities created by the end of the Cold War to achieve common security and sustainable development through better global governance" (Commission on Global Governance, 1994: 6). The commission released its first report in January 1995. Building on its members' visions of "global neighborhood" and "planetary security," the commission called for phased reforms of the U.N. system to promote expanded humanitarian relief, demilitarization and greater conflict prevention, elimination of permanent memberships and veto powers on the Security Council, creation of an "apex" global economic council within the U.N., expanded and compulsory jurisdiction for the World Court, a strengthened international civil service, and the establishment of strict U.N. custodianship of the global commons (Commission on Global Governance, 1995).

A summary of proposed reforms of the U.N. system and its environmental policy mechanisms is provided in table 6-1. While some of the proposals border on utopian visions, it is important to note that many ideas that seemed outlandish less than a decade ago now wear the look of respectability, plausibility, and, their supporters would even say, logical inevitability. What imperils their development is not some massive denial of status quo deficiencies, but rather disarray about what can be done to repair them. Despite a flurry of suggested changes, there is no elite or mass consensus to propel major reforms at the present time.

Consider the evidence from a 1993 *Los Angeles Times* survey of 649 elites representing high-level positions in American government, business and finance, academia, religion, science and engineering, foreign affairs, the arts, and the news media (McManus, 1993: H3). Each interviewee was asked to choose which of six challenges facing the world—nationalism and ethnic hatred, proliferation of weapons of mass destruction, international trade conflicts, environmental pollution, religious fanaticism, and overpopulation—was the most dangerous to world stability. Only members of one elite, science and engineering, were able to reach a bare consensus (51 percent) on the most important issue—in their case, overpopulation. No other elite managed a 50 percent vote on any of the six issues tested. A parallel survey of the American general public by Princeton Research Associates revealed even less consensus than was achieved among elites (McManus, 1993: H2). While it is possible that both surveys overlooked more important issues, and that the subjects surveyed were not representative of either elite or non-elite world opinion, one potential lesson for would-be reformers seems clear: Where there is no consensus on the priority of needs, it will be difficult to find consensus on the direction of reform. Without that consensus, the entrenched power of sovereign states and U.N. bureaucracies is likely to make institutional reform at best an ad hoc and incremental process.

In trying to strengthen the U.N., reformers must bear in mind that a state's right of secession will act as an ever-present check on the scale and pace of political change that can realistically occur. Even a crisis-driven transition to a world constitutional order would presumably be tempered (initially, at least) by the right of secession of any member state. While concerns about issue linkage and lost political leverage may make the option to defect very difficult for some states to exercise, the mere threat of defection is nevertheless a powerful limiting factor in attempts to strengthen international environmental institutions. Such conditions of political feasibility may weaken over time, but for the foreseeable future,

TABLE 6-1. *Proposed Reforms of the United Nations by Major Function*

Generic Policy Making
- Alter the Security Council by expanding or changing its membership, and limiting the five permanent members' veto power
- Create a U.N. federation with a bicameral world legislature composed of a House of States (appointed government representatives) and a House of Representatives (citizens who are directly elected)
- Create a second U.N. Assembly, subsidiary to the General Assembly, composed of representatives from nongovernmental organizations
- Form a World Consultative Council composed of leading world citizens appointed on the basis of their prominence outside of government
- Arrange a global summit for the purpose of systematic U.N. charter reform
- Extend limited mandatory jurisdiction of the International Court of Justice

Environmental Policy Making
- Elevate the Commission on Sustainable Development (established in 1992)
- Establish an Environmental Security Council, or add global environmental protection as one of the existing council's chief security functions
- Establish a permanent intergovernmental panel of global environmental experts
- Strengthen environmental treaty secretariats, including the right to perform independent monitoring of national implementation efforts

Environmental Funding and Capacity-Building
- Achieve the U.N.'s goal of persuading donor nations to give 0.7% of their GDPs for official development assistance
- Expand the Global Environmental Facility to increase environmental funding under the direction of UNEP, UNDP, and the World Bank
- Elevate the role of CIDIE in development assistance
- Create limited U.N. taxing authority (e.g., taxes on international sales of cigarettes, transfers of hazardous materials, etc.)
- Create regional environment and development agencies

Environmental Monitoring and Analysis
- Establish at U.N. headquarters a Center for Environment and Development Analysis
- Strengthen UNEP's Earthwatch Program
- Develop a U.N.-level "Mission to Planet Earth," based on the US model
- Expand the use of GIS and computerized data retrieval systems, and provide improved links between U.N. and nongovernmental organizations

Intergovernmental Environmental Coordination
- Expand UNEP's role as a clearinghouse and organizer of international fora
- Increase the contact and communication levels of the interagency program for Designated Officials on Environmental Management

Sources: Maurice Bertrand, *Some Reflections on Reform of the United Nations* (Geneva: United Nations, 1985); *Common Responsibility in the 1990's*, The Stockholm Initiative on Global Security and Governance (April 22, 1991); Commission on Global Governance, *Our Global Neighborhood* (Oxford University Press, 1995); Johan Galtung, "International Organizations and World Decision-Making," *International Transnational Associations, Transnationales* 1986, No. 4; Mikhail Gorbachev, Address to the 43rd session of the U.N. General Assembly, December 7, 1987; Lee A. Kimball, *Forging International Agreement: Strengthening Intergovernmental Institutions for Environment and Development* (World Resources Institute 1992); Pamela Leonard and Walter Hoffman, *World Federalist Proposals to Strengthen the Role of the U.N.* (World Federalist Association 1990), Marc Nerfin, "The Future of the United Nations System: Some Questions on the Occasion of an Anniversary," *Development Dialogue* No. 1 (1985).

reform will be limited by the potential of any state to reassert its formal sovereignty whenever international institutions are perceived to threaten one of its core interests. Hence, global environmental governance may remain a function of national foresight and voluntary international cooperation well into the next century, and perhaps beyond.

For those who are convinced that this will be the case, a strategic retreat from world order objectives is necessary. In their minds, the appropriate goal of environmental design or intervention must be much smaller and simpler than world federalism or reform of the U.N. system (French, 1992a,b). It is a goal that is much more likely to be achieved by piecemeal engineers than by global systems architects. In its most common depiction, the goal is to expand and strengthen the use of issue-specific, negotiated regimes for environmental management. Such regimes form the backbone of today's system of international environmental governance.

Green Regimes

While planetary thinkers worry about reforming a complex, interlinked set of international institutions, political pragmatists (pessimists?) focus on multilateral policy responses to particular problems. For those interested in environmentally pragmatic action, regime formation and maintenance have become the key objectives of multilateral policy making. A regime, as defined by Gareth Porter and Janet Welsh Brown (1991: 20), is a "system of norms and rules that are specified by a multilateral legal instrument [e.g., treaty] among states to regulate national actions on a given issue." Regimes that are principally designed to regulate national environmental behavior that affects other nations or the global commons can be defined as "green" regimes. Some of the most important of these regimes are derived from the environmental treaties listed in table 6-2. At present, approximately 150 green regimes are in operation. This is in addition to more than 500 bilateral environmental agreements that have been successfully negotiated during this century (von Moltke, 1988: 87).

Unlike an international governing institution with broad authority over issues of transnational environmental quality, green regimes are constructed to deal with one issue at a time. Because they often function more like marginal adjustments than structural reforms, regimes constitute a less threatening political means for strengthening environmental governance. They arise in ad hoc proceedings, under the design of ad hoc bodies of negotiators, and develop as outgrowths of existing international law. They address transboundary threats from pollution, resource consumption, and ecosimplification without directly challenging the state-

TABLE 6-2. *A Chronology of Major Multilateral Treaty Instruments Used in the Creation of Green Regimes*

1911	"Big Four" Convention for the Preservation and Protection of North Pacific Fur Seals (Russia, Great Britain/Canada, United States, Japan)
1940	Washington–OAS Convention on Nature Protection and Wild Life Preservation in the Western Hemisphere
1946	Washington Convention for the Regulation of International Whaling
1949	Rome Agreement for the Establishment of the Central Fisheries Council for the Mediterranean
1950	Paris Convention for the Protection of Birds
1951	Rome International Plant Protection Convention
1954	London Convention for the Prevention of Pollution of the Sea by Oil
1957	Washington Interim Convention on North Pacific Fur Seals
1957	Geneva–European Agreement Concerning the International Carriage of Dangerous Goods by Road
1958	Geneva Convention on Fishing and Conservation of the Living Resources of the High Seas
1959	Washington Antarctic Treaty
1963	Vienna Convention on Civil Liability for Nuclear Damage
1963	Moscow Treaty Banning Nuclear Weapon Tests in the Atmosphere, in Outer Space, and Under Water
1964	Copenhagen Convention for the International Council for the Exploration of the Sea
1966	Rio International Convention for the Conservation of Atlantic Tunas
1967	Treaty on Principles Governing the Activities of States in the Exploration and Use of Outer Space (London, Moscow, Washington)
1968	Algiers African Convention on the Conservation of Nature and Natural Resources
1969	Brussels International Convention on Civil Liability for Oil Pollution Damage
1969	Brussels International Convention Relating to Intervention on the High Seas in Case of Oil Pollution Casualties
1969	Bonn Agreement on Cooperation for Control of North Sea Oil Pollution
1971	Ramsar Convention on Wetlands and Waterfowl Habitat
1971	Brussels International Convention on the Establishment of an International Fund for Compensation for Oil Pollution Damage
1972	London Convention on the Prohibition of the Development, Production, and Stockpiling of Bacteriological and Toxin Weapons, and on their Destruction
1973	Washington Convention on International Trade in Endangered Species of Wild Fauna and Flora

1973	London International Convention for the Prevention of Pollution from Ships (MARPOL)
1974	Geneva Convention Concerning Prevention and Control of Occupational Hazards Caused by Carcinogenic Substances and Agents
1974	Paris Convention for the Prevention of Marine Pollution from Land-Based Sources
1976	Convention on Protection of the Rhine Against Chemical Pollution
1976	Barcelona Convention for the Protection of the Mediterranean Sea Against Pollution
1977	Geneva Convention Concerning Protection of Workers against Occupational Hazards in the Working Environment Due to Air Pollution, Noise, and Vibration
1978	Nairobi–Principles of Conduct in the Field of the Environment for the Guidance of States in the Conservation and Harmonious Utilization of Natural Resources Shared by Two or More States
1978	Ottawa Convention on Future Multilateral Cooperation in the Northwest Atlantic Fisheries
1979	Geneva Convention on Long-Range Transboundary Air Pollution
1979	Bonn Convention on Conservation of Migratory Species of Animals
1980	Nairobi Provisions for Cooperation between States on Weather Modification
1980	Canberra Convention on the Conservation of Antarctic Marine Living Resources
1981	Abidjan Convention for Cooperation in the Protection and Development of the Marine and Coastal Environment of the West and Central African Region
1982	Montego Bay Convention on the Law of the Sea (not in force)
1983	Geneva International Tropical Timber Agreement
1983	Rome International Undertaking on Plant Genetic Resources
1983	Bonn Agreement for Cooperation in Dealing with Pollution of the North Sea by Oil and Other Harmful Substances
1984	Geneva Protocol (1979 LRTAP) for Long-Term Financing of Monitoring and Evaluation Programs
1985	Nairobi–Montreal Guidelines for the Protection of the Marine Environment against Pollution from Land-Based Sources
1985	Vienna Convention for Protection of the Ozone Layer
1985	Helsinki Protocol (1979 LRTAP) for Reduction of Sulfur Emissions
1985	Rome International Code of Conduct on the Distribution and Use of Pesticides

(Continues)

TABLE 6-2. *(Continued)*

1986	Vienna Conventions on Early Notification of a Nuclear Accident, and on Assistance in the Case of a Nuclear Accident or Radiological Emergency
1986	Geneva Convention Concerning Safety in the Use of Asbestos
1987	Nairobi–London Guidelines for the Exchange of Information on Chemicals in International Trade
1987	Montreal Protocol (1985 Vienna Convention) on Substances That Deplete the Ozone Layer
1988	Sophia Protocol (1979 LRTAP) for Control of Nitrogen Oxide Emissions
1989	Basel Convention on the Control of Transboundary Movements of Hazardous Wastes and Their Disposal
1990	London Amendments to 1987 Montreal Protocol
1991	Bamako Organization of African Unity Convention on the Ban of the Import into Africa and the Control of Transboundary Movement and Management of Hazardous Wastes within Africa (not in force)
1992	Rio Biodiversity Convention
1992	Rio Climate Change Convention
1993	Copenhagen Amendments to 1987 Montreal Protocol
1993	London Dumping Convention to Ban Nuclear Waste Disposal in Oceans (replaces voluntary moratorium adopted in 1983)

centric system. For all of these reasons, self-proclaimed pragmatists argue that the path to an improved global environment is through stronger, policy-driven regimes, not through fundamental changes in political institutions.

Figure 6-1 presents a simple conceptual model of international regime formation and adjustment, based on a cyclical process of problem recognition, interest articulation, national response, coalition building, application of international norms and voting rules, policy adoption and financing, ratification, implementation, and enforcement. The swirl of activity portrayed in the model takes place around a secretariat that is responsible for arranging meetings of the parties, coordinating implementation, and serving as a regime's "headquarters" or information clearinghouse. The cyclical portrayal is necessary because many regimes have to be renegotiated at the margin as new protocols and new interpretations of regime authority are proposed.

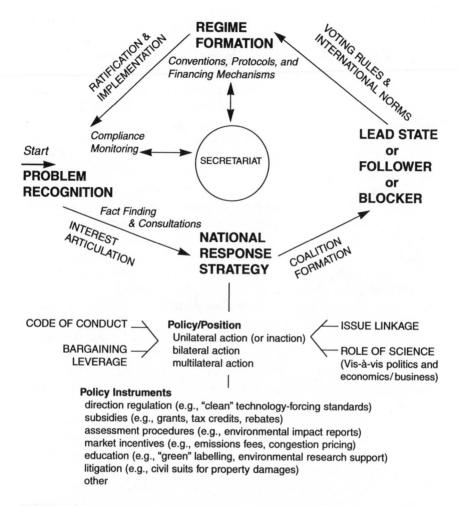

FIGURE 6-1. *International regime formation and adjustment.*

The process of regime formation, like all voluntary attempts at collective action, permits state actors to adopt one of three basic roles: to lead, follow, or oppose proposed agreements. Some actors may initially choose to be "swing states" (Porter and Brown, 1991: 36), taking no position in support or opposition until other actors have given them a good reason to do so. Because most proposed regimes represent very modest concessions of state power, the stakes in regime negotiation often have more to do with national prestige, strategic posturing, and avoidance of "slippery-slope" precedents than with substantive environmental problem solving.

In the case of the 1992 biodiversity convention, for example, many negotiators from industrial countries shared the U.S. government's concerns about the treaty's provisions for intellectual property and financing mechanisms, but unlike the United States they chose to support the regime at the Earth Summit, calculating perhaps that the potential gains in cooperation and national prestige would more than offset the political and economic concessions implied by the treaty.

The question of how to create stronger international regimes in a community of sovereign states has been vigorously debated in recent years (Camilleri and Falk, 1992; French, 1992b; Lipschutz and Conca, 1993). There appear to be many ways to accomplish this objective, some that seem anathema to a strict interpretation of national sovereignty. The most important approach, perhaps, centers on the voting rules that are adopted for bringing a particular regime into existence. The old approach of requiring unanimity among participating states virtually ensured that regime formation would be shaped by lowest-common-denominator politics. Increasingly, however, qualified majority voting (e.g., agreement by two-thirds of the nations participating) has been adopted to prevent one or a few blocking states from continually steering policy. The 1992 convention on biodiversity, for example, went into force upon ratification by thirty states. The 1992 climate convention required only fifty state ratifications to take effect. Although states refusing to sign initial agreements often declare their immunity from majoritarian regimes, in practice, many continue to comply out of concern that they will be perceived as outcasts or penalized indirectly in lost political leverage or credibility. In the International Whaling Commission, which uses qualified majority voting, Japan, Norway, the former Soviet Union, and Peru all said they would defy the 1986 moratorium on harvesting, but none of the states openly followed through on their previous declarations of immunity.

Additional ways to strengthen regimes include development of (1) innovative financing mechanisms, such as earmarked environmental trust funds; (2) the creation of standing international bodies to replace ad hoc negotiators; (3) development of trade sanctions for noncompliance; and (4) monitoring and evaluation programs that require regular reports by states, while permitting unintrusive, independent inspection by representatives of treaty secretariats.[10] The idea here is to have sufficient data to undertake state-by-state performance and compliance evaluations, with any poor showings brought to the attention of the world press and appropriate NGO watchdogs. If we have learned anything about what makes regimes work, it is that a state's concern with its international image (e.g., avoidance of embarrassment) may be at least as important as its respect for international law, thus inviting grudging state participation in regimes that it does not truly favor.

The theory behind international environmental regime formation is relatively straightforward, since it is derived from theories of the state. The multilateral norms and rules that make up green regimes create obligations on behalf of states and their agents to limit or prevent certain types of environmental harm. Such arrangements become necessary to reduce transboundary environmental impacts and the political conflict that such impacts generate. In political ecology terms, green regimes help determine the degree to which homeostasis or ecological balance will be legally recognized and protected across states or the commons they share. The regimes also help determine what might be called the economic "trophic" levels that competing states, as natural resource consumers, will be allowed to occupy. Most important of all, they help determine how asymmetries in political interdependence and in environmental relations between states will be redressed.

For instance, consider states whose quality of surface water or air depends heavily on the pollution-prevention practices of their upstream or upwind neighbors. Next, consider a world in which all states are vulnerable to global pollutants that each state emits in varying amounts. In the first case, regional regimes, such as river-basin authorities, can redress the asymmetry of state relationships with respect to the environment by allowing injured or potentially injured states to invoke previously agreed upon and codified norms and rules, in the form of multilateral treaties. These treaties protect them from such harm or at least provide grounds for seeking compensation if it occurs. In the second case—global emissions of carbon dioxide, for example—comprehensive regimes must include all states as both causes of injury and as potentially injured parties.

To properly address differences in state contributions and in their environmental risks, a globally effective regime would have to incorporate the historical emissions record of each state, the per capita emissions record, and perhaps the population growth record. It would then have to deal with the political and economic asymmetries that arise when states suffer different levels of absolute loss due to global environmental changes, leaving some states to conclude that they are in a position of relative gain with respect to their competitors and potential enemies. For example, conventional notions of national security and prestige may encourage some states to perceive global damage from climate change as an acceptable cost if it is disproportionately concentrated among their enemies. Under these circumstances, global regimes are likely to form only where environmental crises impose absolute losses on a state that appear greater, in the near term, than the sum of relative gains (e.g., trade and security advantages) created by the losses experienced by competing states. In other words, as long as nations value their futures in the immediate terms of international political economy, instead of in the long-range terms of political ecology, there can be little prospect that sufficient portions of state sovereignty will be surrendered to provide for the common good.

Conclusion

We began this assessment of environmental governance with bold visions of what *could be* and ended with incremental variations of what *is*. The apparent staying power of nationalism seems to drive thinking in that direction. It would be unwise, however, to argue that what is past will continue to be prologue. Institutions and policies can change in unexpected and nonincremental ways, as recent studies of "punctuated equilibria" in politics make clear (e.g., Baumgartner and Jones, 1993). Moreover, the pragmatic preference for policy reform over institutional reform relies on a distinction that is much sharper in theory than in practice. Policy changes are necessary, but not sufficient, elements of effective global environmental governance. They must be combined with institutional reform and innovation.

Environmental treaties offer disoriented reformers a means of sharp focus, timely response, and sometimes a rewarding sense of closure. Although they are accorded most of the attention by today's scholars, practitioners, and advocacy coalitions, attempts to design new institutions and political orders, however scattered and open-ended they may seem, are probably much more important in the long run. Granting that state-level adjustments at the margin are, and will continue to be, the most favored response of governments, the task for environmental NGOs will increasingly become one of persuading their governments and fellow citizens that the most pressing challenges we face are largely glocal problems that require nonincremental, glocal responses. If the precepts of political ecology are correct, neither unitary world government nor nation-state confederations will be adequate for meeting those challenges.

The design of stronger confederations through a revitalized United Nations and World Court offers a promising way in the short run to elevate the rule of law in international relations, but it is unlikely to prove any more sustainable in the long run than the economic development plans of its sovereign members. Utopian as it may seem, a constitutionally based world federation that can link communities and regions, without either decimating or strengthening nation-states, may be the only way to ensure that the policy and institutional responses needed for effective global environmental governance do not undermine the world's growing but fragile impulse for democracy.

Notes

1. While the author has used the term "glocal" since the late 1980s, the word appears to have originated—or was popularized, at least—in Japan. In any event, others apparently used the term earlier—some, perhaps, like the author, deriving it from the popular expression "Think globally and act locally."

2. Like its biological counterpart, the political ecosystem can be described in terms of its flows of energy and cycling of nutrients and materials. Although it strains the analogy to do so, one can imagine a myriad of political entities coexisting in competing niches. Energy, in the form of influence, votes, and authoritative symbols, courses through channels of power and public acquiescence, forming the basic political "food chain" that determines "who gets what, where, when, and how" (Lasswell, 1936). Nutrients and materials, in the form of money, staffs, and access to information, perpetuate the cycle of incremental growth, decay, and renewal that characterizes modern bureaucratic politics. Although cynics might choose predator–prey imagery to represent the essence of political life, the more fitting image may be that of *symbiosis*—the association of different organisms engaged in what political scientists would call "coalition behavior."

3. For a discussion of postmaterialist ideas, see Ronald Inglehart, "Post-Materialism in an Environment of Insecurity," *American Political Science Review* 75 (1981), 880–888. The distinction between quantitative and qualitative growth is developed in Mihajlo Mesarovic and Eduard Pestel, *Mankind at the Turning Point: The Second Report of the Club of Rome* (New York: Dutton, 1974), pp. 1–9.

4. See, for example, Gilpin (1981, 1987), Clark and Dear (1984), and Ruggie (ed.) (1993).

5. For a description and discussion of these goals, see Falk, Kim, and Mendlovitz (1982).

6. The ability of powerful corporations to exploit tensions between the center and the periphery of federal systems is well documented in the literature on air pollution and toxics regulation. See, for example, Charles Davis and James P. Lester, *Environmental Politics and Policy: Theories and Evidence* (Duke, 1989), 57–84.

7. The list of federal states currently includes Argentina, Australia, Aus-

tria, Brazil, Canada, the Comoros, Germany, India, Malaysia, Mexico, Nigeria, Pakistan, Russia, Switzerland, United Arab Emirates, the United States, and Venezuela.

8. Maurice Strong, for example, in "What Place Will the Environment Have in the Next Century—and at What Price?" *International Environmental Affairs* 2, 3 (Summer 1990), p. 212, has argued that U.N. organizations and programs represent "not the precursors of world government, but the basic framework for a system of world governance."

9. According to Secretary General Boutros-Ghali, in 1992–93 more than 24,000 troops and civilians under U.N. control were dispatched to the former Yugoslavia, another 28,000 to Somalia, and 22,000 to Cambodia.

10. For a discussion of many of these measures, see Hillary French (1992a,b).

CHAPTER 7

Political Economy

This chapter is concerned fundamentally with the ways in which economics and politics come together in environmental governance. It presents the political economy of environmental protection as a field of inquiry that is parallel and complementary to that of political ecology. Unlike the "glocal" perspective of political ecology, however, the political economy approach is primarily concerned with *national* economic power and capacity. International political economy (IPE) expands the purview to cross-border expressions of economic development and state capacity, but the focus remains on national practices and strategies.

Essentially, IPE is concerned with the ways in which geography and resources combine with policy decisions and structural imperfections to determine comparative economic advantage among nations. From this perspective, failures and successes in environmental governance are usually attributed to a combination of incentive and exchange structures that shape and perpetuate the struggle for advantage among nations. Terms of trade, economic competitiveness, monetary policy, and the political interests that influence them are said to lie at the heart of international power, leaving everything from environmental regulation to national education policy to be explained as epiphenomena. Theories of national competitive advantage can be used to explain why the Montreal Protocol took the form that it did, why the United States initially opposed a tough climate convention and refused to sign the biodiversity treaty, and why the Law of the Sea convention has failed thus far to gain the necessary signatures for implementation.

By examining the interaction of political and economic decisions and consequences, IPE scholars provide a powerful glimpse of the forces that shape today's international system. Among the key questions they study are the effects of tariffs and other restrictions on trade, the influence of unstable exchange rates, concerns about intellectual property rights, debt and structural adjustment programs, market distortions caused by government subsidies, and barriers to market entry or economies of scale caused by excessive or inadequate regulation.

From a global environmental perspective, nearly every major threat to the health of the biosphere can be explained in terms of some failure (or should we say "qualified success?") in political economy. As explained in chapter 3, environmental costs are seldom internalized in market prices, and environmental property rights are rarely defined, assigned, and enforced. Government subsidies and other market distortions, which encourage environmentally harmful manufacturing and agricultural practices, often result in oversupply or overconsumption of nonrenewable natural resources. The incentive structures of contemporary political economy—tax rates, price supports, depreciation schedules, etc.—generate ecologically tragic decisions about the uses of land, energy, water, and fisheries. They promote excessive reliance on private automobiles, pesticides, packaging materials, and assorted objects of conspicuous consumption. In short, they foster behaviors and trade practices that are inextricably linked to the fate of the biosphere.

This chapter explores the diverse ways in which the structure of political economy is evolving to accommodate changes in technology, ecology, and capital flows. At the macro level, it describes how economic trade and the pursuit of comparative advantage have contributed to environmental destruction, and how reforms in trade and development practices can be used to help resolve environmental problems. At the micro level, it offers an examination of the role played by multinational corporations in making environmental reform both necessary and possible. The chapter ends with a discussion of some promising tools for greening the global economy.

Trade and Environment

The 1990s are likely to be remembered as the decade in which environmental protection became a key consideration in cross-border investment and trade policy. Much of the initial interest grew out of the struggle over European integration and harmonization, and the changes in political economy that created the European Union (EU). It became more sharply defined in the debate over the North American Free Trade Agreement (NAFTA), particularly with respect to the effects of free trade on environmental conditions in Mexico and on domestic environmental standards in the United States. Less visibly, but more importantly, it surfaced late in the Uruguay round of negotiations over the General Agreement on Tariffs and Trade (GATT)—negotiations that affected more than 90 percent of world trade and that are helping to determine the fate of environment and natural resource endowments in more than one hundred countries.

Prior to the 1990s, trade liberalization and its implications for future governance received little attention in the environmental literature. Although some environmentalists have been active for many years in defending environmental standards that inadvertently impede interstate trade, most have shied away from the complex legal and economic issues that characterize the trade–environment debate. The Uruguay round of negotiations on GATT reform, which began in 1986, represented the first major opportunity to infuse global trade negotiations with environmental considerations. The negotiations, however, proceeded without any significant involvement by environmental groups until a year or two before their completion in December 1993. Although a few writers, notably Charles Pearson (1974), Ingo Walter (1975), Seymour Rubin and Thomas Graham (1982), and Herman Daly and John Cobb (1989), called attention to the environmental implications of trade liberalization, it was not until the bruising struggle for European integration—symbolized by the 1992 Mastrecht Treaty and the parallel debates about NAFTA and GATT in 1993—that the significance of free trade policies began to figure prominently in the thinking of many environmentalists.

Trade liberalization, which has long been a leading goal of economists and many government leaders, became a topic of considerable interest at the 1992 Earth Summit. Even in that setting, however, environmental concerns appeared to take a back seat to concerns about economic fairness and equity. It was not until the following year that the issues of trade and environment became fully joined in overlapping debates about the European Community (now "Union") Single Market, U.S. ratification of NAFTA, and international completion of the Uruguay Round of GATT negotiations. By the end of 1993, the trade and environment nexus had been defined on both a regional and a global basis, and the environmental challenges implicit in that definition could no longer be ignored.

The European Experience

The faltering steps toward political and economic integration of Europe in the 1980s and early 1990s provided one of the first and most instructive cases of the potential incompatibility of certain trade and environmental goals. Although many Western Europeans take pride in their history of regional cooperation on transboundary water and air pollution problems, they have seldom made environmental harmony a condition for intracommunity trade. The freedom of the region's exporters and importers to be cleaner or dirtier than their trading partners has only recently become a matter for protracted debate.

Under the Single European Act, differences in product standards between trading nations have been permitted in cases where national policies for health and environment would otherwise be undermined. In effect, member nations have been given the freedom in carefully defined circumstances to set higher environmental standards than their neighbors and to apply those standards to imported goods and services. A major precedent for this form of environmental sovereignty was established in September 1988, when the European Court of Justice ruled in favor of a 1981 Danish law requiring that all beer and soft drink bottles, foreign and domestic, be recycled and include a mandatory deposit at point of sale. Nations without container deposit and recycling programs, but wishing to export bottled drinks to Denmark, vigorously opposed the container law, arguing that it constituted a barrier to trade. Similar trade disagreements arose over efforts by the Dutch to mandate the use of catalytic converters in all cars sold or registered in their country.

The European Court's decision opened the way for a number of subsequent attempts by members of the EU to adopt packaging, recycling, and ecolabeling standards that were more demanding than those of other members. Germany, for example, passed a controversial law requiring firms doing business in Germany, along with foreign distributors, to provide for the collection of 80 percent of their packaging waste by 1995 and to recycle 80–90 percent of that amount. Named for Germany's environmental minister, the "Töpfer Law" brought strong complaints from Britain, France, and Belgium, who insisted that the law was too demanding and that it represented a green-shaded form of protectionism. Some criticism even came from environmentally friendly companies operating outside of Germany. The head of Britain's largest recycling firm, for example, charged that the packaging law was designed to allow Germany to dominate the European recycling market (*Economist*, 1992: 60).

In a related trade dispute, the European Court's advocate general called on Germany in 1994 to remove its ban on the pesticide pentachlorophenol (PCP), following a complaint by the French government that the ban constituted an unfair barrier to intra-EU trade and that it was not a "proportionate" measure in terms of the negligible health and environmental benefits that the ban would achieve. Because Germany's ban applied to both indigenous production and imported products, the advocate general's finding was criticized by many environmentalists as a step backwards toward the practice of "lowest common denominator" environmental standards. The finding called renewed attention to the problems of determining environmental virtue in the context of free and fair trade.

NAFTA

Interest in the relationship between trade and environment became more sharply defined in the debate over the North American Free Trade Agreement (NAFTA), particularly with respect to environmental conditions in Mexico. Environmentalists contended that Mexican pollution control and resource protection, especially near the border, had to be strengthened substantially before implementing any new trade agreements. Although trade negotiators in both countries were quick to point out similarities between U.S. and Mexican environmental law, pronounced differences remained between the countries' monitoring and enforcement capacities. While the United States budgeted $24.40 per capita on environmental enforcement in 1991, the figure for Mexico was $0.48 (Lewis et al. 1991: iii).

Many U.S. environmental groups, often acting in concert with organized labor, opposed NAFTA on grounds that it would expand unsustainable development in Mexico, undermine U.S. environmental sovereignty, and promote industrial flight to "pollution havens" in Mexico at the expense of U.S. workers. From a legal perspective, the most important of these concerns was the perceived assault on environmental sovereignty. Under free-trade rules, stringent national environmental standards are often characterized as indirect means to protectionist ends. Environmentalists fear that efforts to harmonize differences between trading partners will result in a lowest-common-denominator approach to environmental standard setting for cross-border goods and services. And even if the standards remain high, they fear the weakening effects of harmonized enforcement.

In the case of NAFTA, grounds for these fears developed quickly with the infamous 1991 GATT Dispute Resolution Panel ruling on the use of trade sanctions to protect dolphins. The dispute arose over a U.S. embargo of imported Mexican tuna caught in purse seine nets that caused the inadvertent death of thousands of dolphins. Commercial fishermen operating in U.S. waters, who were required by the U.S. Marine Mammal Protection Act to develop "dolphin-safe" fishing practices, complained bitterly that Mexican fisherman, unfettered by U.S. law and industry practices, were profiting from differences in domestic standards that rewarded them with a competitive advantage in the tuna market. Invoking the sanctions provisions of the Marine Mammal Protection Act more than a decade after its passage, the United States declared a ban on the importation of Mexican tuna. Mexico appealed to the GATT panel to declare the U.S. action a non-tariff trade barrier, and the three-man panel responded with a non-binding ruling upholding Mexico's claim. At this point, political appeasement entered the picture. Mexico, despite having won the initial round in the GATT hearing process, proceeded to adopt voluntarily many of the dolphin-safe tuna fishing practices of the U.S. fishing fleet. Environmentalists and animal rights groups responded to the move with great reserve and outright skepticism. They were convinced that a dangerous precedent had been set by the GATT panel, and that Mexico's voluntary efforts to protect dolphins were driven by public-relations concerns rather than a genuine change in environmental consciousness.

GATT Reform

Although the international environmental community was awakening to the implications of NAFTA disputes like the tuna-dolphin case, most members did not understand the far greater environmental implications—both good and bad—that proposed changes in GATT represented. North American environmentalists, in particular, seemed so preoccupied with NAFTA that the changes taking place in GATT were largely ignored, initially. Ironically, NAFTA was in part a political strategy developed by the United States to push other countries into accepting a stronger GATT.

The history of GATT goes back to 1947, when, in an attempt to suppress the protectionist tendencies of nations emerging from the World War II, a broad set of agreements was drafted by twenty-three countries to regulate the use of international quotas, tariffs, and other trade restrictions. Although environmental concerns appear to have been peripheral at best in the initial design of GATT and in its subsequent revisions, contracting parties were permitted to restrict trade in a few narrowly defined environmental circumstances in order to conserve "exhaustible resources" (Article XX,g) or where it was "necessary to protect human, animal or plant life or health" (Article XX,b). Such restrictions also had to apply to domestic production if they were to be justified under GATT, hence a party that wanted to restrict trade on the basis of environmental risk had to demonstrate that foreign and domestic sources of the risk were treated exactly alike.

Prior to the 1986–1993 Uruguay Round of GATT negotiations, seven other rounds were completed without any significant effort to tie environmental protection to trade objectives. During the Uruguay Round, however, Austria, Sweden, and Switzerland attempted to forge such a link, only to be rebuffed by other countries, mostly G-77 members, who feared the possibility of extraterritorial implementation and enforcement of "First World" environmental standards. In their eyes, the reform efforts of these three small European countries represented an attempt by the North to use its comparative advantage in environmental regulation as a means of restricting imports from the South.

The arrival of the GATT panel's tuna–dolphin decision during the preparations for the Earth Summit may have allayed some of the G-77's fears about extraterritoriality, but it also sharpened the resolve of many environmental organizations to become more involved in trade negotiations. Environmental groups quickly set out to show the degree to which proposed trade reforms were at odds with the concept of sustainable development. Many concentrated on what they perceived to be the anti-environmental bias of past multilateral trade agreements and of the dispute-resolution procedures they relied on. Virtually all of the major international environmental organizations developed strategies to transform the GATT negotiations into instruments for not only preserving but strengthening international environmental standards. At a minimum, they wanted a permanent environmental commission to be created under GATT. Some wanted to remove trade barriers, such as the Multi-Fibre Agreement, that restricted labor-intensive exports from developing countries and thereby pressured those countries to export their precious natural resources in an unsustainable manner. Many also wanted an end to government agricultural and water subsidies, and other forms of protectionism that had resulted in overfarming and inappropriate conversion of forests and hillsides to agricultural uses. Above all, they wanted GATT reforms that would recognize the legitimacy of trade sanctions in clear cases of violations of international environmental law.

At the same time that environmentalists were contemplating ways to harness the power of GATT for ecological purposes, Uruguay Round negotiators were voicing growing concern about the degree to which environmental regulations were interfering with trade. By the end of 1993, more than twenty international environmental regimes in force included provisions for managing cross-border trade or for imposing trade sanctions against countries that failed to comply with regime policy. The best known of these—the Convention on International Trade in Endangered Species (CITES), the Montreal Protocol on Substances That Deplete the

Ozone Layer, and the Basel Convention on the Control of Transboundary Movements of Hazardous Waste—were viewed by many trade negotiators as a direct challenge to the authority of GATT. In the case of CITES, for example, critics of environmental trade measures feared that illegal trade by China and Taiwan in rhinoceros and tiger parts would lead to the imposition of trade sanctions against both countries. Similarly, they worried that the Montreal Protocol went too far in authorizing trade sanctions against nonsignatories involved in the production or exchange of ozone-depleting substances. Of particular concern to free-trade supporters was the protocol's provision for a feasibility study of import bans on products manufactured with processes that used CFCs— even if the products themselves contained no substances regulated by the protocol. Finally, free-trade advocates pointed to the precedent-setting trade restrictions of the Basel Convention. The convention, which previously limited trade in hazardous waste, was amended in March 1994 to ban all hazardous waste shipments to developing countries, although much of the waste could still be shipped to Eastern Europe. Since some developing countries were apparently pleased to accept money in exchange for toxic risks, free-trade advocates questioned what they saw as undue interference in voluntary contracts, resulting in unfair restraint of trade. The dispute provided an early test of environmental priorities under the proposed GATT reforms.

On December 14, 1993, representatives from all 117 nations engaged in the Uruguay Round agreed to overhaul the GATT framework and further reduce tariffs by as much as 50 percent. The reduction of tariffs and expansion of import quotas was expected to add $270 billion annually to world income by the end of the decade (Passell, 1993: A1). The representatives also created a new World Trade Organization (WTO) and empowered it with "the exclusive authority to adopt interpretations of [the GATT reforms] and of the Multilateral Trade Agreements." Article XVI, section 4, of the WTO states that national laws must conform with all GATT provisions, raising concerns in some quarters that the state-centric world was indeed succumbing to global trade imperatives. Ironically, the Uruguay Round "Final Act, " as the WTO agreement was known, appeared to require the surrender of far more national sovereignty than even the most demanding international environmental agreements had required to date.

The implications of the Final Act were very mixed. The undeniable benefits of liberalized trade for multinational corporations and many national economies had to be tempered by a general concern that the economic growth fostered by greater trade would far exceed trade-induced growth in environmental protection. While many environmental economists cheered the assault on subsidization and protectionism as a necessary step toward establishment of environmentally sound price signals, some foresaw a difficult transition period in which environmental conditions would deteriorate due to trade before they got better. This claim was informed, in part, by research showing that gains from trade liberalization realized under NAFTA would exacerbate many environmental problems in the early going but in the longer term bring net improvement.[1]

While the Final Act contained no provision for the creation of a permanent committee on environment and trade, it left the door open for further negotiations on this and many other proposals. Of special concern for environmentalists was the act's provisions to treat stringent health and environmental safety standards as trade barriers unless they could be justified on a scientific basis. By continuing to place the burden of proof for environmental regulation on countries with the highest standards, the trade negotiators effectively undermined "high-end" harmonization (which is based on a precautionary philosophy of erring on the side of environmental protection) in favor of a "low-end" approach based on accepted scientific evidence. With large amounts of scientific uncertainty to be surmounted and even larger differences in the economic and political capacities of nations to protect territorial environments, few observers expected international standards to move rapidly toward the high end. Thus, environmental organizations were not able in most cases to leverage stronger protection out of the 1993 GATT reforms. They did, however, manage to imbue discussions about the design of the WTO with considerations about sustainable development and the need for participation by nongovernmental organizations. More important, they made the establishment of a permanent committee the centerpiece of an international lobbying effort at the April 1994 Ministerial Meeting of the WTO in Marrakesh.

A Sustainable Trade Order

The Uruguay Round Final Act established the basic principles and directions for future international trade policy, but it left many basic issues and questions of implementation unresolved. Perhaps the most important of these, from an environmental perspective, was the future viability of retaliatory trade barriers or tariffs applied against countries that failed to comply with international environmental standards or with the domestic standards of a national trading partner. Environmental groups in the United States, for example, fought to preserve the provisions for unilateral trade sanctions contained in Section 301 of the U.S. Trade Act of

1974. They warned that once the Clinton administration's signing of the Uruguay Round Final Act was ratified by the Congress, many U.S. environmental standards would become vulnerable to challenges by GATT partners on the grounds that they appeared to be impediments to trade.

Another issue of great importance for environmental protection involves the right of nations to impose export controls for the purpose of conserving important natural resources. Limiting the export of tropical hardwoods, for example, may be an important way to preserve rainforest habitat, although few nations appear ready to value their forests over the foreign exchange that can be had for raw timber and wood products. The challenge facing the WTO is to prevent the arbitrary use of national measures to restrain trade, while at the same time recognizing the proper role of limited national export controls for environmental protection.

In order to afford adequate environmental protection in the future, additional reform of the world trade system will be necessary. Sustainable trade, like sustainable development, will require glocalized policies and institutions that foster greater public participation in the design of markets, and stronger environmental commitment to managing the flows of investment, technology, and resources that markets attract. Embracing the principle of sustainability represents a critical first step in reforming the global trade system, but other principles will be needed. In keeping with the philosophy of glocalization, future trade policies will need to incorporate global objectives and imperatives, while encouraging more decision-making at the local community level or as low on the political ladder as circumstances permit. Because of the information-management and communications revolution, global organizations that encourage local decision-making are likely to thrive in the next century. This is true for government and business sectors. The principle of subsidiarity—keeping the locus of decision-making as close to the people and their direct representatives as possible—has become an important design feature of the European Union in recent years, and its extension worldwide may be essential for developing a system of glocal decision-making that successfully joins trade and environmental concerns.

The principles of sustainability and subsidiarity represent, respectively, the substantive and procedural "guidestars" of future trade reform; but there are many other principles that must be added in order to make trade reform truly beneficial for the environment. Table 7-1 provides a summary of some of the most important principles. Many can be thought of as prerequisites for achieving the overarching principle of sustainability. The first principle to consider in terms of urgency, however, is that of *precautionary action*. The precautionary principle argues that environmental prudence, in the face of scientific uncertainty, requires cost-effec-

TABLE 7-1. *Ten Principles to Make the World Trade System More Compatible with Environmental Goals*

1. *Sustainability*	Trade policy should preserve meaningful choices, opportunities, and environmental experiences for future generations.
2. *Subsidiarity*	Decision-making should be kept as close to the grassroots level of governance as circumstances permit.
3. *Polluter pays*	Pollution abatement is the responsibility of the polluter and should not be subsidized by governments.
4. *Lifecycle cost*	Goods and services should be evaluated not only on the basis of initial cost but also on the basis of lifetime operation and maintenance costs, hidden energy and environmental costs, and the costs of product disposal or recycling.
5. *Limited harmonization*	Efforts to foster upward harmonization of national environmental standards should be tempered by the ability of poor countries to pay for higher standards.
6. *Precautionary action ("no regrets" strategy)*	Actions that reduce the risk of large and irreversible environmental changes should be taken in advance of scientific proof wherever they can be justified by known cost-effective side benefits (e.g., energy efficiency).
7. *Priority of prevention*	Future policy should focus on preventing additional environmental destruction, rather than constantly responding to damage that has already occurred.
8. *National environmental treatment (NET)*	Foreign and domestic goods and services should be treated equally under national environmental regulation (environmental nondiscrimination).
9. *Participation and transparency*	Public access to, participation in, and continuous monitoring of rule making and implementation should be encouraged.
10. *Common heritage*	Open access and joint ownership of the global commons and its resources should be protected.

Sources: OECD (1972), Moss (1993:116), Esty (1994: 216–224).

tive actions and limitations on trade wherever there are reasonable grounds for suspecting that the trade activity will result in serious environmental damage. Waiting for scientific certainty before acting, according to this principle, is tantamount to reckless endangerment of the planet in the mistaken belief that the burden of proof should lie with those who favor environmental action, rather than with those who risk irreversible harm by its deferment. Without observance of the precautionary principle, environmental arguments for reforming world trade may attain legitimacy and support too late to avert global disasters. This would not only violate the *priority of prevention* principle—that it is usually much cheaper to prevent environmental problems than to "solve" them—but it might also make the goal of sustainability unattainable in any meaningful sense.

In terms of market signals and direct trade incentives, the principles of greatest significance are *lifecycle cost, national environmental treatment,* and *polluter pays.* The principle of lifecycle costing argues that environmental damage from a good that is being traded should be assessed on the basis of not only what it represents at point of sale, but on the basis of its lifetime use, and the materials and energy that are expended in its manufacture, transport, packaging, and disposal. The principle of national environmental treatment holds that each nation must apply the same environmental standards to imported goods and services that it applies to domestic production. This is simply a way of saying that environmental protection must not be used as a "mask" for trade protection. Finally, the polluter pays principle, which was introduced by the OECD in 1972, puts polluting firms on notice that *they,* not their governments, are responsible for pollution-abatement costs, and that government cleanup of private pollution sources constitutes an illegitimate subsidy because it creates an unfair trade advantage for the offending firm. Although many firms pass their pollution-control costs on to their customers, the principle nevertheless seeks to assign responsibility where it will do the most good—at the source.

The Role of the Corporation

However lofty and correct the principles, the problem of how to operationalize them in day-to-day trade activities remains daunting. In part, this is because of profound changes that are occurring in the corporate management of world trade. Alliance formation among multinational corporations is quietly diminishing the power of governments to determine how trade shall be conducted. Thus, at the same time that global environmental threats are calling into question the legal and political viability of national sovereignty, cross-border investment activities of large multinational corporations are calling into question its economic viability.[2]

In 1970, the United Nations identified seven thousand multinational corporations (MNCs) in operation, a majority of them based in the United States and Britain. In a little more than two decades time, that number has increased to over thirty-five thousand—many of them controlled from gleaming new headquarters in Japan, Germany, and Switzerland. Another 170,000 firms serve as foreign affiliates for these MNCs. The top one hundred MNCs are believed to control nearly half of the total foreign assets represented by cross-border trade and direct corporate investment (*Economist*, 1993: 6). In the United States, the top one thousand corporations, most of them MNCs, account for nearly two-thirds of GNP, with the remainder of GNP drawn from eleven million smaller firms. The average size of these MNCs is 16,500 times larger than the average small- to medium-scale business in America (Hawken, 1993: 8).

From an environmental perspective, the development of the multinational firm has been a very mixed blessing (Choucri, 1991). On the one hand, MNCs tend to be more advanced or sophisticated than many domestic, small- to medium-sized firms in their environmental management. They can transfer environmental technology quickly, draw on large R&D programs and international information networks for developing waste-management and pollution-control programs, and they can compare notes on the most promising environmental innovations developed by the countries in which they do business. In addition, they are often in a better financial position than local firms to absorb new environmental mandates, and their environmental impacts are more likely to be scrutinized by host countries (not to mention the countries in which they are headquartered), making them more conscious of their environmental reputations (Choucri, 1993: 205-253; Leonard and Duerksen, 1979: 23).

On the other hand, MNCs have created an enormous integrated market for goods and services that has had the effect of greatly accelerating the extraction and consumption of natural resources and the pollution output of industrial manufacturing and agriculture. MNCs make possible the massive, coordinated development of heretofore wild or remote parts of the world. They are involved in patterns of exploitation and trade that, in the eyes of many Third World observers (e.g., Raghavan, 1990), amount to nothing less than recolonization. Moreover, their mobility, corporate secrecy, financial leverage, and ability to exploit ambiguity in national laws often make it possible for them to evade regulation and avoid accountability for their actions. Although there is little evidence today that large numbers of MNCs are actively seeking pollution havens in developing countries (Harrison, 1994), many environmentalists fear that such exploitation will grow in the future as regulation within developed countries is strengthened. Table 7-2 summarizes the most common regulatory tools and strategies employed to manage the environmental practices and impacts of MNCs.

It is usually assumed that strict environmental standards place firms at a competitve disadvantage and eliminate jobs in regulated industries. While environmental regulation is clearly costly for some firms and industries, empirical studies reveal that the correlation between environmental stringency and economic performance for most industrial sectors is extremely weak and, if anything, positive (Repetto, 1995). Some studies suggest that strict environmental regulation may be a major factor in promoting economic competitiveness (Hall, 1994). This finding can be explained, perhaps, by the tendency of firms to develop greater efficiencies and money-saving innovations in responding to new environmental mandates (Porter, 1990). It may also reflect the rapid growth of "green technology" industries, now estimated to comprise a world market valued at nearly $200 billion.

Despite the growing evidence that environmental measures contribute to strong economies, many MNCs seem to view environmental goals as major impediments to economic progress. Some have devoted major portions of their public relations and advertising budgets to challenging what they perceive as unreasonable national environmental standards. In these contests of business and government influence, it is not the power or scale of particular MNCs that matters so much as it is their collective ability to form strategic alliances that effectively place them beyond the reach of many national governments. In fact, with increasing trade liberalization and technological advances in worldwide communication and computing, today's strategic alliances of MNCs typically represent more power and influence over particular commodities or services than is wielded by the vast majority of nations in which they do business. The development of these alliances, aided by trade policy and technology, has fostered a subtle transformation of MNCs into TNCs—transnational corporations—and, in a few cases, into SNCs—supranational corporations.[3]

A supranational world is a borderless world, and consequently peoples' sense of loyalty is drawn to something larger and separate from the nation-state. To be supranational today, in practical social and economic terms, really means to be glocal. A supranational corporation is one in which economic development is tied to local labor pools, global capital flows, and regional investment opportunities. Consequently, SNCs may perceive existing political institutions and boundaries largely as potential

TABLE 7-2. *Regulating the Environmental Practices of Transnational Corporations*

National governments	TNC self-regulation	International authority
Pollution standards	Corporate codes of conduct	International codes and guidelines (e.g., OECD guidelines for MNCs)
Land-use controls	Site selection	Cross-border consultation and notification
Disclosure rules and reporting requirements	Corporate health and safety rules	Conventions and protocols (e.g., Montreal Protocol)
Import restrictions	Project- and product-planning goals	Information exchanges and registries (e.g., IRPTC: International Toxics Registry)
Customs inspections	Management contracts and licensing agreements	Trade policy
Liability for damages	Industry performance objectives and monitoring	Environmental review by international panels/commissions
Impact assessment and audit requirements	Voluntary audits	Global monitoring and compliance audits
Enforcement programs	Inspection and maintenance reviews	Citizen action campaign (e.g., Pesticide Action Network)
Penalties/Fines	Promotion and hiring practices	International sanctions

Sources: Charles S. Pearson (1987: 3–31), Nazli Choucri (1991, 1993: 205–253), Stephan Schmidheiny et al. (1992), Frances Cairncross (1992), and Paul Hawken (1993).

barriers to growth. They will be prone to view international law and diplomacy as costly and inefficient means for protecting cross-border investment and contract enforcement. In the eyes of many SNCs, governance—to the extent it is needed to protect market economies—may have to be entrusted to the World Trade Organization. It is strategic alliances based on trade, rather than the military alliances of nations, that drives SNC expectations about world affairs in the next century.

National governments, for their part, are confronted with a rising tide of cross-border investment, managed by so-called "stateless" corporations that have developed "chameleon-like abilities to resemble insiders no matter where they operate," along with abilities to customize their global product line to conform with local tastes (Holstein,1990: 98, 102). Although few corporations are truly stateless in either design or operating philosophy, an increasing number are making decisions without regard to national boundaries and interests, except as they affect the business climate. This trend has prompted some environmental groups to push for stronger MNC codes of conduct, such as the CERES principles, established in the aftermath of the 1989 *Exxon Valdez* oil spill,[4] and the Global Environmental Management Initiative (GEMI), which promotes greater environmental openness and self-monitoring by its corporate members.[5] These initiatives go beyond past attempts by governments to regulate the international behavior of corporations, such as the U.N. Code of Conduct on Transnational Corporations, the OECD Guidelines for Multinational Enterprises, and the International Labor Office's Tripartite Declaration of Principles Concerning Multinational Enterprises and Social Policy.

Fortunately, some corporations are beginning to see environmental protection as a value-added factor in production and service. Concepts such as Total Environmental Quality Management (TQEM) and Industrial Ecology are slowly making their mark on the management philosophies of major corporations.[6] As a consequence, the people who run TNCs are becoming much more aware of the environmental opportunities arising from global interdependence. They are also beginning to realize that the ability to provide stable climates for business and trade depend increasingly on the stablity of the earth's physical climate and of its ecological and geochemical systems. In order to understand how the business environment and the natural environment affect each other, a number of private sector leaders have called for changes in the way that nations and corporations define and measure their political economies (e.g., Schmidheiny, 1992; Hawken, 1993). They favor the use of market-based environmental indicators and investment indices that will help business, government, and consumers make better informed decisions about economic activities that harm the environment.

Designing Green Markets

One of the most promising ways to make decisions about political economy more in keeping with ecological thinking is to incorporate ecological services and the costs of their loss into the design of markets. Although it is customary to speak of market forces in terms of spontaneously arising natural laws and "invisible hands," the fact is that all markets are the design products of governments, business entrepreneurs, and financiers. There are no truly *free* markets; only designed markets. Unfortunately, most market designs to date have encouraged the systematic destruction of nature's ecological services in return for fleeting forms of profit and capital accumulation. In the future, however, it will be much harder for market designers to hide or defer ecological costs merely by discounting them into oblivion or promising artificial replacements as compensation. Too many ecosystems have been irreparably damaged, and too much of the world's remaining capacity for wealth creation is dependent on a healthy biosphere to risk a continuation of past practices.

Green Accounting

If sustainable development is to become more than just a fashionable term, ecological and economic "fund" balances will have to be tightly integrated in the accounting practices of individuals, firms, and nations. A major push in this direction has been provided by the new field of "natural income" accounting. Protecting ecological wealth in practical terms requires the preservation of natural capital, as distinct from man-made capital. Natural capital includes a variety of ecological services and vital resources, such as forests, topsoil, breathable air, and drinkable water. Because no distinction was made in the past between natural and man-made capital, much of what counted as growth in GNP and other forms of national income accounting actually represented the destruction of natural capital. Destroying a rainforest for its scattered mahogany resource, for example, increased GNP for the moment, but at a staggering loss in ecological wealth. Likewise, mining topsoil as a result of intensive agricultural practices led to vast improvements in short-term economic performance, while impoverishing a nation's future ability to grow food. The result has been an economic accounting system that highlites short-term benefits and conceals deferred costs. For instance, the severe contamination of hundreds of major groundwater basins represents an enormous deferred cost of modern agriculture and manufacturing. Because natural capital, unlike man-made capital, is seldom reproducible or recoverable by human technology, its loss is irreplaceable and represents a potentially massive constraint on future human development.

Today, as much as one-third of GNP in some countries represents the squandering of natural capital (Heuting, 1990). Studies of Costa Rica (Repetto et al., 1991) and Indonesia (Repetto et al., 1989) suggest that national income and economic growth indicators will have to be substantially revised in order to reflect the natural resource depletion associated with timber, energy, agricultural, and fisheries development. Costa Rica, for example, which is widely regarded as relatively progressive in its environmental thinking, loses 5 percent of its GNP each year due to overexploitation of natural resources (Repetto et al. 1991: 1). The opportunity costs of unsustainable development are increasingly apparent in the degradation of streams and forest lands, which in turn threaten Costa Rica's lucrative ecotourism industry. In many other regions of the world (e.g., East Africa, the Amazon Basin, South Asia) the sustainable development opportunities foregone because of excessive resource exploitation appear to be much greater. Ultimately, most of the world risks severe ecological impoverishment unless the indicators that nations employ to measure economic health are revised to account for natural capital depletion and then acted on. As economist David Pearce observes, sustainability requires that natural capital resource stocks be held constant over time (Pearce and Turner, 1990: 23–58). The implication for future generations is clear: Irreversible processes and irreplaceable uses of natural capital are taking place in ways that entail an unsustainable future and a loss of freedom for those who will inherit the planet.

Market-based Incentives

Modern environmental protection programs have relied heavily in some countries on government regulations that specify both the standards to be met and the acceptable technologies or other means to meet them. This is especially true of many U.S. pollution-abatement programs. With the rise of so-called "free-market environmentalism" (Anderson and Leal, 1991), a variety of market-based, "flex-tech" approaches to environmental protection have begun to be employed on a pilot basis, often with favorable results (see, for example, Tietenberg, 1985 and 1991). Using the conventional dichotomy of command-and-control regulation versus market-based incentives, economists and other analysts have argued strongly that "carrots" (incentives) are more effective than "sticks" (regulatory enforcement) for protecting the environment. But governments frequently prefer sticks to carrots, and even when carrots are selected, they often end up looking more like orange-colored sticks. According to most economists, environmental control measures that demand extensive governmental coordination and enforcement are likely to fail, while those that rely on the invisible hand of the market have a good chance of succeeding. A preponderance of economic evidence appears to support this conclusion, but it is by no means clear that market-based solutions alone can resolve major environmental problems in a timely fashion. Some combination of regulation, taxes, and market mechanisms may indeed be optimal.

The controversy over emissions trading as a pollution-abatement strategy illustrates the kind of arguments that arise over the use of green market instruments. Emissions trading operates on the principle that wide differences in pollution-abatement costs make it more efficient for those for whom abatement is very expensive to pay those for whom it is relatively cheap to make additional abatement efforts above and beyond what is required by law. Thus polluters facing steep marginal cleanup costs will buy credits from firms that can reduce emissions cheaply until the net reduction in total pollution is equal or greater than what would be required of each firm acting alone. The conventional economic wisdom suggests that markets for emissions trading will usually work better than across-the-board regulation in achieving pollution reductions at the lowest cost. A study of seventeen emissions control programs, in which compliance costs were compared with simulated, market-induced abatement costs, found that emissions trading alternatives in almost all cases produced large savings over command-and-control measures (Tietenberg, 1985). According to some economists, emissions trading could reduce the costs of pollution abatement by at least one-third, without adding any net emissions to the environment (Blinder, 1988)

Mandatory standards, on the other hand, have the advantage of concentrating the attention of polluters on quantifiable objectives and timetables. If consistently and evenly applied, they make it easier to forecast and to plan. Moreover, they are often faster than market approaches in getting results. Emissions trading, by contrast, subjects participants to the changing risks and opportunities of a dynamic market. Some power-plant operators, for example, may prefer known regulatory constraints to uncertain opportunities for emissions trading. Another advantage of mandatory standards, theoretically, is that they define the duties and responsibilities of citizens in relatively unambiguous and virtuous ways, while emissions trading is often perceived as a "license to pollute" and motivated by greed.

While there are serious limitations on the use of market-based tools in some environmental problem areas (trade in endangered species, for example), there are many other applications in which such tools appear to offer a promising means of improving environmental conditions at relatively low cost. To illustrate how market-oriented policies can be used to prevent or reduce global environmental problems, two of these tools have been selected for closer examination. Both represent partial solutions to global problems of atmospheric change. The first—international carbon emissions offsets (ICEOs)—was designed to reduce atmospheric emissions of carbon dioxide, while the second—the "golden carrot" program for green technology innovation—was established to attack greenhouse, ozone, and energy efficiency problems simultaneously.

International Carbon Emissions Offsets

Perhaps the most ambitious of the market-oriented greenhouse solutions proposed thus far is the use of international carbon emissions offsets (ICEOs) as a tradeable currency for use in financing energy efficiency improvements, afforestation, and low-impact logging programs. Since approximately three-quarters of global CO_2 emissions are produced by fossil energy combustion, efforts that are successful in getting more work out of each unit of fossil energy will be repaid with proportionate reductions in carbon emissions. For example, doubling the fuel efficiency of the average American automobile would reduce annual CO_2 emissions by nearly 2.5 metric tons per vehicle (a total of more than 400 million tons/year). Trees become important in this regard because annual deforestation releases 6.4 billion metric tons of CO_2 each year to the atmosphere (22 percent of global emissions). Because trees sequester ("scrub") excess CO_2 from the atmosphere, at least until they decompose or are burned, afforestation and forest protection provide attractive investment targets for offsetting carbon emissions from energy use, logging, and slash-and-burn agricultural development. A single acre of tropical hardwood forest, for example, can sequester up to 7 metric tons of CO_2 per year. Some fast-growing species of tropical pine and eucalyptus are estimated to sequester 12–16 metric tons of carbon per hectare annually (Marland, 1988).

The first ICEO program was initiated in 1989 by Applied Energy Systems (AES) of Virginia. With the help of the U.S. Agency for International Development (AID), the Peace Corps, and the international relief agency CARE, AES embarked on a voluntary program to plant more than fifty million trees in Guatemala over a ten-year period in order to offset the carbon emissions from a new, 183-megawatt coal-fired power plant being built in Connecticut. The plan called for enough surviving trees to scrub all of the CO_2 emitted by the power plant over its expected forty-year lifetime, at a total cost estimated at less than $0.25 per ton. Subsequent ICEO projects, most of them forest-based, have been developed or proposed for Malaysia, Thailand, Panama, Costa Rica, Mexico, Nepal, Russia, and the Amazon. The most interesting of these, perhaps, involve efforts to protect existing forests through the financing of reduced-impact logging and through the extension of property rights and agroforestry development for indigenous forest peoples.[7]

The objective of ICEO policies is to permit carbon emitters to find the least expensive way to offset their emission impacts. By assigning a monetary value to CO_2 reductions, emissions trading would enable carbon emitters to compare the cost of making emission reductions at the source (e.g., installing power-plant scrubbers) with the cost of offsetting emissions through energy conservation, tree planting, or renewable energy programs at other locations. Ideally, carbon emitters would be able to offset their CO_2 emissions at any participating location in the world where equivalent carbon savings could be purchased through the currency of ICEOs. In most cases, this would result in a shift in investment toward developing countries with large and untapped potential for energy efficiency improvements, alternative energy development, and stable opportunities for reforestation and forest protection. Developing countries with significant debt problems could be encouraged to trade their ICEO services for debt relief.

In practice, many developing countries have been wary, even hostile, to the concept of international offsets out of fear that they would be exploited by rich industrial giants who would "buy up" all the best offset sites, lock them in as long-term carbon sinks, and continue development-as-usual in their home countries. Their fears crystallized with the signing of the global climate convention in 1992. Article 4.2a, known as the "joint implementation" section, explicitly allows parties to the convention to work jointly with other parties in managing greenhouse gas emissions. Because the parties are divided into three groups or "annexes," and only the Annex I nations (essentially OECD members) have obligated themselves to contain emissions in the year 2000 at or below 1990 levels, other parties fear that the most inexpensive carbon-reduction opportunities will be monopolized by Annex I powers, leaving the developing nations with the prospect that only expensive options will remain at some future time when Annex II and III members are mandated to stabilize their own emissions. From this perspective, carbon offsets are a cheap way for rich Northern nations to continue their profligate consumption of fossil fuels and forest products while tying up potentially valuable land in the South for low productive use as carbon sequestration sites.

One promising way out of this North–South dilemma would be to permit developing countries hosting a joint implementation project to double count the carbon benefits for the duration of the project. For example, assume that a power company from an OECD nation wished to offset its carbon emissions by signing a thirty-year contract with a tree-planting organization in a developing country. Assume further that fifteen years into the contract, carbon-reduction targets were established for the host country. From that point on, after calculation and verification of carbon savings, both parties would be allowed to count the savings in its carbon inventory. While assigning double credit plays havoc with accounting practices used in monitoring the global carbon budget, from the perspective of international cooperation it may be a vital incentive for encouraging highly efficient carbon savings to be undertaken in developing nations, even those that have not yet become parties to the climate convention.

The initial participants in such a program would presumably be a small subset of the world's nations. As a market for carbon-saving services developed, a new group of energy and forest conservation entrepreneurs could be expected to develop, some in the role of project developers and others in the role of international emissions-trading brokers, whose job it would be to help carbon emitters find promising carbon offsets (i.e., carbon saving or sequestering projects). While political instability in regions where offsets take place could result in wrenching dislocations in project implementation and contract enforcement, the risk of ICEO investments will decline as the practice becomes institutionalized. Properly designed, ICEO projects that focus on the South could end up transferring billions of dollars and green technology where it potentially can do the most good.

Golden Carrots

The golden carrot idea is based on a program started in 1992 as a joint effort of twenty-four electric utilities and the U.S. Environmental Protection Agency (EPA) to assist refrigerator manufacturers in developing and marketing a highly energy efficient, CFC-free refrigerator. The incentive, or carrot, was a $30 million prize to be awarded to the manufacturer of the best prototype that met the criteria of being ozone friendly, moderately priced, and at least 25 percent more energy efficient than the 1993 U.S. appliance efficiency standard. The carrot strategy was intended to provide a mechanism for surmounting technical and resource barriers to green technology innovation—especially innovation needed for demand-side management in the energy sector.[8] The theory was that it would be much cheaper to finance refrigerator manufacturing innovations that saved energy than to build new power plants to run inefficient refrigerators. To these savings were added the avoided costs of abating CFC and other greenhouse gas emissions, as well as the avoided costs of tropospheric pollution from additional power plants.

The winning refrigerator, a 21.6-cubic-foot Whirlpool, was designed, built, and tested in less than four months. Nearly 30 percent more efficient than the 1993 standard, its speedy development owed a great deal to the company's prior R&D investments in improved fan motors, compressors, lubrication and insulation, and refrigerants. The first unit off the assembly line was sent to the Clinton White House in February 1994. Backers of the program expect sales of the refrigerator to reach $2 billion.[9]

As a result of the success with refrigerator technology, other golden carrot targets are being identified for future sponsored competitions. These include air conditioners, clothes washers, lighting systems, and even water conservation devices. The Consortium for Energy Efficiency (CEE), a nonprofit group of utilities and environmental organizations that grew out of the superefficient refrigerator program, is promoting a wide range of demand-side management programs that will benefit from technological improvements in these target areas. Because the membership includes utilities serving twenty-five million households and commercial establishments, CEE's efforts to combine technology-push and market-pull strategies are potentially very important means for reducing atmospheric emissions of carbon, CFCs, and many other pollutants. What remains to be seen is whether the idea is transferable to other economic sectors and other countries, especially those in the Third World.

There are, of course, many other promising ideas and market-based methods that could be employed on behalf of global environmental protection. For example, in the automotive sector alone there are dozens of attractive green market measures that are ready to be tested or already being demonstrated in industrialized countries. These include congestion pricing or roadway pricing, pay-as-you-drive auto insurance, emission-based registration fees, carbon taxes on gasoline, and "feebate" systems, which tax vehicles with higher than average pollution and fuel consumption levels and rebate the revenue proportionally to buyers of vehicles that perform better than these averages. The common feature of all of these measures is a reliance on pricing signals to discourage environmentally destructive purchases and behaviors and to reinforce actions that prevent or mitigate environmental harm.

Distributional Effects

While there is little doubt that market incentives can be effective in nations where disposable incomes are relatively high, the suitability of such measures for bringing about major environmental gains in developing countries is much less clear. In general, equity concerns about market-driven environmental solutions have tended to become polarized along North–South lines. This is not surprising, given the obvious differences in wealth and the fact that distributional effects of environmental policy are one of the least studied aspects of international political economy.

Green fees and pollution taxes often add to the regressivity of existing pricing and taxing systems. As a result, progressive advocacy coalitions that are typically in the forefront of environmental action have sometimes campaigned against market tools, even when their membership is in broad agreement that the application of these tools would result in positive net benefits for society and the environment.[10] The net social benefits criterion, so revered by beginning policy analysts, usually proves on closer examination to be impractical. What is appealing in economic theory may turn out to be irrelevant in practice. This is because scientific rationality has very limited utility in the distribution of power and wealth, and in the cultivation of constituencies. "Who gets the cookies?" always trumps the question, "How shall we make more cookies?"

In formulating public policy, even innovative market-based policy, it is often difficult to tell the difference between developing a solution and creating someone else's problem. A fine line separates problem solving from problem *shifting*. While game theorists cherish positive sum games and economists celebrate the achievement of Pareto optimality, true win–win situations, including the Kaldor–Hicks variety,[11] are seemingly in short supply in the real world of international political economy. Even the decision rules employed in benefit–cost analysis ensure, based on the choice of discount rate, that today's problems can be shifted to future generations.

Viewing one group's policy solution as another group's (or future gerneration's) problem, for all of its prosaic qualities, remains an important source of tension in international environmental governance. Environmental problem shifting becomes easier to spot when national environmental policies, or the lack thereof, become matters of regional or global concern, as in the cases of transboundary acid rain pollution and CFC emissions. Exporting a nation's problems becomes even more visible when the act is exposed in the searchlights of the global news media and telecommunications industry, as exemplified by infamous attempts to dump toxic wastes from the North into poor countries of the South.

The fact remains, however, that most global environmental destruction escapes such notice and occurs in complex ways that are hard to trace to a particular nation or source. Political responsibility has not kept pace with scientific abilities to detect and measure environmental damage, and governments have not found (or perhaps *wanted* to find) an acceptable way to internalize the costs of that damage in the marketplace. In political economy terms, this means that the destruction of natural capital is being documented with increasing precision and complexity, but the failure of political will to stop this destruction is somehow justified as noble observance of the principle of nonintervention in the marketplace.

Conclusion

The increasingly open architecture of the world's economy is proving far more responsive to global change than the relatively closed architecture of world politics. Perhaps the allure of money and trade is simply stronger than the allure of national sovereignty. That is why command-and-control regulation will probably prove inadequate to the task of global environmental protection and why new and additional market-based incentives may be needed to supplement such regulation. It also suggests why defenders of national sovereignty, so intent on fighting environmental globalism, are more likely to fall prey to its economic counterpart.

Like Rousseau's distinction between the general and the particular will, the distinction between global polity and national constituency weighs heavily in the formation and legitimation of international environmental policy. The changing political economy has altered, probably forever, the relative size and significance of the global and national policy spheres. It has left transnational corporations, with their strategic alliances and cross-cutting agendas, propitiously wedged between these spheres. Business and trade, and the development activity that they engender, have emerged as the real driving forces behind globalism—much more so than ecological thinking. Unfortunately, the growth of the global political economy may be no less threatening to the biosphere than the state-centric system that it is slowly replacing.

Almost forgotten is the role of local communities and the possibility of glocalism, as opposed to globalism. The precarious counterbalancing act that unites the state, the corporation, and the international governing institutions too often draws attention away from the possibility of a more representative and less bureaucratic system of governance built upon revitalized communities and environmentally designed markets. Trading away government size for effectiveness in dealing with transboundary environmental and security problems sounds like a wise choice. But it remains an elusive one. How to get more governance out of less government is a challenge fit for a political Einstein. Getting more governance at the global *and* the local level out of less government at the national level makes the challenge even greater. Not even Einstein's leap to quantum physics can match the conceptual breakthrough that is required for glocal political institutions to flourish in a political economy dominated by corporate alliances and nations determined to preserve their sovereignty. To point out the difficulty of this reconceptualization, however, is not meant to justify a retreat into academic equivocation. The hope expressed here is that the breakthrough will come from the reintegration of political ecology and political economy, and from a profound reorientation of market forces to support public values of sustainability and sufficiency. Precisely how that could happen and what form of public philosophy will be needed to legitimize it are questions that no one can answer with much confidence. They are questions, nevertheless, that warrant exploration in a systematic fashion. The following chapter represents one such attempt at exploration.

Notes

1. Grossman and Krueger (1991: 35–36), for example, argue that if per capita income in Mexico begins to grow due to enhanced trade it will probably result, initially, in net environmental damage; but as it reaches levels of approximately $4,000–5,000, discretionary spending on environmental quality improvements will increase, yielding net benefits thereafter.

2. For a discussion of these trends, see Richard J. Barnet and John Cavanagh, *Global Dreams: Imperial Corporations and the New World Order* (New York: Simon and Schuster, 1994).

3. Although the terms *multinational* and *transnational* have been used interchangeably for many years, a subtle difference in meaning can be noted for purposes of this discussion. The term multinational refers to a state-centric system that permits multilateral ties; the term transnational refers to a system that places less emphasis on the state and more attention on cross-border activity. *Supranationalism* moves beyond the state, or a particular group of states, altogether.

4. Developed by the Coaltion for Environmentally Responsible Economies in 1990, the CERES Principles (formerly called the *"Valdez* Principles") have been adopted by thirty-four firms to date—mostly social investment firms and relatively small companies known for their progressive management styles. Among the ten principles are provisions for the voluntary disclosure of pollution incidents and potential environmental hazards, performance of annual environmental audits, and the appointment of an environmental representative to each company's board of directors.

5. Members of GEMI include Allied Signal, Amoco, Apple Computers, AT&T, Boeing, Browning-Ferris, Digital, Dow Chemical, Kodak, DuPont, Merck, Occidental Petroleum, Procter & Gamble, and Union Carbide. Unlike the CERES Principles, GEMI does not demand strong public disclosure policies or annual environmental audits.

6. TQEM is an extension of the Total Quality Management (TQM) movement that W. Edwards Deming and others introduced in Japan following World War II. It is a business strategy that seeks to incorporate environmental protection and energy efficiency in all aspects of business operations,

at all levels of the firm, in the belief that both environmental quality and product quality are directly linked to long-term company profits. Industrial ecology is a management approach that assumes that "cradle-to-grave" product planning (lifecycle analysis) can eliminate much of the waste and pollution of conventional production processes by increasing on-site recycling and by treating one firm's by-products as another firm's feedstock for production.

7. For an analysis of recent and proposed ICEO projects, see Lamont C. Hempel et al., *Forest-Based Carbon Offsets for Climate and Habitat Protection*, (Policy Clinic Report, The Claremont Graduate School, May 1994); and Paul Faeth, Cheryl Cort, and Robert Livernash, *Evaluating the Carbon Sequestration Benefits of Forestry Projects in Developing Countries* (World Resources Institute and U.S. EPA, February 1994).

8. Initially proposed in 1989 by the Natural Resources Defense Council, the golden carrot strategy was officially known as the Super Efficient Refrigerator Program (SERP). Most of the $30 million "carrot" was provided by participating electric utility companies.

9. The $2 billion sales forecast was made in early 1994 by Ray Farhang, president of the Consortium for Energy Efficiency.

10. One of the best examples of this phenomenon can be drawn from the controversy over international carbon emission offset trading and its perceived effect on income distribution. Many other promising solutions to environmental problems (e.g., green taxes, congestion pricing) have been abandoned over the years on grounds that they would place an undue burden on people living in poverty. Judging by their writings and public comments, many environmentalists are deeply ambivalent about what they perceive as unavoidable trade-offs between environmental progress and social justice.

11. The Kaldor–Hicks principle promotes redistributions of wealth that increase the net welfare but reduce the welfare of some individuals so long as those individuals can be compensated (i.e., have their welfare restored) from the gains made by everyone else. For a discussion of this concept, see J. R. Hicks, "The Foundations of Welfare Economics," *The Economic Journal* 49: 196 (December 1939): 696–712.

CHAPTER 8

An Ethical Framework for Glocal Action

Any understanding of the political ecology and political economy perspectives of environmental governance will be incomplete without a clear conception of the normative goals and principles on which they are based. Legal and political frameworks for making environmental or other types of policy depend on ethical frameworks for their legitimation. Ethical frameworks, in turn, depend on norms that can be ordered and arranged in terms of appropriate context and priority. Recalling the arguments presented in chapter 3, the principal norms of the modern era that have governed human behavior toward the natural environment are anthropocentrism and contempocentrism. The rules of political ecology and political economy that have arisen from those norms—for example, national sovereignty, the denial of property rights to nearly two billion women, the use of high discount rates—all reflect acceptance of values that are incompatible in the long run with the goals of a sustainable society.

In this chapter, we will explore alternative norms that can be applied cross-culturally and cross-temporally to achieve such a society. First, we will examine the communitarian norms needed to guide environmental action; then we will turn to the norms of democratic deliberation needed to legitimize that action in ways that improve both environmental sustainability and social justice among human beings. By treating norms and the governing rules they support as part of an indivisible goal of social and environmental improvement, we shall attempt to show that glocal institutions and policies offer one of the most promising ways to reconcile environmental imperatives with democratic governance.

Although norms and rules usually develop interactively, policy makers frequently downplay normative analysis in their rush for politically advantageous rules. Moral values and principles may be loudly proclaimed, but economic self-interest and coalition politics usually dictate the choice of rules. It follows that global environmental agreements are much more likely to result from a fortuitous alignment of domestic political pressures than the negotiators' collective sense of moral responsibility. International norms of environmental behavior tend to be addressed only to the extent that they can be linked to popular symbols and broad, often vacuous, ethical precepts. Slogans often drive policy. Saving whales has become a towering symbol of ecological virtue, while the slaughter of sharks has been permitted to expand without so much as a sigh from most environmentalists. Similarly, millions have rallied to save African elephants and Asian tigers and pandas, but few people appear to be very concerned about the hippopotamus or the fate of thousands of endangered plants and insects. In such circumstances, the ambiguous and sometimes contradictory values embraced by ordinary citizens end up being applied selectively to justify triage measures. Large sums of money can be raised to save rhinos, but not crocodiles. Scientists and international diplomats have succeeded admirably in developing policies to protect Antarctica, but no comparable policy successes have arisen to stop the environmental devastation of Madagascar, Haiti, South-Central Los Angeles, Jakarta, or thousands of other places that lack powerful environmental defenders.

As some policy preferences get transformed into legal rights and duties, the development of norms comes full circle, albeit with ambiguous results. At the Earth Summit, for example, the "right" to a clean environment competed with the "right" to economic self-determination, the outcome depending on whether advocates of sustainable development emphasized the word "sustainable" or "development." The need for consensus on the concept of sustainable development made it necessary to avoid precision in defining what the concept meant. Thus, the strategic use of ambiguity appears to be as important for the development of ethical consensus as it is in forging political agreement.

The principles presented in the 1992 Rio Declaration help to illustrate how strategic ambiguity can facilitate policy agreement by bringing together conflicting norms. Echoing the famous Stockholm Declaration of 1972, the Rio Declaration assured participating states that environmental progress would not be achieved at the expense of their sovereign rights and economic interests. Principle 2, which closely resembles Principle 21 of the Stockholm Declaration, declares:

> *States have, in accordance with the Charter of the United Nations and the principles of international law, the sovereign right to exploit their own resources pursuant to their own environmental and developmental policies, and the responsibility to ensure that activities within their jurisdiction or control do not cause damage to the environment of other states or of areas beyond the limits of national jurisdiction.*

Like the tendency to deemphasize the action in "action plan," the nations subscribing to Principle 2 have tended to neglect the "responsibility to ensure" clause (environmental protection) in favor of the "right to exploit." Granting at present the political necessity of reaffirming sovereign rights in declarations of this type, it is nevertheless hard to reconcile such affirmations with many of the other principles adopted at the Earth Summit. States endorsing the declaration, for example, pledged to "cooperate in a spirit of global partnership to conserve, protect and restore the health and integrity of the Earth's ecosystems" (Principle 7); "enact effective environmental legislation" (Principle 11); rely on "international consensus," where possible, when addressing transboundary or global environmental problems (Principle 12); "cooperate in an expeditious and more determined manner to develop further international law regarding liability and compensation for adverse effects of environmental damage" (Principle 13); and "promote the internationalization of environmental costs and the use of economic instruments" (Principle 16).

Most if not all of these last principles tend to limit or threaten the notion of national sovereignty. However, the fact that they appear in the same declaration as the sovereignty principle is not surprising. The apparent inconsistency only strengthens the argument, introduced in chapter 1, that the world is indeed undergoing a global transition in which elements of both twentieth- and twenty-first-century thinking are woven into major decisions and policy choices. Part of the historic importance of the Earth Summit was its significance as a symbolic dividing line between these two conceptions of environmental politics.

Without a credible environmental ethic, no conception of environmental politics can claim enough legitimacy to invite adequate global action. But who can say what constitutes a credible environmental ethic? The central importance of ethical frameworks is disputed by those who insist that careful policy design and institutional reform can be accomplished without resorting to murky investigations of values. Their resistance is understandable, given the difficulty of establishing universal norms and codes of conduct that can be extended from individuals to nations, and then across nations. The fact remains, however, that international law can thrive only where there is agreement on norms. Since the only legitimate coercion at the international level is that to which states have previously and voluntarily subscribed, future international cooperation is likely to depend more on national leaders' perceived interests and acceptance of norms than on collective threats of force. As the framers of the Rio Declaration probably recognized, norms form the rhetorical foundation of policy, but the strength of that foundation is more a function of strategic ambiguity than of coherent ethical persuasion. International norms are full of contradictions that are reflected in competing policies. The challenge for advocates of glocal environmental governance will be to develop broad support for environmental and other norms that, however ambiguous, foster and legitimate the voluntary surrender of carefully delineated portions of state sovereignty in return for vital environmental benefits.

No single environmental ethic is likely to win adherents across the myriad of cultures and political environments that influence international policy making. However, there may be some shared elements among different environmental ethics that can provide a basis for developing and strengthening supranational norms. Many promising norms have already been proposed and others could be adapted for this purpose, but three in particular stand out as crucial to the development of an ethical framework for global environmental action. For the sake of brevity, they will be identified here as the norms of *common heritage*, *common equity*, and *common security*. The use of the word "common" is included to suggest that the norms apply across political jurisdictions, cultures, and generations— both living and unborn. A fourth norm, *deliberative democracy*, represents the procedural standard by which common heritage, equity, and security must be applied in order to have lasting legitimacy. Together, these norms represent the irreducible minimum for achieving forms of environmental governance that are effective, just, participatory, and sustainable.

Common Heritage

The first environmental norm we will consider was proposed in 1967 by Malta's ambassador to the United Nations, Dr. Arvid Pardo. Addressing the thorny issue of access to and ownership of deep-seabed resources in the Law of the Sea negotiations, Pardo proposed that such resources be regarded as "the common heritage of mankind." By the use of the word "common," Pardo meant to imply both open access and joint ownership of the resource by rich and poor nations alike. He even suggested that most of the immense wealth represented by seabed minerals be distributed to countries that lacked any prospect of developing a deep-sea mining program of their own. Since nearly three-quarters of the earth's surface can be regarded as a commons, the implications of Pardo's proposals were indeed far-reaching.

Common heritage represents an extension of an earlier concept, "province of mankind," which was introduced in the 1959 Antarctic treaty and reaffirmed in the 1967 Outer Space treaty. In practice, the province envisioned by the earlier treaties was restricted to an elite group of nations that had mapped and explored the Antarctic and portions of outer space. Pardo's proposal was to globalize the right of entry and use of the commons. In the words of Malaysia's U.N. ambassador, who was objecting at the time to the Antarctic treaty's exclusion of developing countries, "Henceforth all the unclaimed wealth of this earth must be regarded as the common heritage of all the nations" (United Nations General Assembly, 1982).

Taken out of context, the common heritage doctrine appears decidedly anthropocentric. Environmentalists may cheer the principle of globalism over nationalism with respect to the commons, but many decry the environmental exploitation that open access and joint ownership seem to imply. In the Law of the Sea negotiations, for example, "common heritage" was broadly interpreted as a license for exploiting marine resources. The anthropocentric outcome was predictable in this case, but there was also a vexing case of contempocentrism at work. Pressures on resource exploitation increase rapidly if nations lacking the financial and technological capabilities to extract certain resources are suddenly in a position to benefit directly from the labors of those who already have such capabilities. Of what good is an international norm that merely hastens Hardin's tragedy of the commons in the name of equity?

Perhaps the only adequate way to answer such a question is to challenge its premise that common heritage means a shared inheritance of property that can be consumed or exchanged for money by the current beneficiaries. Part of the inheritance, after all, is a planetary life-support system that cannot ethically be appropriated or stripped of parts to be pawned. Another form of the inheritance consists of ecological services and aesthetic features that add immeasurably to the quality of human life, and thus must be preserved if future generations are not to be short-changed or impoverished. Clearly, the notion of heritage must incorporate the notion of sustainability if it is to become a supporting pillar of global environmental governance. It must be applied in perpetuity or else subsumed under some larger norm of planetary stewardship. Each generation must accept moral responsibility for passing along nonrenewable portions of its environmental inheritance to the next generation. Otherwise, the declining value of each successive inheritance becomes a measure of the previous generation's failure to practice sustainable development (i.e., to meet today's needs without diminishing the opportunities for our descendants to meet theirs).

Although this principle of common heritage in perpetuity appears to be a worthy ideal on which to construct an international norm, the present realities of disparate state power and political capacity make movement in this direction very difficult. For one thing, norms based on common heritage principles violate the "first come, first served" rule that is customary in capitalist societies; they challenge the Lockean notion that the ownership of a common pool resource is awarded to the first person to expend his or her labor in exploiting it.[1] It is largely on this basis that the United States and several other industrial powers have rejected Ambassador Pardo's joint-ownership arguments. What incentive is there, they ask, for developing the financial and technological wherewithal to exploit a common pool resource, such as manganese nodules, if the rewards are divided among all nations while the risks are confined to the lead appropriator? Economists, of course, would respond that risk-taking appropriators should proceed whenever their marginal benefits exceed their marginal costs—including the costs of any relative trade disadvantages created by the windfalls their activity produces for other firms or nations. While this has the virtue of maximizing material wealth, it leaves unanswered questions about transgenerational appropriation rights and environmental justice.

Despite the opposition of free marketeers, the common heritage doctrine has retained a strong following during the past twenty-five years, particularly among developing countries. The Group of 77 (now approximately 130 countries), capitalizing on their numerical voting strength in the U.N. General Assembly to compensate for their political weakness in the Security Council and in other key international institutions, have repeatedly sought to incorporate the common heritage principle into international environmental agreements. For the most part, they have been unsuccessful. Starting with proposals for an international regime to govern the seabed, one after another common heritage initiatives have foundered on the issue of redistributive politics. Even an initiative by the Nixon administration to apply common heritage principles failed—largely because the concept was being pursued in order to expand U.S. navigation rights.

Attempts have been made to define everything from genetic information to telecommunication frequencies in space as part of the common heritage doctrine. In the case of genetic resources, G-77 countries tried in the early 1980s to have wild germ plasm that was used in the development of commercial biotechnology products declared a common heritage property. They succeeded initially in getting the U.N.'s Food and Agricultural Organization (FAO) to press their case, but the biotechnology industry quickly enlisted the help of powerful governments, led by the United States, who forced FAO to back down and to rescind its declarations by withholding a major portion of the agency's funding.

The issue of common biological heritage arose once again in the preparations for the 1992 Earth Summit. Many participants wanted to develop a biodiversity convention based on the principle of common heritage. Negotiators, however, decided to avoid the politically charged issue and settled instead for a treaty in which biodiversity became merely a "common concern," remaining firmly under the control of each state. This decision arguably may have made the resulting treaty worse in some respects than having no treaty at all.

Ironically, the common heritage principle long embraced by G-77 members has increasingly been promoted by environmentalists in ways that developing countries find threatening to their own national interests. For example, American and European environmentalists have argued that major rainforest habitat for threatened and endangered species, which is found almost entirely in G-77 countries, should be regarded as common heritage sites. The implication is that the host countries would have the responsibility of becoming onsite caretakers, managing a resource "owned" by humanity. Some G-77 countries—Brazil, for example—have rejected such implications in no uncertain terms.[2]

Virtually every attempt to strengthen the concept of common heritage involves a mechanism for creating what amounts to a severance tax on the use or extraction of common pool resources. One of the more imaginative and comprehensive of such schemes is a proposal by legal scholar Christopher Stone (1993) for a Global Commons Trust Fund (GCTF). Stone's idea is to impose modest tax levies on activities that exploit or damage the commons and then earmark the revenue for the protection and restoration of common heritage sites. Revenues for the GCTF, totaling well over $6 billion a year, would come from a proposed 1.5 percent tax on the commercial value of marine fish harvests, a $0.10-per-ton tax on CO_2 emissions (or CO_2-equivalent greenhouse gas emissions), a $1-per-ton tax on waste and dredge disposal in the ocean, token rate taxes on oil and gas development in commons areas, fees for the rights to scarce geostationary orbits for satellites and scarce frequencies in space for telecommunications, perhaps royalties from biotechnology and pharmaceutical industries that exploit genetic information, and legal charges assessed for violation of treaties protecting commons areas.

Stone proposes that the revenue be used solely for managing the commons under the auspices of international authority. He argues against dividing the revenue among nations or allowing it to be used for nonenvironmental purposes (with the exception of famine and disaster relief). Appropriate activities to be funded would include global environmental monitoring programs, inventorying and collecting precious genetic material, environmental education about conservation and waste-minimization behavior, technology transfers that assist in the management and repair of common heritage sites, and development of international quick-response teams for major oil spills and nuclear accidents.

While there are many practical and political objections to the idea of a global environmental trust fund, the single most important criticism has to do with the perceived inequities involved in its funding. Poor countries would be especially resistant to paying for the use of the commons, particularly in light of the historical fact that many of their richer neighbors helped finance their own rise to economic power by treating the commons as either a free source of commodities (e.g., marine fisheries) or a free waste depository (e.g., atmospheric carbon emissions). Representatives of G-77 countries are prone to regard pollution of the global atmosphere or genetic manipulation of wild seeds as proper targets for trust fund levies, since at present these activities are predominantly the handiwork of wealthy countries. But when it comes to other common heritage resources, the arguments tend to flow in the opposite direction. For example, there is strong opposition among developing countries (not to mention among certain developed nations) to proposals for imposing conservation levies on ocean fisheries or on economic development activities that destroy biological "hot spots" of international significance. Given that most of the developed countries are just as inclined to avoid paying for use of the commons, the heritage doctrine is likely to remain a vague and weakly constructed norm unless concerns about fairness and national self-interest are satisfactorily incorporated into its structure. Perhaps the best way to accomplish this is through the development of "companion" norms for equity and security.

Common Equity

Although related to the principle of common heritage, the principle of common equity is fundamentally concerned with broad questions of distributive justice across political units and human generations. In a sense, the achievement of either norm implies the achievement of the other. In order to preserve nature's bequest of ecological wealth from generation to generation there must be a transcendent notion of equity operating, one that is held in common by different cultures and generations (Brown, 1989). Likewise, in order to secure the promise of *common* equity (e.g., non-overlapping, intergenerational equity), there must be a sense of common heritage that transcends the notion of common ownership, and its emphasis on divisible property. In the absence of a concern with heritage, we are back to the problem of creating a tragedy of the commons in the mistaken pursuit of equity.

The principle of common equity is intended to apply primarily to communities and states across time and space. It is not aimed at the individuals within those societies, for to do so would be to reinforce the individualism that progressive political ecology condemns, while denying the diversity that political ecology celebrates. The goal is not equality, as Herman Daly and John Cobb (1989: 331) point out, but limited inequality:

> *Complete equality is the collectivist's denial of true differences in community. Unlimited inequality is the individualist's denial of interdependence and true solidarity in community.*

Common equity is measured in the political arena by the degree to which the legitimate interests of communities and states are fairly represented and addressed in international policy agreements. Where large gaps in income, wealth, technology, or coercive power permit one community to impose its will on another (present or future), the principle of common equity is violated. Similarly, the balance struck between global, regional, national, and local community interests is only equitable where limitations on inequality prevent a particular community from benefiting at the expense of humanity and the biosphere as a whole. In other words, glocal equity arrangements must balance the need for a redistribution of wealth with the need to preserve the common heritage. Allowing the poor to profit temporarily from the exploitation of common property resources (e.g., overfishing) may represent a major step toward equity, but it can hardly be seen as a step toward ecological sustainability.

Global environmental pressures are changing this economic–ecological balance, not to mention the balance of regional power between North and South and East and West. Because the prospects of environmental danger are not viewed with equal alarm across nations or regions, some of the poor countries engaged in international environmental negotiations have demanded compensation from the rich for any environmental protection services they are asked to provide. China and India, for example, served notice to the industrialized nations of North America, Japan, and Europe that protecting the ozone layer could not come at the expense of their future economic development. By taking advantage of Western anxieties about chlorofluorocarbons (CFCs) and other ozone-depleting chemicals, China and India have employed their differential risk assessments as leverage to exact funds from the West for CFC substitutes and other forms of technology transfer.

Similar leverage has been employed by Brazil in seeking debt relief in return for forest protection services in the Amazon. Brazil's message to anguished environmentalists in the North is simple: If you can afford to care so much about saving rainforests, then compensate us to forego the same kind of exploitation of nature that your own countries profited from and that rapid industrialization seems to demand. In eastern Europe, already choked by heavy industrialization, a slightly different refrain is heard. If the West wants (even more than the East) to reduce the transboundary impacts of acid rain and greenhouse warming resulting from eastern Europe's heavy reliance on lignite (soft coal) for energy, then it will have to pay for many of the fuel-switching and energy-efficiency measures that environmental improvement requires. While wealthy nations may view this as environmental extortion, poor nations are likely to regard any noncompensatory alternative as a form of environmental imperialism.

Achieving development without destruction—progress without poverty—will require rich and poor nations to cooperate in bold and clever ways. Because of growing educational and technological disparities, the poverty that drives the agendas of North and South in incompatible directions is certain to increase in the absence of strong norms for common equity. The "geriatric" societies of the rich and the "pediatric" societies of the poor (Djerassi, 1992) will have to work fast to bridge the growing gaps between North and South—or, more precisely, between temperate and tropical interests. Countries in which the average age is around fifteen years may be understandably more concerned about job creation than, say, climate protection; while countries with a mean age of over thirty years may profess or harbor more environmental concern but lack the youthful idealism needed for bold solutions. Unfortunately, neither young nor old, poor nor rich, appear ready to bridge the generational and socioeconomic gaps that divide them in order to pursue a viable and indivisible ecological order. As a consequence, global cooperation remains a fragile hope, one that may not survive the politics of scarcity and the climate of indifference that continue to confound awareness of an interdependent world.

In a world where 60 percent of humanity holds less than 7 percent of the wealth, securing the cooperation of many poor nations will require at a minimum the promise of debt relief, improved terms of trade, and technology transfers that effectively compensate them for the short-term losses they may absorb in cooperating to bring about shared long-term gains. In order to provide technologies in the numbers and quality that are needed to make a significant contribution, increased foreign assistance will be required of industrial nations, much of it bypassing government-to-government channels. In addition, periodic training programs to accompany the technology transfer will be necessary. While the technologies themselves may soon be available and affordable—for example, CFC substitutes, biomass gasifiers with aeroderivative gas turbines, efficient compact fluorescent lamps, and advanced photovoltaics (solar electricity)—the financing and training mechanisms involved in their transfer and eventual indigenous manufacture may require a scale of planning and financial assistance that is unprecedented in human history, dwarfing even the monumental program of the German Treuhand in rebuilding eastern Germany. It is in this area that the development of transnational institutions may prove to be most important.

Financing for such institutions could come from global environmental trust funds (such as those proposed by Christopher Stone), transfers from military budgets, or surcharges on imports of scarce natural resources (such as tropical timber). Much greater reliance would almost certainly have to be placed on nongovernmental organizations for project sponsorship and investment. Not only would enormous debt burdens of the poor have to be lifted, but the traditional world banking and investment system would have to be radically altered to render the discount rates used in benefit–cost analysis less injurious to the environmental interests of future generations.

These equity-building tasks can be viewed as impossible dreams or as activating challenges that provide an unequaled opportunity to restructure our thinking about the next human frontier. Political risk taking is needed, but so is economic restructuring to provide incentives that will make environmental investments attractive in the short run. Funding for major environmental initiatives is currently constrained by greed, economic recession, and foreign assistance burdens that have sapped the ability or willingness of donor countries to respond to external natural disasters and ethnic or regional conflicts, especially those spawned by the disintegration of the Soviet empire. Serious action is still awaiting the elusive "peace" dividends and the vaunted trade dividends that were supposed to follow from earlier gains in Western military security and global economic liberalization. But even as national leaders prepared to address the costs of environmental cooperation at the Earth Summit, their governments were collectively spending nearly $1 trillion a year on military programs—nearly two hundred times what they pledged to finance implementation of Agenda 21. The momentum behind this massive spending imbalance is likely to persist long after credible justifications for it have dissolved. And even if spending priorities are somehow swiftly reversed, the institutional changes needed for implementation will take many years to achieve. It is as if we had finally recognized the need to redress the imbalance between military and environmental security without stopping to think about whether our present institutions could accept and promote the international cooperation needed for the switch.

Common Security

If the twentieth century is remembered as an era in which national security interests overshadowed those of the local and global community, perhaps the twenty-first century will mark the ascendance of common security over national security. Common security, the idea that human welfare depends on a delicate balance between international interdependence and community self-sufficiency, is by current standards a very idealistic notion, one that draws heavily on the proposition that future security will depend more on glocal thinking and ecological foresight than on national military preparedness.

National security is being rapidly redefined to incorporate ecological threats and relative deprivation conflicts as major sources of international instability (Mathews, 1989; Myers, 1993a). In today's global village, the fortress image of national defense seems anachronistic and dangerously out of step with the realities of transnational corporatism and subnational conflict. Increasingly, ecological scarcity is a cause, and not just a consequence, of violent confrontations. Although past conflicts over natural resources have occasionally developed into interstate wars, such incidents have been relatively rare (see, for example, Westing, 1986, and Durham, 1979). In the future, however, interstate conflicts based on control of oil, fisheries, fertile land, water resources, and so forth, are likely to become more common as the pressures of population and technology on the resource base grow.

Developing countries are especially susceptible to political stress arising from the ecological marginalization of their rural populations. Near-term regional problems, such as border conflicts over riparian rights in some of the more than two hundred multinational river basins as well as long-term problems, such as global climate change, are likely to take their heaviest toll on the Third World. In the case of greenhouse warming, for example, developing countries tend to be much more vulnerable than industrialized nations to changes in the quality and availability of water, reductions in agricultural productivity, and increases in sea level triggered by climate change (Gleick, 1989: 336).

Many analysts see the security issue not so much as a matter of North–South or interstate tension, but rather intrastate conflict. While downplaying the prospects of "scarcity wars," they have warned of growing civil strife and ethnic unrest arising from the effects of rapid environmental deterioration on economic productivity and human migration patterns. Thomas Homer-Dixon, Jeffrey Boutwell, and George Rathjens (1993: 38), for example, argue that one of today's greatest sources of subnational political instability is the rapidity of environmental deterioration: "Entire countries can now be deforested in a few decades; most of a region's topsoil can disappear in a generation; and acute ozone depletion may occur in as few as twenty years." The resulting demands for resource imports, substitution, and conservation behavior may impose widespread pressures to abandon notions of common heritage, common equity, and even common decency. China's current loss of natural capital from air and water pollution, soil erosion, flooding from deforestation, and other resource losses from poor harvesting techniques is estimated to represent at least 12–15 percent of its gross national product, and this percentage is expected to increase sharply in the next two decades (Smil, 1992: 30). During this same period, China's per capita availability of arable land has been forecast to decline by more than 25 percent (Goldstone, 1992: 42).

This process of ecological marginalization is in no nation's interest, since it triggers massive movements of ecological refugees to places where they may not be politically welcome, or absorbable by the host area's carrying capacity, thus spreading the problem of marginalization (Myers, 1993b). In a world of high mobility, the principle of common security holds that any conditions that force hundreds of millions of people to abandon their homelands represent a clear and present danger to the rest of humanity. No amount of immigration control will be sufficient to contain the ripple effects of attempted movements by such massive populations of people. Moreover, in a world of sophisticated instruments of terrorism, no country will be secure if it allows other peoples to become marginalized to the point where they have little or nothing to lose by engaging in violence. The first step toward achieving common security is the recognition that our security as individuals is ultimately tied to perceived improvements in the welfare of potentially desperate people.

Deliberative Democracy

As important as the norms of common heritage, common equity, and common security are for guiding environmental action, they are incomplete without the addition of procedural norms that determine how concerns about heritage, equity, and security are to be incorporated in environmental governance. Procedural norms confer legitimacy in political decision-making. Although political decisions may be made on the basis of force, bribery, fraud, or democratic deliberation, only the last appears politically sustainable and morally acceptable. Hence, democratic norms provide a very attractive procedural foundation on which to build environmental norms. Democratic standards of legitimacy are successfully sweeping much of the world, and it is difficult to imagine a reversal of this trend that could persist in the absence of widespread anarchy or public mind control. Less encouraging, however, is the fact that much of what passes for democracy has been achieved with little or no meaningful deliberation on the part of most citizens. Without greater public deliberation on today's important issues, democratic norms may erode into empty slogans of majority rule, aided by dangerous procedures for eliciting instant opinions from an uninformed citizenry.

Deliberative democracy is a form of popular government in which citizens are directly engaged in the challenge of self-rule through their participation in educative public debates about policy issues and processes. The essential feature is open engagement in a contest of ideas in order to make informed choices about policy or about representatives who are delegated to make policy. All true democracies are deliberative to some extent, but the goal of popular deliberation has often given way to situations in which nearly all of the deliberating is done remotely by representatives, both elected and unelected.

The problem has been that as the population, territorial size, and managerial scale of democratic states has increased, the opportunities for face-to-face deliberation have declined. The ancient Athenian ideal of participatory democracy was long ago replaced by a complex system of representative democracy. While the replacement can be described as a necessary choice, dictated by large-scale collective security and economic development interests, the perceived diminishment of democracy has deeply troubled many political thinkers (e.g., Dahl and Tufte, 1973). For some, the only solution to the problem of increasing scale and complexity may lie in the use of telecommunications technology to construct the electronic equivalent of face-to-face deliberation, or "teledemocracy" (Etzioni, 1972). Some futurists envision the day when virtually the entire adult population of the world will register their preferences on politics and policy with the use of instant electronic referenda using interactive computing and telecommunication capabilities. It is unclear, however, what could be done to ensure genuine deliberation in such circumstances.

Most scholars have argued that deliberation is best accomplished in small group settings that can be used to sample the views of ordinary citizens as they become informed about a particular policy issue. James Fishkin (1994: 27), for example, has pioneered a new form of public opinion polling that, in his words, "attempts to model what the public *would* think, if it had a better opportunity to consider the question." Unlike the "snapshot" provided by electronic referenda or conventional public opinion polls, deliberative polls require a random sample of citizens to be scientifically surveyed both before and after they have participated in an intensive group study and assessment of a specific policy issue. Following completion of a baseline survey, using a representative sample of the citizenry, the respondents are invited to participate in a deliberative forum with a subsample of other respondents. The participants engage in a face-to-face process of small-group discussions, briefings, and opportunities to cross-examine experts and politicians. They are then polled again to determine if, how, and why their opinions may have shifted. The results are then communicated to the general public, ideally in the form of a televised summary of the deliberations. Although a great deal of care and attention is involved in the design and management of this process, the basic idea is disarmingly simple: deliberate before rendering an opinion. The goal is to replace the sound-bite approach of today's pollsters with a more thoughtful one that overcomes some of the rational ignorance and apathy that cloud modern democratic decision-making.

The first major test of deliberative polling was conducted in Britain in April 1994, and a video record was presented to millions of British viewers in the following month by Grenada Television. The two-day deliberative forum and polling, which focused on the issue of government responses to crime, revealed large and significant shifts in the participants' views of major policy responses as a result of deliberation (Fishkin, 1994: 28). One can imagine similar exercises focused on environmental problems and controversial issues of environmental policy. Although the cost of such deliberation can be high, particularly if the process is recorded and communicated via television to the citizenry at large, the added understanding and legitimacy afforded by deliberation may render the costs negligible in the larger scheme of things. What remains to be seen is whether such a deliberative process could be used in matters of bilateral, regional, multilateral, or global environmental controversy. The obstacles would presumably be enormous, but then again, so would the potential benefits of encouraging transnational deliberation on key environmental issues by a representative sample of ordinary citizens from different countries. International experiments with deliberative polling might prove extremely useful for determining what citizens of participating countries would want their collective governments to do about environmental problems, if the citizen representatives understood more about what is at stake and about the trade-offs involved in choosing a response. Among the key questions to be answered in such experiments would be:

1. How are cultural differences among participants to be treated?

2. Who gets to frame the issues and what safeguards can be used to prevent biasing of information given to participants?

3. How can bias be minimized in the selection of experts, politicians, and group moderators employed in deliberative forums?

4. How should the *intensity* of participants' preferences be addressed?

5. Is deliberative polling suitable for environmental issues with high levels of technical complexity?

6. How stable and persistent are shifts in opinion due to deliberation, and do they provide a legitimate basis for policy reforms?

7. How critical is news media coverage—especially internationally televised coverage—for making deliberative polling results known to the general, attentive public?

8. Is vicarious participation in deliberative forums by TV viewers important to deliberative polling's political success? If so, how should North–South differences in access to television be dealt with?

9. How efficacious is "face-to-face" deliberation compared with electronically mediated deliberation of citizens?

10. What is the likelihood that forum participants will be truly representative of the large baseline survey sample?

11. How will the site selection for forums affect participation and how might the use of cash inducements for participation affect survey results?

Is it too fantastic to imagine global deliberative fora being held in the year 2000 for the purpose of addressing the environmental, social, and economic challenges of the coming century? If it is true that glocal thinking is weakening the barriers to interjurisdictional mobility of opinion and policy, the time to experiment with global deliberative fora and deliberative polling may have arrived, especially in the context of preparations to celebrate a new millennium. Deliberative democracy appears both possible and highly desirable under glocal forms of environmental governance. From the standpoint of political legitimacy, it is essential. Like the concept of supranational federalism presented in chapter 6, democratic glocalism seeks to bridge the conflicting ideals of unity and diversity, promoting centralized global action on the one hand and decentralized, community-based action on the other.

Deliberative polling is a powerful instrument for building and maintaining the bridge from diversity to unity. The single strongest argument for glocalism is the need to connect local policy-making processes that are conducive to deliberative democracy with environmental strategies that must sometimes be global, or at least regional, to be effective. Communities that foster face-to-face interaction, informed by a sense of place and bioregional knowledge, are essential ingredients in the formation of an environmental ethic that can simultaneously guide policy making at the local, regional, and global levels.

The value of close-knit communities in the midst of globalizing markets and giant technological networks is principally that individuals can discover a sense of connection with place in what is otherwise an overwhelmingly complex and fragmented world. As explained in the next chapter, the reestablishment of civic community is one of the most fundamental prerequisites for developing a healthy system of environmental governance. For billions of uprooted human beings, there appears to be a diminishing sense of political engagement and social belonging outside the increasingly fragile structure of family life. This is what makes deliberative democracy socially therapeutic, as well as politically liberating. Ecologically, there is a parallel loss of connection being experienced in much of the world that undermines traditional values of land stewardship, communal pride of place, and a sense of interconnectedness with nature. It is important to note that while communal organization is still strong in many places, especially in the village cultures of the South, it is under assault from the growing forces of geographic mobility, individualism, and cultural assimilation or homogenization.

Radical individualism, at least in the United States, has clearly undermined the ideal of humanly scaled communities living in harmony; but that ideal was probably doomed from the start by the dual advance of technology and human population growth. What is needed is not a renunciation of individualism, but an accommodation with the needs of real and imperfect communities. Community ideals, after all, can be carried too far. As noted in chapter 1, one can see in many communal goals the shadows of conformity, parochialism, and erosion of individual accountability. There is no denying that community life, in extreme circumstances, can choke individual expression and create more harm than it alleviates. It can narrow one's vision and scope of concern and at the same time change the locus of responsibility from the individual to some faceless group. What it can provide, however, is an appreciation for the interdependence of life and the civic role of human beings in collectively protecting that life.

Conclusion

There is, as previously noted, a strong element of idealism in the hope that norms of common heritage, common equity, common security, and deliberative democracy will somehow replace the exploitative ideals of personal aggrandizement, nationalism, and military industrialism that characterize so much of today's world. Without a change in norms, however, any well-intended program for global environmental action is likely to offer only temporary or symptomatic relief. Effective environmental governance requires ecological "literacy," meaningful citizen participation, and allegiance to a common code of conduct that enhances the moral authority of political institutions, elevates debates about policy, and structures action plans for the common good of present *and* future generations. Only where knowledge, participation, and ethics can be fully combined is governance truly legitimate. Ecological literacy, which is examined in the next chapter, is the form of knowledge most needed for applying the ethical norms promoted in this chapter. Participation in spatially defined civic communities is the most needed form of environmental mobilization. As for ethics, it appears that given growing ecological literacy and democratic participation, what is most needed is *time*.

The Race to Save the Planet, the title of a popular television documentary series about the environment, captures the sense of urgency that is needed but fails to convey any sense of the ethical learning handicaps that limit the human runners. In a race between Pandoran technology (e.g., ozone-depleting chemicals) and ecological literacy there is little reason to expect that learning about our responsibility for pollution prevention or mitigation will outpace the environmental impacts of new technology. The same can be said about the race between population growth and learning about the ethics of family planning. It bears repeating: Time is short; change is slow. A serious global examination of the ideals of common heritage, common equity, common security, and deliberative democracy is unlikely to come about in time to prevent vast amounts of additional environmental damage, particularly in the case of the biological experiment introduced in chapter 1. The race, in a sense, cannot be won. It is less like a sprint than a marathon without a clear finish line. It is in truth a holding action that is needed to buy time for reflection and environmental education.

The goal of sustainable development, which is something of a compromise between a true environmental ethic and a political slogan, may provide an organizing principle on which to base future environmental norms and education. It conceivably can encompass all of the important elements of common heritage, equity, and security and democracy. As a way to connect environmental policy with environmental justice, it offers one of the most promising conceptual links available. But it also suffers from abstraction and oversimplification in day-to-day usage. In order to do justice to the norms of common heritage, equity, and security, the concept needs further development and refinement. To be truly sustainable, development must entail more than a compromise between economic and environmental needs. It must reflect the expandable but ultimately limited nature of ecological carrying capacity.[3]

These notions of sustainability are merely a starting place for guiding environmental action. Skeptics are right to question how such lofty ideals can be put into operation or made politically feasible. They must be reminded, however, that the ideals sketched here are attempts at reconceptualization, not prediction. The only thing harder than forging international consensus around such ideals will be developing adequate environmental protection in their absence. Fortunately, a perceptible movement toward what has been called "postmaterialist values" is already taking place in many different countries (Inglehart, 1990 and 1979). What remains to be seen is whether this so-called "silent revolution" will ultimately succeed in reforming the policies and institutions that govern our world in time to prevent most of the planet's ecological wealth from being squandered.

Notes

1. Locke, in his Second Treatise (No. 6), goes on to warn against appropriating so much of a resource that some of it goes to waste and prevents others from sharing it.

2. Brazil, backed by seven other South American nations that make up the Amazon Pact, strongly objected in 1989 to the "foreign meddling" of envi-

ronmentalists in their internal affairs. Meeting in Ecuador, members of the pact reaffirmed their sovereign right to develop and manage their natural resources free from interference by industrialized nations promoting supranational environmental regimes. Similar sentiments were proclaimed at the Earth Summit by Malaysian Prime Minister D. S. Mahathir Mohamed. For descriptions of these views, see Mac Margolis, "Amazon Nations Back Brazil on Rain Forest," *The Washington Post*, March 9, 1989, p. A32; and "Rich North Must End Eco-Imperialism," *The Toronto Star*, June 7, 1992, p. B1.

3. As used here, carrying capacity is a combined function of nature's limited absorptive and regenerative capacities, and humanity's limited techno-scientific capacity to artificially replace or substitute for natural ecological processes and services. In terms of human time frames, only the technoscientific capacity is expandable.

CHAPTER 9

Cornucopians, Catastrophists, and Optimizers

What we do today largely depends on how we interpret the past, and our interpretation of the past will, to a considerable extent, be shaped by the futures that our desires have already created.

—Michael Schwartz and Michael Thompson[1]

The most popular symbol of the 1992 Earth Summit was an artificial tree whose leaves were fashioned from pieces of paper bearing the personal environmental pledges of over one million individuals from all over the world, most of them children. The Tree of Life, as it was called, symbolized the hopes and fears of today's youth, who are destined to live most of their lives in the twenty-first century. It also signified the importance of individual commitment and grassroots participation in the conduct of international diplomacy.

Prospects for effective global environmental governance depend heavily on how today's youth—tomorrow's leaders—envision the future. Their sense of what is possible and desirable will no doubt be influenced by their interpretations of the past and by the visions of their elders; but it may be influenced even more by the prospect of impending global changes in ecology and technology, and in the international political economy. To the extent that environmental improvements can be derived from improvements in technology and from the creation of man-made capital, the traditional and familiar visions of human progress can be expected to persist. But where progress itself becomes implicated in the assault on the biosphere, the images of the future held by today's young people are likely to depart significantly from those of their parents. For example, two-thirds of sixteen- to twenty-four-year-old Americans surveyed in 1989 said that they worried more about the environment than did their parents (Brown, 1989). How and why this matters will become clearer if we examine the idea of progress in terms of its unintended consequences.

The Risks of Progress

It would be comforting to think that threats to environmental quality represent temporary setbacks in the inexorable progress of modern civilization. Technological progress alone, some say, will soon rescue society from its deepest environmental fears. Today's problems will diminish in importance as soon as we recognize the virtual inevitability of tomorrow's solutions. For example, cost-effective breakthroughs in solar energy, biodegradable plastics, and zero-emission cars may lie just around the corner. Some, like CFC substitutes, are already here. Together with advances in science and public education, such progress in technology could help reverse the widespread process of ecological destruction. Who could deny that humanity today has the capacity to innovate in these ways? The standard view is that inequitable distribution, not innovation, is the limiting factor in humanity's advance.

Like the belief in life after death, the idea of progress appeals to both our noblest hopes and our basest fears. It is an extremely powerful idea that affects not only our understanding of history and our expectations about the future but also our sense of personal responsibility for present conditions. On the one hand, the belief in progress promotes a healthy expectation for higher standards of decency and an improved quality of life; on the other, it seems to justify neglect in the way human beings prepare for their descendants' future. The champions of progress argue that whatever problems we create for our children—or, for that matter, great, great grandchildren—will be offset or mitigated by the enhanced means (e.g., the fruits of technological progress) they will have at their disposal to solve them. If industrial pollution leads to increased cancer risks, it is expected that industrial wealth and scientific know-how will help the next generation discover and afford a cure for the disease. Many of the negative, unintended consequences of progress in this way become the stimulus for more progress, which in turn becomes a form of compensation awaiting a new generation of human beings. Attending to the principal engines of progress—science and economic growth—will in this view accomplish more in the long run than will spending huge sums of money to prevent or mitigate the unwanted impacts of progress as they emerge.

Such views treat environmental casualties like expendable soldiers in a military campaign. While no one wishes the losses to occur, they are nevertheless accepted as unavoidable costs of victory. That the object of victory is often less clear in campaigns of social and economic progress does not seem to diminish the force of the argument. Progress, at almost any cost, seems preferable to stagnation. What does call the argument into question, however, is the ideological character of the claim that social and economic progress requires the sacrifice of other species, not to mention the risk of harm that is involuntarily imposed on disadvantaged groups of human beings. In deontological terms, the importance of victory (progress) can never justify casualties among the innocent or among those who have not consented to the risks of progress. But such an ethical standard is seldom defended with any vigor outside of religious and academic circles. A more telling objection involves the undefined ends for which progress is desired. Since the goals of progress are seldom specified in advance, there is often no legitimate basis for calculating how much sacrifice may be warranted. "Progress toward what?" remains the vexing question that must be answered before acceptable costs can be determined.

Progress as an ideology remains as paradoxical today as it was in the late sixteenth and early seventeenth centuries, during the celebrated battle between the ancients and the moderns (Nisbet, 1980: 151–155). The greatest paradox, perhaps, is that human faith in the inevitability of progress is in decline at the very moment in history that advance in technology and political economy make possible a truly global assessment of the ends for which progress is most needed. It appears that a mature form of progress is needed to rescue modern societies from the unacceptable risks produced by earlier adolescent forms (i.e., physical growth as progress). Unfortunately, the confidence in social and political institutions that is required in order for that maturation to take place is rapidly ebbing away. Fundamental human choices about reproduction, economic security, and the uses of technology, land, and other natural resources have long been influenced by the belief that progress is inevitable. Now that the belief is being questioned by large portions of humanity, the challenge of how to reinvent the idea of progress and tie it to the goal of sustainable living will be among the most pressing issues of our future.

Contrasting Visions

The simultaneous acceleration of technoscientific progress and ecological regress has begun to have a powerful effect on popular images of the future. While there are a wide variety of images to choose from, certain clusters have emerged to represent contrasting visions or outlooks that individuals use to characterize their expectations about the future and their confidence in human ingenuity or adaptability to manage it. At least three such visions appear to figure prominently in disagreements about global environmental governance. Those who hold them shall be referred to here as *cornucopians, catastrophists,* and *optimizers.* [2] The cornucopian's vision is an expression of almost unlimited confidence in the human capacity to achieve ecological balance and economic prosperity, although not necessarily at the same time; it represents the ultimate test of the idea of progress. The catastrophist's sharply contrasting vision is derived from the persistent doubts of radical environmentalists about the very survivability of the biosphere as we know it. A renunciation of the idea of progress, it reflects the concerns of the deep ecology movement and the twentieth century's literary trend away from utopian visions and toward those of a dystopian character. The optimizer's vision expresses the guarded optimism of "knee-deep" ecologists, who believe that there is still a little time and enough political will to avoid ecological disaster. It represents the pragmatic, almost fatalistic, notion that progress is more of a cyclical than a linear phenomenon. While the terms for each vision have been chosen with dramatic license to emphasize differences in future environmental scenarios, it is worth noting that many, perhaps even most, people weave elements of all three categories into their own personal visions of the future.

Cornucopians

An example of a twenty-first-century cornucopian is someone who eagerly anticipates the prosperity of a free-market global village, tightly linked by communication, education, and trade activity and powered by technoscientific innovation. Such individuals are apt to conclude that there are no environmental limits of carrying capacity that will surpass the intellectual limits of human coping capacity. Smarter, wealthier, healthier, and happier are the core expectations of the cornucopian, and not even the catastrophists' growing hard evidence of a biodiversity crisis will shake his or her confidence in the power of human progress to rescue the environment from its collision course with development.

Julian Simon, one of the best-known cornucopians, argues that nearly all of the environmental handwringing of the past few decades can be attributed to "an oversupply of false bad news" (1980: 1431). In his view, human development activities, including population growth, are positive forces in improving quality of life, and those who worry about their impact on the environment are grossly underestimating the human capability to employ technology, resource substitution, and market-based management skills to minimize negative consequences. Others, such as the late Herman Kahn, have argued that development-induced environmental impacts could be troublesome for a while, but that they will recede as the tide of human progress manages to undo much of the damage inflicted by earlier, unsophisticated forms of economic development.

Although cornucopians regard themselves as realists with a modicum of faith in humanity, their environmental critics often brand them as dangerous utopians. Dismissed as inventors of statistical perpetual-motion machines (i.e., the "infinite earth" fallacy), cornucopians respond by challenging the modeling inventions of their arch rivals, the ecological catastrophists. Their favorite targets include the Club of Rome's famous study, *Limits to Growth* (Meadows et al., 1972); the Carter administration's *Global 2000 Report* (U.S. Council on Environmental Quality, 1980); and the World Commission on Environment and Development's report (1987), *Our Common Future*. Each of these studies, in the view of cornucopians, presents a profoundly pessimistic view of the future, one that is so preoccupied with problems that it fails to take into account the tremendous expansion that is occurring in human capacities to develop and implement solutions.

Catastrophists

For those whose images of the future are drawn from their experience of urban squalor or the grinding poverty of village life, questions about future quality of life or about the promise of environmental governance are likely to appear remote, if not altogether irrelevant. Ironically, their views may be shared by many fortunate individuals at the other end of the income distribution who have become convinced that the world is locked on a course of ecological ruin, and that it is too late to avoid a global disaster. Regardless of personal wealth, the vision is of a future colored by despair. The catastrophist vision, however, need not end with catastrophe. Catastrophe often provides the impetus for genuine reform.

There are basically two kinds of catastrophists: those who believe that human beings will cooperate at the last moment to avert an impending ecological disaster and those who argue that such cooperation, if it comes at all, will only be undertaken after it is too late to repair large portions of the biosphere. Both visions of the future are crisis driven and steeped in apocalyptic symbols. In the first case, the scale and immediacy of the crisis is enough to bring about environmental cooperation. In the second, the severity and proximity of the crisis serve only to paralyze initiative and reaffirm the futility of action. Only after the catastrophe occurs are people ready to listen and learn, and then only temporarily.

A blending of the two perspectives has been attempted by many "new-age" environmentalists, who envision life in the next century as the product of a desperate spiritual transformation or paradigm shift that eventually results in environmental harmony and a radical decentralization of political and economic power (e.g., Callenbach, 1975). A series of regional or national catastrophes typically serves as a prelude to the actions needed for averting global disaster. Some new-age thinkers argue that environmentally induced social change is most likely to occur in the aftermath of global atmospheric crises likely to take place initially in high-latitude regions of the world. Others foresee a growing crisis of the human spirit brought on by the loss of diversity in the world and by the declining marginal satisfaction that is said to accompany rapid growth in material consumption. According to some new-age prophets, humans victimized by such crises quickly discover who among their fellow citizens escaped serious damage and then set out to emulate their behaviors or lifestyles (Brand, 1975: 155). New agers who have preadapted to the new ecological realities (e.g., learned to become more self-reliant and environmentally informed) assume that they will be the ones whose way of life will be emulated. Their values arguably permit them to thrive in a world that has lost its faith in the inevitability of growth as progress.

The problem with most catastrophist accounts is that they are large-scale, event-oriented stories about ecosuicide rather than incremental, process-oriented stories about insidious but curable cancers of the biosphere. Catastrophists are not equipped to see that the most sinister of environmental threats is not wholesale destruction of ecosystems but rather the incremental adaptation of human beings to the incremental deterioration of nonhuman nature. René Dubos (1965, 1972), the famous microbiologist, correctly diagnosed the core problem: Human adaptability to environmental stress is so great that the warning signals of environmental collapse are likely to be ignored and thresholds exceeded before any meaningful preventive action is taken. Even if human innovation permits the species to survive handily in an artificially created world, the chronic, degenerative changes in the human psyche that are likely to result may forever change what it means to be human. Dubos's warning takes us back to a point made in the first chapter: The catastrophe envisioned for our species is not necessarily one of biological disaster but spiritual disaster.

Optimizers

Optimizers like to use the symbols of catastrophists while stressing the diplomatic achievements that are helping to make the arrival of ecological catastrophe less likely. Richard Gardner, for example, wrote a book about the Earth Summit with the dramatic title *Negotiating Survival*, but in his text he praises incremental diplomacy and occasionally criticizes the scare tactics and uncompromising attitudes employed by some of the environmental NGOs in Rio. Politicians are optimizers almost by occupational choice. Vice President Al Gore, for example, operates rhetorically at the catastrophist level—"earth in the balance"—but politically his actions have been those of an optimizer. Such a characterization would fit most political leaders, not to mention ordinary citizens, who are active in day-to-day environmental politics.

When pressed by the bad news about changes in the global environment, optimizers are likely to adopt the behavior of triage officers. Having written off large areas of natural habitat as impossible to save, they concentrate on saving biological "hotspots"—areas of a few square kilometers known to contain vast numbers of species (Myers, 1990). Similarly, they favor carbon-offset programs to reduce greenhouse warming rather than bold proposals for a worldwide ban on coal combustion. In recognition of the apparent futility of managing rapid, large-scale policy changes, optimizers often settle for improvements at the margin. "Muddling through" is one of their slogans, although they might prefer "doing more with less" or the author's previously stated axiom: "time is short; change is slow." In essence, optimizers recognize sufficient potential in both the cornucopian's hopes and the catastrophist's fears to justify an intermediate position that is sometimes referred to as the maxi-min strategy. They wish to strike a balance and maximize potential gains up to the point that potential losses can no longer be minimized.

While accepting the catastrophist's claim that humanity's economic, if not physical, security is imperiled by environmental destruction, they see cultivating a crisis atmosphere as being, at best, a means of getting people's attention rather than a way to avert disaster. In the optimizer's view, the development of widespread and sustained ecological concern is dependent on credible demonstrations of the relationship between ecological virtue and economic self-interest. Helping billions of people to understand and appreciate that relationship will require a time-consuming educational process and an unprecedented effort to raise the prices of many goods and services to reflect their environmental costs. To argue that there is not sufficient time to educate the masses or design markets that are environmentally sound misses the point, say the optimizers.

While it is clear that ecological wealth is a prerequisite for sustainable *economic* wealth, it is also clear that in much of the world perceived economic progress is a prerequisite for preserving ecological wealth. Without reaching some minimal threshold of economic security, however tenuous, a majority of the people on this planet will simply not invest the time and attention needed to rescue the biosphere. Regardless of the dimensions of the environmental threats we face, humanity cannot be stampeded into effective action without first creating the information and incentive structures needed to sustain the effort. To rely on crisis-activated policies may only buy time; the point is to change the environmental behaviors that produce an unending chain of crises.

Predisposing Orientations

Most people perceive a trade-off between ecological virtue and economic security. One might even say that their assumed roles in society have predisposed them to view the trade-off in a particular way, such as a choice between collective and individual security. Contrasting visions of the future undoubtedly account for some of the differences in how this tradeoff is defined; but what, besides differing experience, accounts for the contrasting visions that people hold? The cornucopian, catastrophist, and optimizer represent stereotypes of how different individuals regard the future. Might there be other, role-dependent stereotypes or social orientations that help to explain differences in how the perceived tradeoff between ecology and economics is viewed?

To answer this question, one must examine the contexts in which individuals choose, however unjustifiably, between economic and environmental objectives. While the choice as posed clearly represents a false dichotomy in the long run, in the contempocentric world of business and policy, the trade-off is both meaningful and sometimes necessary—it lies at the heart of debates over global environmental governance. Like a choice between individual and community interests, or the interests of today and those of posterity, the trade-off creates a clash between the multiple identities that make up the human psyche. It is not so much a contest between three competing visions of the future as it is a contest between three conceptual orientations or "faces" of human behavior that reside within most adult individuals: the *consumer* (individual preference), the *citizen* (collective responsibility), and the *parent* (familial obligation). Each identity is vying to influence the way in which problems are defined and acted upon in decision-making. Whether buying a car, electing a political leader, or starting a family, environmental considerations that go into important decisions are bound to be affected by the multiple, overlapping, and often conflicting roles each of us is capable of playing.

Economists who seek to convert these roles into a single, "rational actor" set of preferences are attempting the impossible, in the eyes of many political ecologists. Mark Sagoff (1988), for example, argues that such attempts will fail for logical and practical reasons:

> Individuals have a variety of often incompatible preference schedules they reveal in the contexts appropriate to each, for example, in markets, family situations, professional contexts, and political circumstances. To try to combine these preference schedules into one is to search for a single comprehensive role the individual plays; it is to ask for the individual to behave not as a parent, citizen, consumer, or the like but in all and none of these roles at once. (p. 55)

The dominant preference orientation for most decision makers continues to be that of the consumer. In buying a car, for example, color and style are far more important in most purchaser's decisions than fuel efficiency or emissions control. Although the roles of parent and citizen are increasingly being injected into such deliberations, there is little immediate prospect that they will replace consumerism as the foundation of popular preference structures. The parent worried about auto safety and the citizen concerned about the effects of auto emissions on clean air or greenhouse warming are likely to act on their concerns only if they have the disposable income necessary to "vote their conscience." This is because zero-emission cars and cars with special safety features tend to cost more than conventional ones.

Overreliance on a consumer identity, even among many environmentalists, still poses the single greatest obstacle to effective action on many environmental problems. Nothing about the goals or behavior of younger generations around the world suggests that this consumerism has waned. If anything, it has accelerated—despite, (and some would say *because* of) a growing conviction that environmental quality will deteriorate further in the future. Why not enjoy life while you can?

In a 1992 worldwide poll conducted by the Gallup International Institute (Dunlap et al. 1992: 45), the percentage of respondents agreeing that the health of their children or grandchildren would be affected a "great deal" or a "fair amount" by environmental problems over the next twenty-five years ranged from 56 percent in Hungary to 92 percent in Chile. Only in Russia was the state of environmental health judged to be worse today than it would be in twenty-five years' time. A similar poll conducted by Louis Harris and Associates in 1988–89 revealed that large majorities of respondents from all but one of sixteen countries surveyed expected the state of the environment to deteriorate in the next fifty years (Harris and Taylor, 1990). Surprisingly for those who equate increased consumption with higher living standards, large majorities in every country said that they preferred lower living standards, if it meant lower health risks, to higher living standards accompanied by significant increases in health risks.

Roots and Wings

A wise parent once advised fellow parents that the most important gift they could provide for their children was a sense of roots and wings: Family and community roots to sustain them in times of adversity, and wings of self-reliance and curiosity to enlarge their individual capacities for discovery and achievement. The challenge was to find the appropriate balance between the two, recognizing that as wings grow more powerful, roots often wither.

Globally speaking, the wings of technology and capital mobility have largely replaced the roots of community and cultural tradition, and the resulting imbalance between individualism and collectivism has made the world more unstable in social terms. But it has also made it more pliable and open to new ways of thinking. Today's youth are being socialized in an era of global change—both hopeful and troubling in character—that may encourage political and social experimentation that goes far beyond what previous generations have tried. Unlike their parents, however, many of these youthful experimenters will lack a reassuring belief in the inevitability of progress. Their experiments, whether tests of global governance or new-age lifestyles, are likely to be conducted without the benefit of expanding optimism about the future and without the uncritical acceptance of change that a firm belief in progress makes possible. In fact, those who equate change with improvement may be in for a long siege of unpleasant surprises.

Barring some catastrophe, nearly two billion teenagers will witness the start of the new millennium—fifty times the number produced by America's celebrated baby boom (Schwartz, 1991: 125). These "global teens" represent the next wave of political experimenters and explorers. They also represent the largest wave of job seekers and would-be immigrants in world history. Unique in their sense of global interconnectedness, especially when it comes to music and fashion, they are the first generation in history to forsake nationalism for the attractions of a borderless world.

Children of the satellite video age, they are avid consumers of news, entertainment, and status goods produced in distant lands. What they have gained in global access, however, has come at considerable cost. In many societies, the idealism of today's global teens is fully matched by their cynicism. Their roots have been damaged. Electronic networks, rather than places, increasingly anchor their identities. Even in the remote villages of the Third World, video verve, rather than local craft or literary artistry, stirs their imaginations.

If present trends continue, most of today's global teens will spend their "golden" years in a world of more than ten billion people. It is likely to be a world of far fewer biological species, less open space and natural resources, a more uncertain climate, much greater social complexity, and rising economic and political volatility. Yes, there will also be new technoscientific marvels and social inventions to help mitigate the impacts of these other changes, but human ingenuity may provide scant compensation for lost ecological services and social disruption. The key challenge will not be one of human inventiveness. Primarily, it will be a test of glocal thinking and community spirit.

Discovering or restoring a sense of place in a shared local landscape will be very difficult for people accustomed to globe-spanning television and telecommunications. Nevertheless, that is what ecological stewardship requires. Revitalized communities, energized by informed citizen participation, are likely to prove more important to the aims of global ecology than the development of, say, a "green" United Nations. Like Archimedes in search of a place to stand in order to move the world, tomorrow's environmental activists will have to rediscover or repair their roots before they can effectively use their wings to repair the planet.

Communities represent the social and physical expression of interdependence. While they can be organized for both good and ill ends, their fundamental purpose is to connect individuals with one another and with the bioregion that envelops them. When designed to promote cooperation for mutual benefit, communities provide what Robert Putnam (1993: 177) calls "virtuous circles" or self-reinforcing stocks of social capital: "cooperation, trust, reciprocity, civic engagement, and collective well-being." Although modern communities have been organized increasingly around the metaphor of the marketplace, they are understood more fruitfully in terms of the Greek ideal of the *polis:* "an entity small enough to have very simple forms of organization yet large enough to embody the elements of politics" (Stone, 1988: 13). By harnessing collective will and effort, communities do for people what ecosystems do for the rest of nature—provide a measure of stability and positive synergy in the otherwise chaotic lives of individual organisms. Moreover, healthy communities provide the bonds of reciprocal obligation needed for the nurture of deliberative democracy.

Lest many environmentalists object that communities are often the organized agents of environmental destruction rather than the means to stop it, we must be clear about what *community* means in this context. Communities are interacting populations whose limited size and collective sense of responsibility and continuity facilitate the achievement of common goals and lasting relationships. While there is no assurance that these goals and relationships will be environmentally sound, overall environmental quality is likely to improve when people take pride in community. Real community provides the only organized level of political interaction in which face-to-face deliberation can flourish. Human scale is very important in this regard. Furthermore, it offers the only form of bioregional interaction in which *ecological literacy*—the local knowledge and sense of place needed for understanding, protecting, and preserving quality of life within biotic communities—can develop and take hold. Ecological literacy promotes the centrality of natural landscapes within the development of human "mindscapes." David Orr (1992: 86), a strong proponent of ecological literacy, describes the joining of landscapes and mindscapes in terms of a connection between knowledge of place and health: "People who do not know the ground on which they stand miss one of the elements of good thinking, which is the capacity to distinguish between health and disease in natural systems and their relation to health and disease in human ones." Orr (1992: 85–140) proposes an ambitious program for integrating environmental education with conventional academic studies, all of it focused on the importance of place and bioregional relationships in human learning. He argues, in effect, for a society that examines its social and biological roots with just as much care as it lavishes on its technological wings.

The creation of a "global village" may complicate this task of reestablishing roots. The electronic interactivity that is featured in the newest wave of information and entertainment technologies promises to engage hundreds of millions of individuals in "virtual" communities and communication networks; but the passive and fragmented character of that experience may only diminish their opportunities for a sense of real community and for direct and unmediated engagements with nature. At the same time, it may set the concept of community adrift in an information ocean linked by fiber optics, with the result that the importance of place, which used to provide an essential basis for community, can only be experienced vicariously through computer networks and the reading of history. The idea of virtual community or "cyberspace" is a logical outgrowth of the emerging information economy (Rheingold, 1994). The

growing preoccupation with electronic information, with its prepro-
grammed choices and borderless geography, tends to obscure the politics
of place. A medium of interaction that can be switched on and off with
the speed of light is a poor means by which to foster social responsibility
and a sense of reciprocal obligation. Although it is easy to imagine positive uses of information technology to strengthen place-centered communities and to protect the environment (for example, telecommuting
and geographic information systems), most forms of human interaction
inspired by this revolution appear to undermine the social cohesiveness
and community spirit that are needed to sustain environmental action
where it counts most—at the roots.

Human impacts on ecosystems and bioregions are probably best managed at the local level, provided that higher levels of political aggregation
exist to coordinate local actions and to harmonize them with legitimate
national, regional, and global interests. No serious environmental mobilization is likely to take place at the international level in the absence of
community-based social learning and commitment to ecological literacy.
Restoration of the role of communities as potential "incubators" of environmental awareness should become one of the primary goals of global
education. Unfortunately, the ties between community revitalization and
ecological literacy will not be easy to establish. Making this connection
will require a means of social learning that is now out of fashion in much
of the world: reverence for place. Reimmersion in physical community—
returning to one's roots—may facilitate social learning of this type, but
for most of today's global teens the challenge and excitement of modern
life is to be found in the global mindscape rather than in the local landscape.

Clearly, the "roots" argument must be qualified and refined to compete with the youthful attractions of a borderless world. To return to
one's roots means to reexperience the socializing patterns and relationships of individuals as members of social and ecological communities. For
most Western societies today, however, these roots are becoming difficult
to trace to a particular geographic place, especially one that has retained
its natural features in the face of development. Nor does the return to
one's roots, assuming they can still be found, lead inevitably to a desire
for civic engagement. Opportunities for intimate involvement in a community's environmental, social, and political life are becoming harder to
discover or resurrect. Overdevelopment, crime, homelessness, and deteriorating public spaces and institutions all add to the challenges of community renewal.

Civic involvement also becomes harder as advances in home-enter-
tainment centers and other isolating technologies of leisure replace col-

lective forms of play and entertainment. Even recreational encounters with local wildlife and other environmental amenities have become more limited with the loss of open space and the resulting need to carefully manage access to what little remains of natural areas. Although hiking, cycling, kayaking, and other healthy forms of outdoor leisure and "eco-tourism" are on the rise in affluent cultures, much of this activity seems focused on getting outfitted with the right equipment and making the right fashion statement rather than on communing with nature. Using one's community as a platform for observing the surrounding bioregion, as in Thoreau's day, is no longer a popular means for ecological learning. Connecting bioregional thinking to an understanding of global environmental problems is just as rare. It seems that community roots continue to be lost in the scramble for global wings.

Revisioning

Conceptions of the future—whether of a simple Arcadian age, George Orwell's *1984*, or something in between—are shaped in large measure by how well we understand the political and economic lessons of the past, by how the technological culture of the present influences our sense of what is possible and desirable, and by our need for a vision or unifying public philosophy, usually born from crisis, that is capable of stimulating the human imagination and perhaps the will to act. We have before us the conditions for building fundamental changes out of crisis-activated community and environmental concerns. Problems such as greenhouse warming call for a mobilizing vision of global environmental steward-ship, one that promises clean, safe energy; healthy air, water, and forests; good top soil; plenty of stratospheric ozone; a wealth of species and habitats; and places to experience nature unmediated by television or crowded tour buses. But even as the vision beckons, world leaders will continue fine tuning at the margins of a creeping disaster. No one wants to tell the emperors of coal, oil, and timber that they have lost their clothes, particularly when enormous profits are still to be made. And with world population likely to double before stabilizing, few will argue publicly that environmental goals must take precedence over efforts to meet soaring demands for human shelter, nutrition, jobs, and health care.

If serious revisioning is to be undertaken, it will almost certainly have to start with a rekindling of community-based public spirit—what Jane Mansbridge (1994: 147) terms "the political form of altruism." Given that there is no guiding public philosophy that commands consensus across much of the world today, there is a pressing need for new leaders and institutions that can inspire the trust and sense of civic community required for public spirit to develop. Because so many political systems have been designed around adversarial approaches and institutions, especially in the United States, the development of "cooperationist" institutions has suffered badly (Kelman, 1992: 180). Environmental politics has become one of the most adversarial fields of modern times. Although new forms of mediation and partnership are being forged in some environmental arenas, the overall trend is one of continued distrust and polarization. We are left to ponder how an ecologically illiterate society about to enter the twenty-first century will fare if it fails to develop a hopeful view of governance, one based on the restoration of civic ideals and the flowering of environmental cooperation.

In order to combat the mulish cynicism that impedes needed reforms in policy and institutional design, a more lucid and focused vision must be cultivated. It must be an orientating vision that sees ecological and community restoration as inseparable goals. Like the concepts of democracy and spirituality, it must be a vision of hope that engages our imagination and ideals, while defying narrow definition. At the same time, it must be sufficiently comprehensible and practical to mobilize grassroots political action. Above all, it must be a vision in which improvements in the quality of human life, the quality of the biosphere, and the quality of civic engagement are inextricably linked.

My candidate for such a vision is based on the concept of *sustainable communities*—humanly scaled and spatially defined communities that are organized to "meet the needs of the present without compromising the ability of future generations to meet their own needs" (World Commission on Environment and Development, 1987: 8). A sustainable community uses resources and services in ways that reflect the full social and environmental cost of their provision. Its members respect ecological carrying capacity and strive to balance the needs of this and future generations for greenspace, economic development, and access to resources. Community sustainability is fundamentally about interdependency, as manifest by the linkages between the long-term health of the polis, the market, and the bioregion. Developing healthy communities is the necessary first step in any strategy to build a sustainable world.

Figure 9-1 depicts a model of sustainable communities in which three basic interrelationships are emphasized: (1) the psychological and physical relationships between the quality of human life and the quality of the biosphere; (2) the social and political relationships between the quality of individual human life and the quality of community engagement and collective self-governance; (3) the local–global relationship between community planning, development, and governance and the overall health of

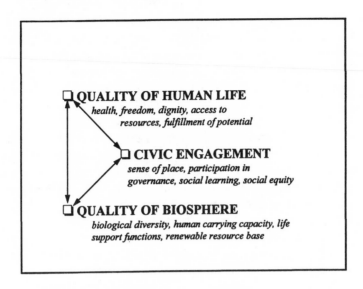

FIGURE 9-2. *The sustainability triangle.*

the planet. Sustainable communities are made possible by this triangle of relationships operating in a balanced and mutually enhancing fashion.

No matter how attractive sustainable communities may be as a long-term goal, the goal will only be of practical use if it can be supported by specific indicators that can be used to reliably gauge social and ecological carrying capacity over time. Developing a set of indicators is crucial for moving the discussion about sustainability from a philosophical plane to one of timely action and policy making. Indicators of social and ecological carrying capacity measure the resilience of communities and bioregions to changes or conditions that threaten their quality of life. Examples of important indicators include population growth rates, levels of pollution and waste generation, per capita natural resource consumption, measures of biodiversity and habitat area, greenspace-to-blackspace ratios (ratios of park and open space area to area of roads and parking lots), changes in ecological productivity and resource quality, community debt and poverty levels, extent of crime, threat of war, economic instability, access to health care and social welfare services, and quality of citizen participation in governance.

These and other indicators of sustainability are slowly being combined with conventional indicators of economic growth and development to allow communities in many different parts of the world to plan their futures. While the vision of sustainable communities is far from being realized, the initiatives being taken by progressive villages, towns, and cities provide hope that practical applications are on the way.[3] The wings of human development are only as strong as its roots. We cannot have sustainable development without sustainable communities. And we cannot build sustainable communities without harnessing both technology and citizen participation for the purposes of informed democratic deliberation.

The reason for including technology in the vision is that it may hold the answer to how public involvement can be strengthened and expanded within real communities. Technology, despite all of its past social and environmental harm, can be used to facilitate a sustainable way of life. Whether it will be applied to this end depends largely on the values that guide its development and use. Sustainable communities need accurate information networks almost as much as they need healthy environments. Perhaps we should be striving to develop sustainable *digital* communities—communities that equipoise a sense of place with global access to quality information; communities that can retain their roots in the face of technologically driven forms of interactivity, such as the Internet.

Whether today's communities can withstand the centrifugal forces of technology and radical individualism remains a troubling question. Almost as troubling, however, is the question of whether the spirit of community, now dissipating in so much of the world, can be revived without undermining or detracting from legitimate global and regional concerns. Neither total absorption in community affairs nor rootless globalism are desirable. Balance is required. The ultimate challenge will be to infuse global awareness and local ecological literacy in the restoration of civic community, and thereby improve both environmental quality and the quality of political engagement in a globalizing society.

Earthkeeping: The Politics of a Sustainable Future

If there is a meaningful way to harness both global and community sensibilities on behalf of environmental concerns, it will most likely involve a blending of the visions of catastrophists and optimizers. The combination of the catastrophist's alarms and the optimizer's bounded rationality may offer the best hope for effective action. Glocal perspectives are more likely to emerge if a proper sense of urgency about world problems is cultivated and accompanied by a pragmatic sense of personal responsibility to act. Personal responsibility and action, however, is best cultivated within families and local communities. Hence the argument for reestablishing roots in community. A strengthened capacity for civic engagement may be absolutely essential for the development of a glocal system of environmental governance.

Beyond civic engagement lies the challenge of establishing a form of "civic environmentalism" (John, 1994) that can supplement and complement other forms of engagement in the social, religious, cultural, and political life of communities. Civic environmentalism represents a bottom-up approach to problem solving that requires decentralized action and innovation within a centralized system of collaboration and coordination. In such a system, communities and other subnational political units would be encouraged to design and implement their own environmental programs, relying primarily on nonregulatory tools of education, grants, monitoring, technical assistance, and public service programs that foster decentralized collaboration. To be sure, national, regional, or global authority and standards must be allowed to override local programs in cases where they conflict with transboundary environmental protection. The burden of proof to justify intervention, however, would be placed on the shoulders of more centralized authorities. Ideally, the principle of subsidiarity, introduced in chapter 7, would remain operative to keep deliberative processes working at the lowest appropriate level of governance.

Implicit in the foregoing discussion is the strong bias of glocal thinking toward a federal structure of governance. Limited experiments with world federalism may offer the best chance for balancing humanity's dual needs for unity and diversity. In such experiments lies the promise of a democratic means for equalizing the power of roots and wings in our lives. As explained in chapter 6, federal designs that are confined to environment and security issues appear to be the most promising experiments for consideration, but even such limited challenges to the sovereign state system are likely to meet with overwhelming opposition. Geopolitics will continue to place enormous obstacles in the way of proposals for glocal governance. The political limbo in which the United Nations is often forced to operate is suggestive of just how deeply the antipathy toward supranational arrangements is felt. Given the United Nations' many failed peacekeeping missions, such as in Somalia and Bosnia in 1994, is there any reason to be optimistic about the United Nations' global capability to conduct successful earthkeeping missions? Developing support for a stronger international confederation, let alone federation, is very difficult at this point in history. But must we assume that "what is past is prologue?" As evidence accumulates that continuation of today's geopolitics may irreparably damage the planet's life-support system, how can it truly be in any state's interest to defend the status quo?

Whether one adopts a cornucopian, catastrophist, or optimizer perspective, the political future of planet earth is likely to be decided by forces that are global in nature but experienced as local problems and opportunities. For many people, concerns about the state of the planet's health are unlikely to seem any more pressing than those related to the economy, crime, ethnic conflict, or many other issues. And for the nearly two billion human beings living at or near subsistence levels, basic needs for food, clothing, and housing may drown out environmental concerns altogether. Policy agendas seem packed with urgent issues requiring action. The shifting attention given to environmental problems by the media and by governments may only reinforce a growing public perception that world events have outrun our political capacity to plan and manage. Rational ignorance may be a predictable result of having so many concerns to deal with. It fosters an understandable tendency for many to retreat from the turbulent world of politics and policy and to "freeride," as economists would say, on the hard work of those who remain engaged in solving the vexing problems of global interdependence. Most people seem weary from the repeated failures of their institutions to keep pace with the changes wrought by technology, politics, and population growth. Many appear deeply cynical about the possibilities of governing under such conditions, particularly when their trust in political leadership is very low and their opportunities for withdrawing from civic responsibilities, at least in the North, are multiplying with the speed of cable television channels. Perhaps catastrophism is an outlook that reflects the popular understanding of politics and government more than it does the perception of trends in global ecology.

The deadly combination of cynicism and consumerism pervading many human societies today threatens to leave us with a world devoid of such things as ancient forests, pure water, clean air, and inspiring landscapes. While it is clear that many people will not rue the loss of such natural amenities, a disturbing question remains: Can humanity afford—economically, psychologically, and politically—to reconstruct the world in ways that systematically destroy the natural heritage on which so much of human aesthetics, identity formation, and general satisfaction depend? Can we in fact be *human*, in the fullest meaning of the term, without a rich and diverse natural environment in which to exist?

Unfortunately for hard-pressed defenders of rainforests, wildlife, and other forms of natural capital, saving the environment may not be possible without first saving the polis. Investments in social capital and the community roots that feed it are key prerequisites in this regard. Global environmental governance is unlikely to succeed without prior and deeper commitments to local forms of deliberative democracy. On the other hand, environmental dilemmas may provide the key stimuli for fostering deliberation about the ways we govern ourselves. The public spirit nurtured by participation in democratic deliberation may be the only viable force behind hope for a sustainable future. That spirit must reflect concerns about both natural and social forms of capital. Their thoughtful integration is vital to the mission of earthkeeping.

Conclusion

In bringing this book to a close, some final observations and summary comments are in order about the main ideas that have been presented and their possible significance. We began with a discussion about global environmental change and the challenge it poses for democratic politics within a nation-state system. The initial focus of examination was on the status quo in environmental governance and on what the author views as its principal problems: overreaching national sovereignty, North–South conflict, and a failure to manage the environmental impacts of anthropocentrism, contempocentrism, technology, population growth, poverty, affluence, market failure, and absent or poorly designed markets. Exacerbating these problems has been the continued erosion of communitarian beliefs and an apparent loss of faith in the promise of governance itself.

In the second half of the book, greater emphasis was placed on future policy directions and institutional reforms that may be needed to prevent catastrophic losses of global ecological wealth. The author's primary goal was to promote a reconceptualization of the environmental problems and opportunities that are likely to help shape twenty-first-century governance. Environmental reconceptualization is ultimately about seeing new connections between economic and ecological wealth, and between individuals and communities. It is about breakthroughs in understanding that occur during the process of becoming ecologically literate. I have argued repeatedly that one of the most important areas for reconceptualization involves the promise and limitations of glocal thinking and its prospects in a state-centric world. I have also called attention to the importance of redefining environmental issues (chapter 3) and rethinking the multiple linkages between environmental policy and political ecology (chapter 6), political economy (chapter 7), and ethical norms (chapter 8). In each case, the conceptual breakthrough involved the reframing of certain problems, establishment of linkages to other problems, and development of fresh combinations of responses.

Of course not all breakthroughs entail sweeping changes in problem definition or issue linkage. Some involve reorientations that, initially, seem much less profound. For example, when conceptualizing the problem of ozone depletion, most people are prone to frame the issue as some faraway threat from outer space. They do not perceive a vertical distance of fifteen to twenty miles—the atmospheric layer where ozone is concentrated—as being nearly as proximate as a horizontal distance of the same magnitude. The conceptual switch in getting people to think about ozone depletion as a "local" problem begins with asking them to think spatially about the ozone layer as they would a favorite town, recreation area, shopping center, or natural attraction lying within a radius of twenty miles from their home. Only by reorienting them to the world in this way can environmental problems arising in "outer space" compete on the same basis with "not-in-my-backyard" problems of the more familiar type (e.g., local toxic waste dumps, nuclear power-plant siting, and various land-use development projects).

The problem with reconceptualization of environmental threats and remedies is that much of it must take place outside the boundaries of scientific analysis and prediction. Critics argue that what makes one conceptual framework better than another is largely a matter of intersubjective agreement. The slippery slope of relativism that threatens established thought when familiar problems and solutions get reframed makes for inevitable controversy in books such as this one. The use of a glocal framework adds to that controversy, especially among political scientists, who assiduously separate their studies into domestic and international categories. Many international-relations specialists prefer to deal with predictable behaviors and expressions of power that can be easily quantified and explained at the nation-state level. They are uncomfortable with the heavy normative content of bioregional and communitarian thinking; and they object to the ideological overtones of glocalism, while usually failing to acknowledge the ideological foundations of nationalism, on which most of their theories are built. The modern nation-state is often viewed uncritically as the climax of a political evolutionary process that began with Stone Age clans and tribes. Stable national preferences about trade, military power, and economic growth, along with measurable utility functions, are central to the predictions of most scholars, while the steeply declining health of natural systems is at best a secondary consideration in their grasp of political reality. As a consequence, they tend to understand and predict future governance needs on the basis of quantitative analyses or models of regime formation, state capacity, hegemonic power, and international political economy.

Perhaps this is how it should be; but if the major arguments advanced in this book are correct in their essential parts, the evidentiary and modeling requirements needed to persuade international scholars and policy analysts of the need for sweeping new environmental actions will not be met in time to avert massive additional damage to the planet's life-support system. And even if natural and social scientists were of one mind on the urgency of the situation, convincing policy makers and the general citizenry might take a very long time. Many people appear to be in a state of profound denial with regard to matters of global environmental risk. Others celebrate each note of scientific uncertainty about a particular environmental threat as either a reprieve or as evidence that unnecessary alarms are being sounded.

The combined influence of psychological denial and indeterminism, however, is only part of the problem. Environmental mobilization does not automatically result from issue recognition and scientific agreement. Whatever one may think about the uncertain probabilities of severe climate change or ozone depletion, convincing evidence of a biodiversity crisis has been available for many years in the literature of conservation biology. However, the evidence that the world is in danger of losing millions of species and thousands of complex ecosystems has not triggered overt denial mechanisms so much as expressions of human indifference. Nature's library is burning, but even some prominent ecologists question whether we need the "books" (Colinvaux, 1978; Norton, 1987: 60). Besides, cornucopians argue, why worry about genetic libraries when new technological marvels, such as virtual-reality devices, will soon be available to fill the void left by the loss of nature's bounty?

The twilight of the twentieth century is a time when instrumental thinking flourishes and constructive critical thought is fading, even in the universities. Learning how to integrate important lines of thought has become harder in the face of determined microspecialization. Ecological thinking—thinking that is synthetic, in the best sense of that term—has found little encouragement in a world shaped by industrial technology, corporate capitalism, and national sovereignty. Global environmental regimes for protecting the atmosphere or other commons may offer a way around the reefs of economics and insular sovereignty, but their formation will require hard choices and, in the short term, inequitable sacrifices. Environmental commitment and cooperation may break down repeatedly in the next century, just as they have in the past. Moreover, the popular perception of environmental threats is likely to ebb and flow with changing perceptions of the political economy, moving in direct relation with economic indicators and in inverse relation with levels of military conflict. Where economies are strong and peace sustainable, environmental issues are likely to command increasing attention. In times of deep recession or rising military conflict, the attention paid to environmental protection is likely to fade. At least, this has been the pattern so far. The single greatest challenge of the transition on which we have now embarked will be to reverse this relationship so that economic performance and the search for multipolar stability can no longer hold global environmental goals hostage. Instead, we must come to see an improved environment as a precondition for lasting improvements in economics and in security.

Despite its drain on public treasuries, the race to the moon provided humanity with at least one timeless and incomparable treasure: the awesome picture of planet earth, one system, rising in blue-and-white splendor above a stark lunar horizon. That picture, more than any other symbol of the high frontier, may yet help to transform a fragmented world into a planetary home. The gnawing question is whether this image can be sustained against a background of unruly nationalism and ethnic pluralism, religious fanaticism, and ruinous disparities in wealth. There simply may not be enough time to sort out all of the problems and opportunities that a rapid transition to glocal environmental governance entails. The twenty-first century is already taking shape faster than our twentieth-century minds are prepared to acknowledge. Whether it will be another century of ecological impoverishment or the beginning of an era of ecological restoration will depend largely on the actions of people already alive. Unless our society makes some wise choices now about the geophysical, biological, and political experiments that we are unwittingly conducting, the children of the next century may have no meaningful choices left to make about how they manage their lives and the planet that must sustain them. Preserving their freedom will require ecological foresight, political courage, and a global commitment on our part to reduce biological and material poverty, and the swelling human population that feeds it. The bridge from twentieth-century crisis to twenty-first-century opportunity can only be crossed in this way.

Notes

1. "Among the Energy Tribes," in *Divided We Stand: Redefining Politics, Technology and Social Change* (Philadelphia: University of Pennsylvania Press, 1990).

2. The basis for this typology is explored in William R. Catton, *Overshoot: The Ecological Basis of Revolutionary Change* (Urbana: University of Illinois Press, 1982).

3. Among the promising applications of the sustainable communities concept is the European Sustainability Index Project. Co-funded by the European Commission, and coordinated by the International Institute for the Urban Environment, the project focuses on efforts to develop sustainability indicators and strategies for fostering sustainable living in twelve European cities—Aalborg, Amsterdam, Angers, Breda, Brussels, Freiburg, The Hague, Hanover, Leicester, Leipzig, Terni, and Valencia.

References

Abrahamson, Dean E., ed. 1989. *The Challenge of Global Warming*. Washington, DC: Island Press.

Abramson, Rudy. 1991. "Ozone Loss Figures Sharply Raised; 200,000 More Deaths Likely." *Los Angeles Times* (April 5): A36.

Adams, W. M. 1990. *Green Development: Environment and Sustainability in the Third World*. London: Routledge.

Alexander, Donald. 1990. "Bioregionalism: Science or Sensibility?" *Environmental Ethics* 12: 161–172.

Almond, Gabriel A., and Sydney Verba. 1963. *The Civic Culture*. Princeton, NJ: Princeton University Press.

Amacher, Ryan C., Robert D. Tollison, and Thomas D. Willett. 1976. "The Economics of Fatal Mistakes: Fiscal Mechanisms for Preserving Endangered Predators." In R. C. Amacher, R. D. Tollison, and T. D. Willett, eds., *The Economic Approach to Public Policy*, pp.187–213. Ithaca, NY: Cornell University Press.

Anderson, Terry, and Donald Leal. 1991. *Free Market Environmentalism*. San Francisco: Pacific Research Institute for Public Policy.

Arnold, Matthew. 1867. "Stanzas from the Grande Chartreuse." Reprinted in *The Poems of Matthew Arnold*. (3d ed., 1963) London: Oxford University Press.

Arrhenius, Svante. 1896. "On the Influence of Carbonic Acid in the Air upon the Temperature of the Ground." *The London, Edinburgh, and Dublin Philosophical Magazine and Journal of Science* (April): 237–276.

Balling, Robert C., Jr. 1992. *The Heated Debate: Greenhouse Predictions versus Climate Reality*. San Francisco: Pacific Research Institute.

Barke, Richard. 1986. *Science, Technology, and Public Policy*. Washington, DC: CQ Press.

Barnet, Richard J., and John Cavanagh. 1994. *Global Dreams: Imperial Corporations and the New World Order.* New York: Simon & Schuster.

Baumgartner, Frank R., and Bryan D. Jones. 1993. *Agendas and Instability in American Politics.* Chicago: University of Chicago Press.

Benedick, Richard E. 1991. *Ozone Diplomacy: New Directions in Safeguarding the Planet.* Cambridge: Harvard University Press.

Berlin, Isaiah. 1969. *Four Essays on Liberty.* New York: Oxford University Press.

Bertrand, Maurice. 1985. *Some Reflections on Reform of the United Nations.* Geneva: United Nations.

Blinder, Allan. 1987. *Hard Heads, Soft Hearts: Tough-Minded Economics for a Just Society.* Reading, MA: Addison-Wesley.

Boo, Elizabeth. 1990. *Ecotourism: The Potentials and Pitfalls.* Washington, DC: World Wildlife Fund—U.S.

Botkin, Daniel. 1990. *Discordant Harmonies: A New Ecology for the Twenty-first Century.* New York: Oxford University Press.

Botkin, Daniel, and R. A. Nisbet. 1992. "Projecting the Effects of Climate Change on Biological Diversity in Forests." In R. L. Peters and T. E. Lovejoy, eds., *Global Warming and Biological Diversity,* pp. 277–293. New Haven, CT: Yale University Press.

Boulding, Elise. 1993. "IGOs, the UN and International NGOs: The Evolving Ecology of the International System." In Richard A. Falk, Robert C. Johansen, and Samuel S. Kim, eds., *The Constitutional Foundations of World Peace,* pp. 167–188. Albany: State University of New York Press.

Brand, Stuart. 1975. "Afterword." In Medard Gabel, *Energy, Earth, and Everyone: A Global Energy Strategy for Spaceship Earth.* San Francisco: Straight Arrow Books.

Branigin, William. 1990. "Mexico Adopts Campaign to Save the Environment." *The Washington Post* (June 6): A18.

Brickman, Ronald, Sheila Jasanoff, and Thomas Ilgen. 1985. *Controlling Chemicals: The Politics of Regulation in Europe and the United States.* Ithaca, NY: Cornell University Press.

Bromley, D. Allan. 1990. "The Making of a Greenhouse Policy." *Issues in Science and Technology* 7, 1 (fall): 55–61.

Brookes, Warren T. 1989. "The Global Warming Panic." *Forbes* (December 25): 96–102.

Brooks, Harvey. 1968. *The Government of Science.* Cambridge, MA: MIT Press.

Brown, Amanda. 1989. "Youngsters Fears for Future Environment." *Press Association Newsfile* (September 11).

Brown, Elizabeth Weiss. 1989. *In Fairness to Future Generations: International Law, Common Patrimony and Intergenerational Equity.* Tokyo: United Nations University and Dobbs Ferry, New York: Transnational.

Brown, Lester. 1984. "Stabilizing Population." *State of the World 1984*, pp. 20–34, Worldwatch Institute. New York: Norton.

Brown, Phil. 1993. "Popular Epidemiology Challenges the System." *Environment* 35, 8 (October 1993): 16–20, 32–41.

Brown, Seyom, Nina W. Cornell, Larry L. Fabian, and Edith Brown Weiss. 1977. *Regimes for the Ocean, Outer Space, and Weather.* Washington, DC: The Brookings Institution.

Bryant, Raymond L. 1991. "Putting Politics First: The Political Ecology of Sustainable Development." *Global Ecology and Biogeography Letters* 1: 164–165.

Burrows, William E., and Robert Windrem. 1994. *Critical Mass: The Dangerous Race for Superweapons in a Fragmenting World.* New York: Simon & Schuster.

Cairncross, Frances. 1992. *Costing the Earth: The Challenge for Governments, the Opportunities for Business.* Boston: Harvard Business School Press.

Caldwell, Lynton K. 1964. *Biopolitics: Science, Ethics, and Public Policy.* New Haven, CT: Yale University Press.

———. 1990. *International Environmental Policy: Emergence and Dimensions.* 2d ed. Durham, NC: Duke University Press.

———. 1990. *Between Two Worlds: Science, the Environmental Movement, and Policy Choice.* New York: Cambridge University Press.

Callenbach, Ernest. 1975. *Ecotopia.* Berkeley, CA: Banyan Tree.

Camilleri, Joseph A., and Jim Falk. 1992. *The End of Sovereignty? The Politics of a Shrinking and Fragmenting World.* Aldershot, UK: Edward Elgar.

Carrol, John, ed. 1988. *International Environmental Diplomacy: The Management and Resolution of Transfrontier Environmental Problems.* New York: Cambridge University Press.

Carson, Rachel. 1962. *Silent Spring.* Boston: Houghton Mifflin.

Catton, William. 1980. *Overshoot: The Ecological Basis of Revolutionary Change.* Urbana: University of Illinois Press.

Charlson, R. J., S. E. Schwartz, J. M. Hales, R. D. Cess, J. A. Coakley, J. E. Hansen, Jr., and D. J. Hofman. 1992. "Climate Forcing by Anthropogenic Aerosols." *Science* 255, 5043: 423–430.

Chayes, Abram, and Antonia Handler Chayes. 1991. "Compliance without Enforcement: State Behavior under Regulatory Treaties." *Negotiation Journal* 7 (July): 311.

Choucri, Nazli. 1991. "The Global Environment and Multinational Corporations." *Technology Review*, 94: 3 (April 1991): 52–59.

———, ed. 1993. *Global Accord: Environmental Challenges and International Responses*. Boston: MIT Press.

Choucri, Nazli, and Robert North. 1990. "Global Environmental Change: Toward a Framework for Decision and Policy." Paper presented at the annual meeting of the International Studies Association (April).

Clark, Gordon L., and Michael J. Dear. 1984. *State Apparatus: Structures and Language of Legitimacy*. Boston: Allen & Unwin.

Clarke, Robin, and Geoffrey Hindley. 1975. *The Challenge of the Primitives*. New York: McGraw-Hill.

Cline, William R. 1992. *The Economics of Global Warming*. Washington, DC: Institute for International Economics.

Coase, Ronald H. 1960. "The Problem of Social Cost." *Journal of Law and Economics* 3 (October): 1–44.

Cobb, Roger, and Charles Elder. 1983. *Participation in American Politics: The Dynamics of Agenda Building* (2d ed.). Baltimore: Johns Hopkins.

Cogan, Douglas. 1992. *The Greenhouse Gambit: Business and Investment Responses to Climate Change*. Washington, DC: Investor Responsibility Research Center.

Cohen, Michael, James March, and Johan Olsen. 1972. "A Garbage Can Model of Organizational Choice." *Administrative Science Quarterly* 17 (March): 1–25.

Colinvaux, Paul. 1978. *Why Big Fierce Animals Are Rare: An Ecologist's Perspective*. Princeton, NJ: Princeton University Press.

Commission on Global Governance. 1994. "What Is Global Governance?" *The Update: September 1994*. Geneva, Switzerland: Commission on Global Governance.

———. 1995. *Our Global Neighborhood: The Report of the Commission on Global Governance*. New York: Oxford University Press.

Commoner, Barry. 1972. *The Closing Circle*. New York: Bantam.

———. 1990. *Making Peace with the Planet*. New York: Pantheon.

Conner, Daniel. 1987. "Is AIDS the Answer to an Environmentalist's Prayer?" *Earth First!* (December 22): 14–16.

Corcoran, Elizabeth. 1992. "Thinking Green: Can Environmentalism Be a Strategic Advantage?" *Scientific American* 267, 6 (December): 44–45.

Costanza, Robert, ed. 1991. *Ecological Economics: The Science and Management of Sustainability*. New York: Columbia University Press.

Cruz, Wilfrido, and Robert Reppeto. 1992. *The Environmental Effects of Sta-*

bilization and Structural Adjustment Programs: The Philippines Case. Washington, DC: World Resources Institute.

Dahl, Robert A., and Edward R. Tufte. 1973. *Size and Democracy*. Stanford, CA: Stanford University Press.

Daly, Herman, and John Cobb. 1989. *For the Common Good: Redirecting the Economy toward Community, the Environment, and a Sustainable Future*. Boston: Beacon Press.

Davis, M. B., and C. Zabinski. 1992. "Changes in Geographical Range from Greenhouse Warming: Effects on Biodiversity in Forests." In R. L. Peters and T. E. Lovejoy, eds., *Global Warming and Biological Diversity*, pp. 297–308. New Haven, CT: Yale University Press.

de la Court, Thijs. *Beyond Brundtland: Green Development in the 1990s*. New York: New Horizons.

Dickson, David. 1984. *The New Politics of Science*. New York: Pantheon.

Djerassi, Carl. 1992. "The Need for Birth Control: Why and What Kind?" *Engineering and Science* 55, 3 (spring): 21–24.

Dryzek, John. 1987. *Rational Ecology: Environment and Political Economy*. Oxford, UK: Basil Blackwell.

Dubos, René. 1965. *Man Adapting*. New Haven, CT: Yale University Press.

———. 1972. *A God Within*. New York: Scribner's.

Dunlap, Riley E., George H. Gallup Jr., and Alec Gallup. 1992. "The Health of the Planet Survey." *The Gallup Poll Monthly* (May): 42–49.

Durham, David F. 1992. "Cultural Carrying Capacity: I = PACT." *Focus* (Carrying Capacity Network) 2, 3: 5–8.

Durham, William. 1979. *Scarcity and Survival in Central America: The Ecological Origins of the Soccer War*. Stanford, CA: Stanford University Press.

Durning, Alan T. 1992. *How Much Is Enough? The Consumer Society and the Future of the Earth*. New York: Norton.

Dyson, Freeman. 1979. *Disturbing the Universe*. New York: Harper & Row.

ECO. 1994. "Surprises in the Developing World." *ECO: Business and the Environment* (January): 90–91.

Economist. 1992. "Environmental Protection in Europe: Abolishing Litter." *Economist* (August 22): 59–60.

———. 1993. "Multinationals: Back in Fashion." *Economist* (March 27): 5–20.

Ehrlich, Paul R. 1968. *The Population Bomb*. New York: Ballantine.

Ehrlich, Paul R., and Anne H. Ehrlich. 1991. *Healing the Planet: Strategies for Resolving the Environmental Crisis*. Reading, MA: Addison-Wesley.

Ekins, Paul. 1991. "The Sustainable Consumer Society: A Contradiction in Terms?" *International Environmental Affairs* (fall).

Epstein, Joshua M., and Raj Gupta. 1990. *Controlling the Greenhouse Effect: Five Global Regimes Compared*. Washington, DC: Brookings Institution.

Esty, Daniel C. 1994. *Greening the GATT: Trade, Environment, and the Future*. Washington, DC: Institute for International Economics.

Etzioni, Amitai. 1972. "Minerva: An Electronic Town Hall." *Policy Sciences* 3: 457–474.

———. 1994. *The Spirit of Community: The Reinvention of American Society*. New York: Simon & Schuster.

Faeth, Paul, Cheryl Cort, and Robert Livernash. 1994. *Evaluating the Carbon Sequestration Benefits of Forestry Projects in Developing Countries*. Washington, DC: World Resources Institute.

Falk, Jim, and Andrew Brownlow. 1989. *The Greenhouse Challenge: What's to Be Done?* New York: Penguin Books.

Falk, Richard A. 1975. *A Study of Future Worlds*. New York: Free Press.

Falk, Richard A., and Samuel S. Kim. 1982. *An Approach to World Order Studies and the World System*. New York: Institute for World Order.

Falk, Richard A., Robert C. Johansen, and Samuel S. Kim. eds. 1993. *The Constitutional Foundations of World Peace*. Albany: State University of New York Press.

Feldman, David L. 1990. *Managing Global Climate Change through International Cooperation: Lessons from Prior Resource Management Efforts*. Oak Ridge National Laboratory (Report ORNL/TM-10914).

Feldman, David L., and Dean Mann, eds. 1991. "Symposium on Global Climate Change and Public Policy." *Policy Studies Journal* 19, 2 (spring).

Feeny, David, Fikret Berkes, Bonnie J. McCay, and James M. Acheson. 1990. "The Tragedy of the Commons: Twenty-Two Years Later." *Human Ecology* 18, 1: 1–15.

Fikkan, Anne, Gail Osherenko, and Alexander Arikainen. 1993. "Polar Bears: The Importance of Simplicity." In Oran Young and Gail Osherenko, eds, *Polar Politics: Creating International Environmental Regimes*, pp. 96–151. Ithaca, NY: Cornell University Press.

Firor, John. *The Changing Atmosphere: A Global Challenge*. New Haven, CT and London: Yale University Press, 1990.

Fischer, Frank. 1990. *Technocracy and the Politics of Expertise*. Newbury Park, CA: Sage.

Fishkin, James S. 1991. *Democracy and Deliberation: New Directions for Democratic Reform*. New Haven, CT: Yale University Press.

———. 1994. "Britain Experiments with the Deliberative Poll." *The Public Perspective* (July/August): 27–29.

French, Hilary. 1992a. "Strengthening Global Environmental Governance," In Lester Brown et al., eds, *State of the World 1992*, pp. 172–173. New York: Norton.

———. 1992b. "After the Environmental Summit: The Future of Environmental Governance." Worldwatch Paper No. 107. Washington, DC: Worldwatch Institute.

Fuchs, Roland, Ellen Brennen, Joseph Chamie, Fu-chen Lo, and Juha Uitto, eds. 1994. *Mega-City Growth and the Future*. New York: United Nations University Press.

Fukuyama, Francis. 1989. "The End of History?" *The Washington Post* (July 30): C1.

Gardner, Richard N. 1992a. *Negotiating Survival: Four Priorities after Rio*. New York: Council on Foreign Relations Press.

———. 1992b. "Practical Internationalism." In Graham Allison and Gregory F. Treverton, eds., *Rethinking America's Security*, pp. 267–278. New York: Norton.

Gilpin, Robert. 1962. *American Scientists and Nuclear Weapons Policy*. Princeton, NJ: Princeton University Press.

———. 1981. *War and Change in World Politics*. Cambridge: Cambridge University Press.

———. 1987. *The Political Economy of International Relations*. Princeton, NJ: Princeton University Press.

Gleick, Peter H. 1989. "Climate Change and International Politics: Problems Facing Developing Countries." *Ambio* 18, 16: 333–339.

Goldemberg, José. 1990. "How to Stop Global Warming." *Technology Review* (November/December): 25–31.

Goldsmith, Edward. 1993. *The Way: An Ecological World-view*. Boston: Shambhala.

Goldstone, Jack. 1992. "Imminent Political Conflict Arising from China's Environmental Crises." Occasional Paper No. 2, Project on Environmental Change and Acute Conflict (December).

Gore, Al. 1992. *Earth in the Balance: Ecology and the Human Spirit*. Boston: Houghton Mifflin.

Goudie, Andrew. 1981. *The Human Impact: Man's Role in Environmental Change*. Cambridge, MA: MIT Press.

Greenberg, Daniel S. 1967 *The Politics of American Science*. New York: New American Library.

Gribbin, John. 1990. *Hothouse Earth: The Greenhouse Effect and Gaia*. New York: Grove Weidenfeld.

Grossman, Gene M., and Alan B. Krueger. 1991. "Environmental Impacts of the North American Free Trade Agreement." Discussion Paper No. 158, Woodrow Wilson School, Princeton University (November).

Grubb, Michael. 1990a (vol. 1), 1991 (vol. 2). *Energy Policies and the Greenhouse Effect*. Brookfield, VT: Dartmouth Publishing Company.

———. 1990b. "The Greenhouse Effect: Negotiating Targets." *International Affairs* 66, 1: 67–89.

Haas, Ernst. 1990. *When Knowledge Is Power*. Berkeley: University of California Press.

Haas, Ernst, Mary Pat Williams, and Don Babai. 1977. *Scientists and World Order: The Uses of Technical Knowledge in International Organizations*. Berkeley: University of California Press.

Haas, Peter M. 1989. "Do Regimes Matter? Epistemic Communities and Mediterranean Pollution Control." *International Organization* 43 (summer).

———. 1992. "Banning Chlorofluorocarbons: Epistemic Community Efforts to Protect Stratospheric Ozone." *International Organization* 48: 1 (winter): 189–224.

Haas, Peter M., Robert O. Keohane, and Marc A. Levy, eds. 1993. *Institutions for the Earth: Sources of Effective International Environmental Protection*. Cambridge, MA: MIT Press

Habermas, Jurgen. 1971. *Toward a Rational Society*. London: Heinemann.

Hall, Bob. 1994. *Gold and Green*. Durham, NC: Institute for Southern Studies.

Hampson, Fen Osler. 1989–90. "Climate Change: Building International Coalitions of the Like-Minded." *International Journal* 65 (winter).

Hansen, James E. 1988. "The Greenhouse Effect: Impacts on Current Global Temperature and Regional Heat Waves." Statement to the U.S. Senate Committee on Energy and Natural Resources, June 23, 1988. (Reprinted in Dean E. Abrahamson, ed. 1989. *The Challenge of Global Warming*, pp. 35–43. Washington, DC: Island Press.)

Hardin, Garrett. 1968. "The Tragedy of the Commons." *Science* 162, 1: 243–248.

Harris, Louis, and Humphrey Taylor. 1990. "Our Planet—Our Health: Attitudes to Environment." *World Health Forum* 11: 32–37.

Harrison, Ann. 1994. "The Role of Multinationals in Economic Development." *Columbia Journal of World Business* 29, 4 (winter).

Hawken, Paul. 1993. *The Ecology of Commerce: A Declaration of Sustainability*. New York: Harper Business.

Hayward, Tim. 1994. "The Meaning of Political Ecology." *Radical Philosophy* 66 (spring): 1–20.

Heuting, Rolf. 1990. "The Ecological Economics of Sustainability." Presentation to the International Society for Ecological Economics, The World Bank, Washington, DC (May 22).

Hogan, W. W., and D. Jorgenson. 1990. *Productivity Trends and the Cost of Reducing CO_2 Emissions.* Cambridge, MA: Harvard University, John F. Kennedy School of Government (May).

Holstein, William J. 1990. "The Stateless Corporation." *Business Week* (May 14): 98–105.

Homer-Dixon, Thomas. 1991. "On the Threshold: Environmental Changes as Causes of Acute Conflict." *International Security* 16, 2 (fall): 76–116.

Homer-Dixon, Thomas, Jeffrey Boutwell, and George Rathjens. 1993. "Environmental Scarcity and Violent Conflict." *Scientific American* (February): 38–45.

Houghton, J. T., G. J. Jenkins, and J. J. Ephraums, eds. 1990. *Climate Change: The Intergovernmental Panel on Climate Change Scientific Assessment.* Cambridge: Cambridge University Press.

Howarth, Richard B., and Richard B. Norgaard. 1990. "Intergenerational Resource Rights, Efficiency and Social Optimality." *Land Economics* 66, 1 (February): 1–11.

Hurst, Philip. 1990. *Rainforest Politics: Ecological Destruction in South-East Asia.* London: Zed Books.

ICJ Reports. 1974. "Australia v. France, 57 ILR 350-600." The Hague, The Netherlands: International Court of Justice.

Inglehart, Ronald. 1979. *The Silent Revolution: Changing Values and Political Styles among Western Publics.* Princeton, NJ: Princeton University Press.

———. 1990. *Culture Shift in Advanced Industrial Society.* Princeton, NJ: Princeton University Press.

Intergovernmental Panel on Climate Change. 1990. *Policymakers' Summary of the Scientific Assessment of Climate Change.* United Nations Environmental Program and World Meterological Organization.

———. 1990–91. *Climate Change: The IPCC Scientific Assessment; The IPCC Impacts Assessment;* and *The IPCC Response Strategies.* Geneva: World Meteorological Organization/United Nations Environment Program.

———. 1992. *Climate Change 1992: The Supplementary Report to the IPCC Scientific Assessment* (J. T. Houghton, B. A. Callander, and S. K. Varney, eds.). Cambridge: Cambridge University Press.

Jacobson, Harold K., and Edith Brown Weiss. 1990. "Implementing and Complying with International Environmental Accords: A Framework for Research." Paper presented at the annual meeting of the American Political Science Association, San Francisco (September).

John, DeWitt. 1994. *Civic Environmentalism: Alternatives to Regulation in States and Communities.* Washington, DC: Congressional Quarterly Press.

Johnston, Ronald John. 1989. *Environmental Problems: Nature, Economy and State.* New York: Belhaven Press.

Kamieniecki, Sheldon, ed. 1993. *Environmental Politics in the International Arena: Movements, Parties, Organizations, and Policy.* Albany: State University of New York Press.

Kasperson, Roger, and Karen Dow. 1991. "Developmental and Geographical Equity in Global Environmental Change: A Framework for Analysis." *Evaluation Review* 15: 149–171.

Kelman, Steven. 1992. "Adversary and Cooperationist Institutions for Conflict Resolution in Public Policymaking." *Journal of Policy Analysis and Management* 11 (spring): 178–206.

Kemeny, John G. 1980. "Saving American Democracy: The Lessons of Three Mile Island." *Technology Review* 82 (June–July): 65–75.

Kemmis, Daniel. 1990. *Community and the Politics of Place.* Norman: University of Oklahoma Press.

Kemp, David D. 1990. *Global Environmental Issues: A Climatological Approach.* London and New York: Routledge.

Keohane, Robert O. 1984. *After Hegemony: Cooperation and Discord in the World Economy.* Princeton, NJ: Princeton University Press.

Kerr, Richard. 1989. "Greenhouse Skeptics Out in the Cold." *Science* 246 (December 1): 1118–1119.

———. 1992. "Pollutant Haze Cools the Greenhouse." *Science* 225, 5045: 683.

Kimball, Lee A., and William C. Boyd. 1992. *Forging International Agreement: Strengthening Inter-Governmental Institutions for Environment and Development.* Washington, DC: World Resources Institute.

Kingdon, John. 1984. *Agendas, Alternatives, and Public Policies.* New York: Little, Brown & Co.

Knorr, Klaus. 1977. "International Economic Leverage and Its Uses." In Klaus Knorr and Frank Trager, eds., *Economic Issues and National Security.* Lawrence: University Press of Kansas.

Kuhn, Thomas. 1962. *The Structure of Scientific Revolutions.* Chicago: University of Chicago Press.

Laing, Jonathan R. 1989. "Climate of Fear." *Barrons* (February 27).

Lamb, Lynette. 1990. "Can Ecotourism Spoil What It Seeks to Save?" *Utne Reader* 41 (September–October): 30–32.

Lambright, Henry W. 1976. *Governing Science and Technology.* New York: Oxford University Press.

Lashof, Daniel, and Dennis Tirpak. 1989. *Policy Options for Stabilizing Global Climate*. U.S. Environmental Protection Agency, Office of Policy, Planning, and Evaluation.

Laski, Harold. 1939. "The Obsolescence of Federalism." *The New Republic* 98 (May 3): 367.

Lasswell, Harold. 1936. *Politics: Who Gets What, When, and How?* (2nd. ed.). New York: McGraw-Hill.

Laszlo, Ervin. 1991. "Cooperative Governance." *World Futures* 31: 215–221.

Lave, Lester B. 1991. "An Economic Analysis of Greenhouse Effects." In Jefferson W. Tester, David O. Wood, and Nancy A. Ferrari, eds., *Energy and the Environment in the Twenty-First Century*, pp. 840–846. Cambridge, MA: MIT Press.

Lean, Geoffrey, and Don Hinrichsen, eds. 1992. *Atlas of the Environment* (2d. ed.). New York: Harper Perrenial.

Leggett, Jeremy, ed. 1990. *Global Warming: The Greenpeace Report*. New York: Oxford University Press.

Leonard, H. Jeffrey. 1988. *Pollution and the Struggle for the World Product: Multinational Corporations, Environment, and International Comparative Advantage*. Cambridge: Cambridge University Press.

Leonard, H. Jeffrey, and Christopher J. Duerksen. 1979. "Environmental Regulations and the Location of Industry: An International Perspective." Paper presented at the Conference on the Role of Environmental and Land-Use Regulations in Industrial Siting, sponsored by the Conservation Foundation, Washington, DC (June 21).

Lewis, Martin W. 1992. *Green Delusions: An Environmentalist Critique of Radical Environmentalism*. Durham, NC: Duke University Press.

Lewis, Sanford J., Marco Kaltofen, and Gregory Ormsby. 1991. *Borders in Trouble: Rivers in Peril*. Boston: National Toxics Campaign Fund.

Lindzen, Richard S. 1990. "A Skeptic Speaks Out." *EPA Journal* 16 (March–April): 46.

Lipschutz, Ronnie D., and Ken Conca, eds. 1993. *The State and Social Power in Global Environmental Politics*. New York: Columbia University Press.

Litfin, Karen. 1994. *Ozone Discourses: Science and Politics in Global Environmental Cooperation*. New York: Columbia University Press.

Lovins, Amory. 1989. "Abating Global Warming—at a Profit." *Rocky Mountain Institute Newsletter* 5: 3 (fall).

———. 1990. *Orion Nature Quarterly* (winter).

Lowi, Theodore J. 1972. "Four Systems of Policy, Politics, and Choice," *Public Administration Review* 32 (July/August): 298–310.

Ludwig, Donald. 1994. "Bad Ecology Leads to Bad Public Policy." *Trends in Ecology and Evolution* 9, 10: 411.

MacDonald, Gordon J. 1991. "Brazil 1992: Who Needs this Meeting?" *Issues in Science and Technology* 7: 41–44.

MacKenzie, James J., Roger C. Dower, and Donald D. T. Chen. 1992. *The Going Rate: What It Really Costs to Drive*. Washington, DC: World Resources Institute.

MacNeill, Jim, Pieter Winsemius, and Taizo Yakushiji. 1991. *Beyond Interdependence: The Meshing of the World's Economy and the Earth's Ecology*. New York: Oxford University Press.

Manne, Alan S., and Richard G. Richels. 1990. *Global CO$_2$ Emission Reductions: The Impacts of Rising Energy Costs*. Palo Alto, CA: Electric Power Research Institute.

Mansbridge, Jane. 1994. "Public Spirit in Political Systems." In Henry J. Aaron, T. E. Mann, and T. Taylor, eds., *Values and Public Policy*, pp. 146–172. Washington, DC: Brookings Institution.

Marland, Greg. 1988. "The Prospect of Solving the CO$_2$ Problem Through Global Reforestation." Report DOE/NBB-0082. Washington, DC: Office of Energy Research, Office of Basic Energy Sciences, U.S. Department of Energy.

Mathews, Jessica T. 1989. "Redefining Security." *Foreign Affairs* 68 (spring): 162–177.

Mathews, Jessica T., et al., ed. 1991. *Preserving the Global Environment: The Challenge of Shared Leadership*. New York: Norton.

———, 1991. *Greenhouse Warming: Negotiating a Global Regime*. Washington, D.C.: World Resources Institute.

Mazur, Laurie Ann, ed. 1994. *Beyond the Numbers: A Reader on Population, Consumption, and the Environment*. Washington, DC: Island Press.

McCormick, John. 1989. *Reclaiming Paradise: The Global Environmental Movement*. Bloomington: Indiana University Press.

McKibben, Bill. 1989. *The End of Nature*. New York: Random House.

McManus, Doyle. 1993. "America's World Role: Divided We Stand." In *Los Angeles Times World Report* (Special Edition), pp. H1–H8. November 2.

McNeely, J. A., K. R. Miller, W. V. Reid, R. A. Mittermeier, and T. A. Werner. 1990. *Conserving the World's Biological Diversity*. Gland, Switzerland: International Union for Conservation of Nature and Natural Resources; Washington, DC: World Resources Institute, Conservation International, World Wildlife Fund—U.S., and the World Bank.

Mdlongwa, Francis. 1989. "Kenya, in Symbolic Gesture, Burns Ivory to Save Elephant." *The Reuter Library Report* (July 18).

Meadows, Donella H., Dennis L. Meadows, and Jorgen Randers. 1992. *Beyond the Limits: Confronting Global Collapse, Envisioning a Sustainable Future.* Post Mills, VT: Chelsea Green.

Meadows, Donella H., Dennis L. Meadows, Jorgen Randers, and William Behrens III. 1972. *The Limits to Growth.* New York: Universe.

Mendlovitz, Saul. 1975. "Introduction." In Saul Mendlovitz, ed., *On the Creation of a Just World Order,* p. xvi. New York: Free Press.

Merchant, Carolyn. 1989. *Ecological Revolutions: Nature, Gender, and Science in New England.* Chapel Hill: University of North Carolina Press.

———. 1992. *Radical Ecology: The Search for a Livable World.* New York: Routledge Press.

Mesarovic, Mihajlo, and Eduard Pestel. 1974. *Mankind at the Turning Point: The Second Report of the Club of Rome.* New York: Dutton.

Milbrath, Lester. 1989. *Envisioning a Sustainable Society: Learning Our Way Out.* Albany: State University of New York Press.

Miller, Alan, Irving Mintzer, and Peter G. Brown. 1990. "Rethinking the Economics of Global Warming." *Issues in Science and Technology* (fall): 70–73.

Miller, Marian A. L. 1995. *The Third World in Global Environmental Politics.* Boulder, CO: Lynne Rienner.

Mishe, Patricia. 1993. "Ecological Scarcity in an Interdependent World." In R. Falk, R. C. Johansen, and S. S. Kim, eds., *The Constitutional Foundations of World Peace,* pp. 101–125. Albany: State University of New York Press.

Mitchell, George J. 1991. *World on Fire: Saving an Endangered Earth.* New York: Scribner's.

Mohammed, Mahathir. 1992. "End of the North's Eco-Imperialism." *Los Angeles Times* (June 2): B7.

Molina, Mario, and F. Sherwood Rowland. 1974. "Stratospheric Sink for Chlorofluoromethanes: Chlorine Atom Catalyzed Destruction of Ozone." *Nature* 249: 810–812.

Moore, Stephen. 1992. "So Much for 'Scarce Resources.'" *The Public Interest* 106, (winter): 97–107.

Moss, Ambler H., Jr., 1993. "Free Trade and Environmental Enhancement: Are They Compatible in the Americas?" In Durwood Zaelke, Paul Orbuch, and Robert F. Housman, eds, *Trade and the Environment: Law, Economics, and Policy,* pp. 109–132. Washington, DC: Island Press

Moynihan, Daniel P. 1993. *Pandaemonium: Ethnicity in International Politics.* New York: Oxford University Press.

Munro, David A., and Martin W. Holdgate, eds. 1991. *Caring for the Earth: A Strategy for Sustainable Living.* Gland, Switzerland: IUCN/UNEP/WWF (distributed by Island Press).

Myers, Norman. 1990. "The Biodiversity Challenge: Expanded Hotspots Analysis." *The Environmentalist* 10, 4: 243–256.

———. 1993a. *Ultimate Security: The Environmental Basis of Political Stability.* New York: Norton.

———. 1993b. "Environmental Refugees in a Globally Warmed World." *Bioscience* 43, 11: 752–761.

Nash, Roderick. 1989. *The Rights of Nature: A History of Environmental Ethics.* Madison: University of Wisconsin Press.

Natural Resources Defense Council. 1993. *One Year after Rio, Keeping the Promises of the Earth Summit: A Country-by-Country Progress Report.* New York: NRDC Earth Summit Watch.

Nelkin, Dorothy, ed. 1984. *Controversy: Politics of Technical Decisions* (2d ed.). Beverly Hills: Sage.

Nisbet, Robert. 1980. *History of the Idea of Progress.* New York: Basic Books.

Nobel Prize Committee. eds. 1971. William Faulkner's 1949 Nobel Prize Acceptance Speech. *Nobel Prize Library: Faulkner, O'Neill, Steinbeck,* pp. 7–8. New York: Alexis Gregory.

Nordhaus, William D. 1990a. "Count before You Leap." *The Economist* (July 7): 21.

———. 1990b. "Global Warming: Slowing the Greenhouse Express." in Henry J. Aaron, ed. *Setting National Priorities.* Washington, DC: Brookings Institution.

———. 1991. "To Slow or Not to Slow: The Economics of the Greenhouse Effect." *The Economic Journal,* 101 (July 1991): 920–937.

Norton, Bryan. 1987. *Why Preserve Natural Variety?* Princeton, NJ: Princeton University Press.

Ohmae, Kenichi. 1990. *The Borderless World: Power and Strategy in the Interlinked Economy.* New York: Harper Business.

Ophuls, William, and A. Stephen Boyan Jr. 1992. *Ecology and the Politics of Scarcity Revisited: The Unraveling of the American Dream.* New York: Freeman and Co.

Oppenheimer, Michael, and Robert H. Boyle. 1990. *Dead Heat: The Race against the Greenhouse Effect.* New York: New Republic Book/Basic Books.

Organization for Economic Cooperation and Development. 1972. "Recommendation on Guiding Principles Concerning Environmental Policies." Reprinted in Bernard Ruster and Bruno Simma, eds., 1975. *International Protection of the Environment: Treaties and Related Documents,* vol. 1. Dobbs Ferry, NY: Oceana Publications.

Orr, David. 1992. *Ecological Literacy: Education and the Transition to a Postmodern World.* Albany: State University of New York Press.

Ostrom, Elinor. 1990. *Governing the Commons: The Evolution of Institutions for Collective Action.* Cambridge: Cambridge University Press

Paehlke, Robert C. 1989. *Environmentalism and the Future of Progressive Politics.* New Haven, CT: Yale University Press.

Palmer, Sir Geoffrey, ed. 1992a. Symposium: "Confronting Global Warming." *Journal of Transnational Law & Contemporary Problems* 2, 1 (spring).

———. 1992b. Interview conducted by Lamont C. Hempel (June 10).

Passell, Peter. 1993. "U.S. and Europe Clear the Way for a World Accord on Trade." *New York Times* (December 15): A1, C18.

Pearce, David. 1990. "Economics and the Global Environmental Challenge." *Millennium Journal of International Studies* 19, 3 (winter): 365–388.

———. 1991. "The Role of Carbon Taxes in Adjusting to Global Warming." *The Economic Journal,* 101 (July): 938–948.

Pearce, David, and R. Kerry Turner. 1990. *Economics of Natural Resources and the Environment.* Baltimore: Johns Hopkins University Press.

Pearce, David, Edward Barbier, and Anil Markandya. 1990. *Sustainable Development: Economics and Environment in the Third World.* London: Earthscan.

Pearson, Charles. 1974. "Environmental Control Costs and Border Adjustments." *National Tax Journal* 27: 599.

———. ed. 1987. *Multinational Corporations, Environment, and the Third World: Business Matters.* Durham, NC: Duke University Press.

Penick, James L., et al. 1972. *The Politics of American Science: 1939 to the Present.* Cambridge, MA: MIT Press.

Plumwood, Val. 1988. "Women, Humanity, and Nature." *Radical Philosophy* 48: 6–24.

Porter, Gareth, and Janet Welsh Brown. 1991. *Global Environmental Politics.* Boulder, CO: Westview Press.

Porter, Michael. 1990. *The Competitive Advantage of Nations.* New York: Free Press.

Postel, Sandra. 1990. "Toward a New 'Eco'-nomics." *World Watch* 3: 5 (September–October 1990): 20–28.

Prescott-Allen, C., and R. Prescott-Allen. 1986. *The First Resource: Wild Species in the North American Economy.* New Haven, CT: Yale University Press.

Pressman, Jeffrey L., and Aaron Wildavsky. 1973. *Implementation: How Great Expectations in Washington Are Dashed in Oakland.* Berkeley: University of California Press.

Price, Don K. 1965. *The Scientific Estate.* New York: Oxford University Press.

Prins, Gwyn, ed. 1993. *Threats without Enemies: Facing Environmental Insecurity.* London: Earthscan.

Putnam, Robert D. 1988. "Diplomacy and Domestic Politics: The Logic of Two-level Games." *International Organization* 42, 3 (summer): 427–460.

———. 1993. *Making Democracy Work: Civic Traditions in Modern Italy.* Princeton, NJ: Princeton University Press.

Raghavan, Chakravarthi. 1990. *Recolonization: GATT, the Uruguay Round and the Third World.* Penang, Malaysia: Third World Network.

Ramakrishna, Kilaparti. 1992. "Interest Articulation and Lawmaking in Global Warming Negotiations: Perspectives from Developing Countries." *Journal of Transnational Law & Contemporary Problems* 2, 1 (spring): 153–172.

Ramaswamy, V., M. D. Schwarzkopf, and K. P. Shine. 1992. "Radiative Forcing of Climate from Halocarbon-Induced Global Stratospheric Ozone Loss." *Nature* 355, 6363: 810–812.

Raup, David M. 1986. "Biological Extinction in Earth History." *Science* 231 (March 28): 1528–1533.

Raven, Peter. 1994. "Biodiversity: Why it Matters." *Our Planet* (United Nations Environment Program) 6,4: 5–8.

Ravetz, Jerome R. 1971. *Scientific Knowledge and Its Social Problems.* New York: Oxford University Press.

Rawls, John. 1971. *A Theory of Justice.* Cambridge, MA: Harvard University Press.

Ray, Dixie Lee. 1990. *Trashing the Planet: How Science Can Help Us Deal with Acid Rain, Depletion of Ozone, and Nuclear Waste (among Other Things).* Washington, DC: Regenery Gateway.

Repetto, Robert. 1990. *Promoting Environmentally Sound Economic Progress: What the North Can Do.* Washington, DC: World Resources Institute.

———. 1995. *Environmental Regulation, Jobs, and U.S. Competitiveness: What's the Real Issue?* Washington, DC: World Resources Institute.

Repetto, Robert, W. Magrath, M. Wells, C. Beer, and F. Rossini. 1989. *Wasting Assets: Natural Resources in the National Income Accounts.* Washington, DC: World Resources Institute.

Repetto, Robert, W. Cruz, R. Solorzano, R. de Camino, R. Woodward, J. Tosi, V. Watson, A. Vasquez, C. Villalobos, and J. Jimenez. 1991. *Accounts Overdue: Natural Resource Depreciation in Costa Rica.* Washington, DC: World Resources Institute.

Repetto, Robert, Roger C. Dower, Robin Jenkins, and Jacqueline Geohegan. 1992. *Green Fees: How a Tax Shift Can Work for the Environment and the Economy.* Washington, DC: World Resources Institute.

Revelle, Roger, and Hans Suess. 1957. "Carbon Dioxide Exchange between Atmosphere and Ocean and the Question of an Increase in Atmospheric CO_2 during Past and Present Decades." *Tellus* 9: 18–27.

Rheingold, Howard. 1994. *The Virtual Community: Homesteading on the Electronic Frontier.* New York: Harper Perrenial.

Roan, Sharon L. 1989. *Ozone Crisis: The 15-Year Evolution of a Sudden Global Emergency.* New York: Wiley.

Rodman, John. 1983. Review of Morris Goran's *Conquest of Pollution* (1981). *Environmental Review* 7, 1 (spring): 98–100.

Rose, Adam. 1992. "Equity Considerations of Tradeable Carbon Emission Entitlements." In U.N. Conference on Trade and Development, *Combatting Global Warming: Study on a Global System of Tradeable Carbon Emission Entitlements,* pp. 55–80. New York: United Nations.

Rosenau, James N. 1990. *Turbulence in World Politics: A Theory of Change and Continuity.* Princeton, NJ: Princeton University Press.

Rosenau, James N., and Ernst-Otto Czempiel, eds. 1992. *Governance without Government: Order and Change in World Politics.* New York: Cambridge University Press.

Rothenberg, Jerome. 1993. "Economic Perspectives on Time Comparisons: Evaluation of Time Discounting." In Nazli Choucri, ed., *Global Accord: Environmental Challenges and International Responses,* pp. 307–332. Cambridge, MA: MIT Press.

Rowland, Wade. 1973. *The Plot to Save the World.* Toronto: Clarke, Irwin & Co.

Rubin, Seymour J. and Thomas R. Graham. eds. 1982. *Environment and Trade: The Relation of International Trade and Environmental Policy.* Totowa, NJ: Allanheld, Osmun.

Ruggie, John Gerard, ed. 1993. *Multilateralism Matters: The Theory and Praxis of an Institutional Form.* New York: Columbia University Press.

Sabatier, Paul A., and Hank C. Jenkins-Smith, eds. 1993. *Policy Change and Learning: An Advocacy Coalition Approach.* Boulder, CO: Westview Press.

Sagoff, Mark. 1988. *The Economy of the Earth: Philosophy, Law, and the Environment.* New York: Cambridge University Press.

Sahlins, Marshall D. 1968. "Notes of the Original Affluent Society." In Richard B. Lee and Irven deVore, eds., *Man the Hunter,* pp. 85–89. Chicago: Aldine Press.

Sale, Kirkpatrick. 1985. *Dwellers in the Land: The Bioregional Vision.* San Francisco: Sierra Club.

Sand, Peter H. 1990. *Lessons Learned in Global Environmental Governance.* Washington, DC: World Resources Institute.

Schaar, John. 1993. Personal communication to Lamont C. Hempel.

Schlesinger, M.E. and X. Jiang, 1991. "Revised Projection of Future Greenhouse Warming." *Nature* 350: 219–221.

Schmidheiny, Stephan. 1992. *Changing Course: A Global Business Perspective on Development and the Environment*. Cambridge, MA: MIT Press.

Schneider, Ann, and Helen Ingram. 1993. "The Social Construction of Target Populations: Implications for Politics and Policy." *American Political Science Review*, 87: 2 (June): 334–347.

Schneider, Stephen H. 1989a. "The Greenhouse Effect: Science and Policy." *Science* 243: 771–781.

———. 1989b. *Global Warming: Are We Entering the Greenhouse Century?* San Francisco: Sierra Club Books.

Schneider, Stephen H., and Randi Londer. 1984. *The Coevolution of Climate and Life*. San Francisco: Sierra Club Books.

Schon, Donald A. 1994. *Frame Reflection: Toward the Resolution of Intractable Policy Controversies*. New York: Basic Books.

Schulman, Paul R. 1980. *Large-scale Policy Making*. New York: Elsevier.

Schwartz, Michael, and Michael Thompson. 1990. *Divided We Stand: Redefining Politics, Technology and Social Change*. Philadelphia: University of Pennsylvania Press.

Schwartz, Peter. 1991. *The Art of the Long View: Planning for the Future in an Uncertain World*. New York: Doubleday.

Science News. 1990. Number 137 (February 10): 95.

Sebenius, James K. 1983. "Negotiation Arithmetic: Adding and Subtracting Issues and Parties." *International Organization* 37: 281–316.

———. 1984. *Negotiating the Law of the Sea: Lessons in the Art and Science of Reaching Agreement*. Cambridge, MA: Harvard University Press.

———. 1991. "Negotiation Analysis." In Viktor Kremenyuk, ed. *International Negotiation: Analysis, Approaches, Issues*, chapter 14. San Francisco: Jossey-Bass.

Seitz, Frederick, Robert Jastrow, and W. A. Nirenberg. 1989. *Scientific Perspectives on the Greenhouse Problem*. Washington, DC: George C. Marshall Institute.

Self, Peter. 1993. *Government by the Market?* London/Boulder: Macmillan/Westview Press.

Shabecoff, Phil. 1989. "Scientist Says U.S. Agency Altered His Testimony on Global Warming." *New York Times* (May 8): 1.

Shafik, Nemat, and Sushenjit Bandyopadhyay. 1992. "Economic Growth and Environmental Quality: Time-Series and Cross-Country Evidence." World Bank Background Paper, Washington, DC.

Shepard, Paul. 1978. *Thinking Animals: Animals and the Development of Human Intelligence*. New York: Viking Press.

Shuman, Michael H. 1992. "Dateline Mainstreet: Courts v. Local Foreign Policies." *Foreign Policy* 86 (spring): 158–177.

Silver, Cheryl. 1990. *One Earth, One Future: Our Changing Global Environment.* Washington, DC: National Academy Press.

Simon, Julian. 1980. "Resources, Population, Environment: An Oversupply of False Bad News." *Science* 208 (June 27): 1431–1437.

———. 1987. *The Ultimate Resource.* Princeton, NJ: Princeton University Press.

Simon, Julian, and Herman Kahn. eds. 1984. *The Resourceful Earth: A Response to Global 2000.* New York: Basil Blackwell

Singer, S. Fred, ed. 1989. *Global Climate Change: Natural and Human Influences.* New York: Paragon House.

Skolnikoff, E. B. 1990. "The Policy Gridlock on Global Warming." *Foreign Policy* (summer): 77–93.

Slater, Philip. 1970. *The Pursuit of Loneliness: American Culture at the Breaking Point.* Boston: Beacon Press.

Smil, Vaclav. 1984. *The Bad Earth: Environmental Degradation in China.* Armonk, NY: M.E. Sharpe.

———. 1992. "Environmental Change as a Source of Conflict and Economic Losses in China." Occasional Paper No. 2, Project on Environmental Change and Acute Conflict (December): 5–39.

———. 1993. *China's Environmental Crisis: An Inquiry into the Limits of National Development.* Armonk, NY: M.E. Sharpe.

Solow, Andrew R. and James M. Broadus. 1990. "Global Warming: Quo Vadis?" *The Fletcher Forum of World Affairs* 14: 2 (summer): 262–269.

Solow, Robert. 1992. "An Almost Practical Step Toward Sustainability." Address on the Occasion of the 40th Anniversary of Resources for the Future (October 8), pp. 1-22. Washington, DC: Resources for the Future.

Soulé, Michael, and B. Wilcox, eds. 1980. *Conservation Biology: An Evolutionary-Ecological Perspective.* Sunderland, MA: Sinauer.

Sprinz, Detlef, and Tapani Vaahtoranta. 1994. "The Interest-based Explanation of International Environmental Policy." *International Organization* 48: 1 (winter): 77–105.

Stein, Arthur A. 1990. *Why Nations Cooperate: Circumstances and Choice in International Relations.* Ithaca, NY: Cornell University Press.

Stern, Paul C. 1992. "Psychological Dimensions of Global Environmental Change." *Annual Review of Psychology* 43: 269–302.

Stolarski, R. S., and Ralph Cicerone. 1974. "Stratospheric Chlorine: A Possible Sink for Ozone." *Canadian Journal of Chemistry* 52: 1610.

Stone, Christopher D. 1993. *The Gnat Is Older Than Man: Global Environmental and Human Agenda.* Princeton, NJ: Princeton University Press.

Stone, Deborah A. 1988. *Policy Paradox and Political Reason.* Glenview, IL: Scott, Foresman and Company.

Strong, Maurice. 1990. "What Place Will the Environment Have in the Next Century—and at What Price?" *International Environmental Affairs* 2, 3 (summer): 212.

Sun, Changjin. 1992. "Community Forestry in Southern China." *Journal of Forestry* 90, 6 (June): 35–40.

Susskind, Lawrence E. 1994. *Environmental Diplomacy: Negotiating More Effective Global Agreements.* New York: Oxford University Press.

Swift, Adam. 1993. *Global Political Ecology: The Crisis in Economy and Government.* London: Pluto Press.

Taylor, Bob Pepperman. 1992. *Our Limits Transgressed: Environmental Political Thought in America.* Lawrence: University of Kansas.

Tietenberg, Thomas H. 1985. *Emissions Trading: An Exercise in Reforming Pollution Policy.* Washington, DC: Resources for the Future.

———. 1991. "Managing the Transition: The Potential Role for Economic Policies." In J.Tuchman Mathews, ed., *Preserving the Global Environment: The Challenge of Shared Leadership*, pp. 187–226. New York: Norton.

———. 1992. *Environmental and Natural Resource Economics* (3d ed.). New York: HarperCollins.

Tobin, Richard. 1990. *The Expendable Future: U.S. Politics and the Protection of Biological Diversity.* Durham, NC: Duke University Press.

Tolba, Mostafa K. 1989. "A Step-by-Step Approach to Protection of the Atmosphere." *International Environmental Affairs* 1, 4 (fall): 304–308.

Tolba, Mostafa K., and Osama A. El-Kholy. 1992. *The World Environment 1972–1992: Two Decades of Challenge.* London: Chapman and Hall.

Union of Concerned Scientists. 1992. *World Scientist's Warning to Humanity.* Washington, DC: Union of Concerned Scientists.

United Nations. 1992. *Agenda 21: Report of the United Nations Conference on Environment and Development* (A/Conf. 151/26/Rev. 1). New York: United Nations.

United Nations General Assembly. 1982. "Speech of the Malaysian Ambassador, September 29, 1982" (A/37PV/10): 17.

United Nations Population Division. 1993. *World Population Prospects: The 1992 Revision.* New York: United Nations.

U.S. Congress, Office of Technology Assessment. 1991a. *Changing by Degrees: Steps to Reduce Greenhouse Gases.* Washington, DC: U.S. Government Printing Office.

———. 1991b. *Improving Automobile Fuel Economy: New Standards, New Approaches* (OTA-0-482). Washington, DC: U.S. Government Printing Office.

———. 1993. *Preparing for an Uncertain Climate—Volumes 1 and 2 (OTA-0-567).* Washington, DC: U.S. Government Printing Office.

U.S. Council of Economic Advisors. 1990. *Economic Report of the President.* Washington, DC: U.S. Government Printing Office.

U.S. Council on Environmental Quality and Department of State. 1980. *The Global 2000 Report to the President.* Vol. 1. Washington, DC: U.S. Government Printing Office.

U.S. National Academy of Sciences (with National Academy of Engineering and Institute of Medicine, Committee on Science, Engineering, and Public Policy). 1991. *Policy Implications of Greenhouse Warming.* Washington, DC: National Academy Press.

U.S. National Science Board Task Force on Global Biodiversity. 1989. *Loss of Biological Diversity: A Global Crisis Requiring International Solutions.* Washington, DC: National Science Foundation.

von Moltke, Konrad. 1988. "International Commissions and Implementation of International Environmental Law." In John Carrol, ed., *International Environmental Diplomacy: The Management and Resolution of Transfrontier Environmental Problems,* pp. 87–93. New York: Cambridge University Press.

Walter, Ingo. 1975. *International Economics of Pollution.* London: Macmillan.

Watts, Ronald L. 1981. "Federalism, Regionalism, and Political Integration." In David Cameron, ed., *Regionalism and Supranationalism,* pp. 3–19. Montreal: Institute for Research in Public Policy.

Weiner, Jonathan. 1990. *The Next One Hundred Years: Shaping the Fate of Our Living Earth.* New York: Bantam.

Westing, Arthur H. ed. 1986. *Global Resources and International Conflict.* Oxford: Oxford University Press.

Wildavsky, Aaron. 1979. *Speaking Truth to Power: The Art and Craft of Policy Analysis.* Boston: Little, Brown.

Williams, Robert H. 1990. "Low Cost Strategies for Coping with CO_2 Emission Limits." *The Energy Journal* 11, 4: 35–59.

Wilson, Edward O. 1985. "The Biological Diversity Crisis." *Bioscience* 35 (December): 701–702.

———. ed. 1988. *Biodiversity.* Washington, DC: National Academy Press.

———. 1989. "Threats to Biodiversity." *Scientific American* 261 (September): 108–112.

———. 1992. *The Diversity of Life.* Cambridge, MA: Belknap Press of Harvard University.

Winner, Langdon. 1986. *The Whale and the Reactor: A Search for Limits in an Age of High Technology.* Chicago: University of Chicago Press.

Wolf, Edward C. 1987. *On the Brink of Extinction: Conserving the Diversity of Life.* Washington, DC: Worldwatch Institute.

World Bank. 1992. *World Development Report 1992: Development and the Environment.* New York: Oxford University Press.

————. 1994. *Making Development Sustainable, Fiscal 1994*. Washington, DC: IBRD/World Bank.

World Commission on Environment and Development. 1987. *Our Common Future*. Oxford, UK: Oxford University Press.

World Meteorological Organization. 1992. *Climate Change, Environment, and Development: World Leaders' Viewpoints*. Geneva: WMO-No. 772.

World Resources Institute. 1992. *World Resources 1992-93: A Guide to the Global Environment*. New York: Oxford University Press.

————. 1994. *World Resources 1994-95: A Guide to the Global Environment*. New York: Oxford University Press.

Worldwatch Institute. 1984. *State of the World 1984: A Worldwatch Institute Report on Progress toward a Sustainable Society*. New York: Norton.

————. 1992. *State of the World 1992: A Worldwatch Institute Report on Progress Toward a Sustainable Society*. New York: Norton.

World Wildlife Fund. 1992. *Impact of the Ivory Ban on Illegal Hunting of Elephants in Six Range States in Africa*. Washington, DC: World Wildlife Fund.

Young, Oran. 1989a. *International Cooperation: Building Regimes for Natural Resources and the Environment*. Ithaca, NY: Cornell University Press.

————. 1989b. "The Politics of International Regime Formation: Managing Natural Resources and the Environment." *International Organization* 43:349–375.

————. 1994. *International Governance: Protecting the Environment in a Stateless Society*. Ithaca, NY: Cornell University Press.

Young, Oran, and Gail Osherenko. 1993. *Polar Politics: Creating International Environmental Regimes*. Ithaca, NY: Cornell University Press.

Zabinski, C., and M. B. Davis. 1989. "Hard Times Ahead for Great Lakes Forests: A Climate Threshold Model Predicts Responses to CO_2-Induced Climate Change." In J. B. Smith and D. Tirpak, eds., *The Potential Effects of Climate Change on the United States, Appendix D: Forests* (EPA-230-95-89-054). Washington, DC: U.S. Environmental Protection Agency.

Zaelke, Durwood, Paul Orbuch, and Robert F. Housman, eds. 1993. *Trade and the Environment: Law, Economics, and Policy*. Washington, DC: Island Press.

Suggested Reading

Environmental Problems and Trends

For an excellent overview of global environmental conditions and trends, see the biennial reports of the World Resources Institute, *World Resources: A Guide to the Global Environment* (New York: Oxford University Press), prepared in collaboration with the U.N. Environmental Program and the U.N. Development Program. The *World Resources* series provides extensive environmental data and statistics arranged by nation and by region of the world. For less data-rich but more issue-focused assessments of the global environment, see the Worldwatch Institute's annual reports, *State of the World* (New York: Norton). The Worldwatch Institute also offers *Vital Signs: The Trends Shaping Our Future* (New York: Norton), an annual summary of important indicators of social, economic, and environmental health. A good geographic guide to global environmental problems is Geoffrey Lean and Don Hinrichsen, *Atlas of the Environment* (New York: Harper Perennial, 2d ed. 1992). For references and short annotations on more than 3,000 environmental books and journals, see Joseph A. Miller et al. (Yale School of Forestry and Environmental Studies), *The Island Press Bibliography of Environmental Literature* (Washington, DC: Island Press, 1993).

Readers wanting more information about the atmospheric and biodiversity crises introduced in chapter 1 will find an excellent journalistic account of these problems in Jonathan Weiner, *The Next 100 Years: Shaping the Fate of Our Living Earth* (New York: Bantam, 1991). For a more technical and comprehensive survey of global warming issues, see Irving M.

Mintzer (ed.), *Confronting Climate Change: Risks, Implications and Responses* (Cambridge University Press, 1992). A good descriptive account of ozone depletion problems is Seth Cagin and Philip Dray, *Between Earth and Sky: How CFCs Changed Our World and Endangered the Ozone Layer* (New York: Pantheon Books, 1993). On the most pressing issues of biodiversity, see Norman Myers, *The Primary Source: Tropical Forests and Our Future* (New York: Norton, 2d ed. 1992) and *Ultimate Security: The Environmental Basis of Political Stability* (New York: Norton, 1993).

International Agenda Setting—Conferences and Commissions

For a lively, if irreverent, description of the first major international environmental conference, held in Stockholm in 1972, see Wade Rowland, *The Plot to Save the World* (Toronto: Clarke, Irwin & Co, 1973). Serving to link the Stockholm conference with the Earth Summit in Rio twenty years later was the work of the World Commission on Environment and Development, summarized in their report, *Our Common Future* (Oxford: Oxford University Press, 1987). Major issues addressed at the 1992 Earth Summit are summarized nicely in Michael Grubb et al., *The Earth Summit Agreements: A Guide and Assessment* (London: Earthscan, 1993), and in Richard Gardner, *Negotiating Survival: Four Priorities after Rio* (New York: Council on Foreign Relations Press, 1992). A more critical review of the summit is provided by Pratap Chatterjee and Matthias Finger, *The Earth Brokers: Power, Politics, and World Development* (New York: Routledge, 1994), and by the Natural Resources Defense Council, *One Year after Rio, Keeping the Promises of the Earth Summit: A Country-by-Country Progress Report* (New York: NRDC Earth Summit Watch, 1993). For ongoing coverage in periodicals of major international environmental conferences and policy forums, see *Earth Times*, *Earth Negotiations Bulletin* (International Institute for Sustainable Development), and *International Environmental Reporter.*

Environmental Politics and Policy

The most comprehensive examination of the development of environmental politics and policy in the international arena is Lynton K. Caldwell, *International Environmental Policy: Emergence and Dimensions* (Durham, NC: Duke University Press, 2d ed. 1990). Mostafa K. Tolba and Osama A. El-Kholy, *The World Environment 1972–1992: Two Decades of Challenge* (London: Chapman and Hall, 1992) is also excellent in this regard. A very helpful reference book on international environmental treaties and policy organizations is the Fridtjof Nansen Institute's (Norway) *Green Globe Yearbook of International Cooperation on Environment and Development* (New York: Oxford University Press, 1995).

For a basic textbook overview of international environmental politics and policy, see Gareth Porter and Janet Welsh Brown, *Global Environmental Politics* (Boulder, CO: Westview Press, 2d ed. 1995). Other useful works for linking problems, theory, and policy responses are Nazli Choucri (ed.), *Global Accord: Environmental Challenges and International Responses* (Cambridge, MA: MIT Press, 1993); Peter M. Haas, Robert O. Keohane, and Marc A. Levy (eds.), *Institutions for the Earth: Sources of Effective International Environmental Protection* (Cambridge, MA: MIT Press, 1993); Sheldon Kamieniecki (ed.), *Environmental Politics in the International Arena: Movements, Parties, Organizations, and Policy* (Albany: SUNY Press, 1993); Ronnie D. Lipschutz and Ken Conca (eds.), *The State and Social Power in Global Environmental Politics* (New York: Columbia University Press, 1993); and Oran Young, *International Governance: Protecting the Environment in a Stateless Society* (Ithaca, NY: Cornell University Press, 1994).

Readers interested in studies of diplomacy and international decision making will find a very practical guide to negotiating strategies and structures for reform in Lawrence Susskind, *Environmental Diplomacy: Negotiating More Effective Global Agreements* (New York: Oxford University Press, 1994). A somewhat dated but still useful collection of writings about diplomacy is John Carrol (ed.), *International Environmental Diplomacy: The Management and Resolution of Transfrontier Environmental Problems* (New York: Cambridge University Press, 1988). For focused case studies of international environmental diplomacy and regime formation, see Richard E. Benedick *Ozone Diplomacy: New Directions in Safeguarding the Planet* (Cambridge, MA: Harvard University Press, 1991); Oran Young and Gail Osherenko (eds.), *Polar Politics: Creating International Environmental Regimes* (Ithaca, NY: Cornell University Press, 1993); Peter Haas, *Saving the Mediterranean: The Politics of International Cooperation* (New York: Columbia University Press, 1990); and James K. Sebenius, *Negotiating the Law of the Sea: Lessons in the Art and Science of Reaching Agreement* (Cambridge, MA: Harvard University Press, 1984).

On the topic of converting environmental science into policy, see Karen Litfin, *Ozone Discourses: Science and Politics in Global Environmental Cooperation* (New York: Columbia University Press, 1994); Lynton Caldwell, *Between Two Worlds: Science, the Environmental Movement and Policy Choice* (New York: Cambridge University Press, 1990); the U.S. National

Academy of Sciences, *Policy Implications of Greenhouse Warming* (Washington, DC: National Academy Press 1991); Cheryl Silver, *One Earth, One Future: Our Changing Global Environment* (Washington, DC: National Academy Press, 1990); and Daniel Botkin, *Discordant Harmonies: A New Ecology for the Twenty-first Century* (New York: Oxford University Press, 1990). Peter Haas's *Saving the Mediterranean* (op cit.) is very useful for understanding how science and technical expertise are organized in "epistemic communities."

Business, Trade, and Economics

For a good textbook introduction to environmental economics, see David Pearce and R. Kerry Turner, *Economics of Natural Resources and the Environment* (Baltimore: Johns Hopkins University Press, 1990); and Tom Tietenberg, *Environmental and Natural Resource Economics* (New York: HarperCollins, 3d ed. 1992). Less grounded in academic economics is Robert Costanza (ed.), *Ecological Economics: The Science and Management of Sustainability* (New York: Columbia University Press, 1991). For a philosophical critique of conventional economic notions about environmental policy, see Mark Sagoff, *The Economy of the Earth: Philosophy, Law, and the Environment* (New York: Cambridge University Press, 1988).

Three very useful studies of applied environmental economics and business strategy are Frances Cairncross, *Costing the Earth: the Challenge for Governments, The Opportunities for Business* (Boston: Harvard Business School Press, 1992); Paul Hawken, *The Ecology of Commerce: A Declaration of Sustainability* (New York: Harper Business, 1993); and Stephan Schmidheiny, *Changing Course: A Global Business Perspective on Development and the Environment* (Cambridge, MA: MIT Press, 1992).

Those who are especially interested in environmental aspects of trade will find a very helpful overview in Durwood Zaelke, Paul Orbuch, and Robert F. Housman (eds.), *Trade and the Environment: Law, Economics, and Policy* (Washington, DC: Island Press, 1993). A more detailed and probing examination of GATT reforms and the new World Trade Organization is provided by Daniel C. Esty, *Greening the GATT: Trade, Environment, and the Future* (Washington, DC: Institute for International Economics, 1994). An earlier but still potent critique of trade practices and their social and environmental consequences can be found in Herman Daly and John Cobb, *For the Common Good: Redirecting the Economy toward Community, the Environment, and a Sustainable Future* (Boston: Beacon Press, 1989).

Readers desiring a brief introduction to environmental issues in international political economy are encouraged to read Jim MacNeill, Pieter Winsemius, and Taizo Yakushiji, *Beyond Interdependence: The Meshing of the World's Economy and the Earth's Ecology* (New York: Oxford University Press, 1991). For a more focused and sophisticated discussion, see William R. Cline, *The Economics of Global Warming* (Washington, DC: Institute for International Economics, 1992).

Environmental Ethics

A good multicultural approach to environmental ethics is featured in J. Ronald Engel and Joan Gibb Engel (eds.), *Ethics of Environment and Development: Global Challenge and International Response* (Tucson: University of Arizona Press, 1990).

A radical and intellectually challenging examination of environmental values can be found in Edward Goldsmith, *The Way: An Ecological Worldview* (Boston: Shambhala, 1993). Also provocative is Carolyn Merchant, *Radical Ecology: The Search for a Livable World* (New York: Routledge, 1992). A thorough and very interesting critique of radical environmental thought is provided by Martin W. Lewis, *Green Delusions: An Environmentalist Critique of Radical Environmentalism* (Durham, NC: Duke University Press, 1992).

Index

Turner, R. Kerry, 89*n*, 274
Tyndall, 104

United Nations conferences
  Conference on the Human Envi-
    ronment (1972), 31, 39, 42,
    74, 89*n*, 91, 207–208
  Conference on Environment and
    Development (UNCED)
    (1992), 29–44, 68, 75, 91,
    115, 117*n*, 174, 181, 207–208,
    212, 217, 226, 232
  Conference on Human Rights
    (1993), 48
  Conference on Population and
    Development, (ICPD) (1994),
    21, 29–30, 37, 45–49,
  Conference on Social Develop-
    ment (1995), 48
  Conference on Women (1995),
    48
  see also Population conferences
United Nations organizations
  Administrative Committee on
    Coordination (ACC), 144
  Commission on Sustainable
    Development, 31, 43, 168
  Conference on Trade and Devel-
    opment (UNCTAD), 102
  Designated Officials on Environ-
    mental Matters (DOEM),
    144
  Development Program (UNDP),
    168
  Economic and Social Council,
    (UNECOSOC), 44
  environmentally active, 145
  Environmental Program (UNEP),
    144, 168
  Food and Agriculture Organiza-
    tion (UNFAO), 141, 212
  General Assembly, 166, 211
  Security Council, 156, 166, 168,
    211

System-Wide-Medium-Term-
    Environment Program
    (SWMTEP), 144
United Nations reform (proposed),
    165–169
United States
  environmental impacts of, 81
  international influence, 35, 156,
    212
  MNCs and, 191
  official development assistance
    and, 36, 47, 50*n*
  role at Earth Summit, 33–36
United States government
  Agency for International Devel-
    opment (AID), 198
  House of Representatives, 126,
    152
  National Academy of Sciences,
    127, 274
  National Center for Atmospheric
    Research, 129
  Senate, 126, 129
  President's Council of Economic
    Advisors, 97
United States Marine Mammal Pro-
    tection Act, 183–184
United States Trade Act (1974), 187

Values, moral and ethical, 160,
    206–209
  see also Ethics
Vatican, the, 131
Vegetarians, 81, 89*n*
Virtual commuity, 7, 237–238

Walter, Ingo, 181
Waste, *see* Pollution
Waste management, 191, 212
Water quality, 76–78, 80, 84, 161,
    175, 195
Weather modification, 66, 109, 111
Weiner, Jonathan, 13, 271
Wetlands, 12, 127

About the Author

Lamont (Monty) Hempel is currently associate professor of political science at The Claremont Graduate School in California, where he specializes in environmental policy.

Previously, Hempel developed and directed model citizen involvement programs for state and local government, served as a project manager in Oregon's Coastal Zone Management Program, and was a candidate for the United States Congress. He has consulted on land-use planning, renewable energy development, and environmental protection in the United States and abroad, and has participated in international conferences on the environment, including the 1992 Earth Summit. In 1995 he was named the first Distinguished Visiting Professor at the newly established Streisand Center for Conservancy Studies in Malibu, California.